The Family in history / Charles E.
Rosenberg ... [et al.] ; edited by
Charles E. Rosenberg. --
[Philadelphia] : University of
Pennsylvania Press, 1975.
210 p. ; 21 cm. -- (Stephen Allen
Kaplan memorial symposium in social
history ; 1) (Haney Foundation
series ; 17)

Includes bibliographical references.
ISBN 0-8122-7703-3

(Cont. on next card)
75-14962

The Family in History

CHARLES E. ROSENBERG

LAWRENCE STONE

WOLFRAM EBERHARD

DAVID LANDES

DIANE HUGHES

JOAN SCOTT

LOUIS TILLY

MICHAEL ZUCKERMAN

The Seventeeth Publication in the
Haney Foundation Series
University of Pennsylvania

The

FAMILY

In

HISTORY

Edited by

CHARLES E. ROSENBERG

University of Pennsylvania Press/1975

Copyright © 1975 by The University of Pennsylvania
Press, Inc.
All rights reserved
Library of Congress Catalog Card Number 75-14962
ISBN: 0-8122-7703-3

Printed in the United States of America

Publication of this book was made possible by a grant from
the Haney Foundation of the University of Pennsylvania.

Contents

The Family in History

☙ CHARLES E. ROSENBERG

INTRODUCTION:

History and Experience

In a fit of rhetorical petulance I referred some years ago to the promised New History of James Harvey Robinson as a half-century-old embryo gestating still. By the mid-1970's, parturition, though hardly complete, seems at least to have begun. The volume of essays presented here must be placed in this general context of contemporary social history.

Our newest social history is made up of varied constituents. One is a growing emphasis on quantitative data. Another is an increasingly self-conscious attempt to employ frameworks of explanation drawn from the social sciences. In some cases, the social sciences have only suggested possibly relevant variables; in others, historians have adopted modes of presenting and evaluating data which differ sharply from those traditionally dominant in history. A third aspect of the new social history is a growing concern with such fundamental human realities as child socialization, disease, death and aging, marriage and kinship structures. A fourth tendency is an increasing interest in the inarticulate and the exploited. (And the study of the peasant and artisan, the industrial worker, women, and ethnic minorities implies the use of novel sources and modes of analysis—as well as changed motivations on the part of the historian.) A final tendency—and one not always consistent with the others—is an increasing use of explanations drawn from psychiatry, thus far Freudian and neo-Freudian in orientation.[1]

1. It is important, I think, to distinguish between the influence of psychoanalytic psychology and that of the social sciences. The two have nevertheless in some ways exerted a parallel influence in shifting historical concern away from traditional public policy areas.

1

Yet, despite such disparity in method and motive, the new social history has a number of unifying characteristics. What binds this new approach to history most firmly together is an implicit rejection of history's traditionally central concern with the reconstruction of particular events (events ordinarily in the spheres of war, politics, and diplomacy). Younger social historians are beginning instead to interest themselves in problems of social structure and the ways in which men have experienced and rationalized their place in that structure; this has meant the increasing prominence of economic, demographic, and ecological approaches, on the one hand, and, on the other, a growing historical concern with world-view, belief systems, and cultural rituals.[2]

A good many historians—some consciously, some not—have begun to seek understanding at another and even more elusive level. What, they ask, was the emotional texture of life for individuals in the past? How did they perceive their world? And their particular social and moral choices? What were the existential consequences of occupying a particular social location? Of being male or female? Of being part of a particular class or ethnic group? That is, how did social structure help shape the emotional reality of individuals?[3]

Such interpretations are not easily made. Though some historians may seek such existential insight, they have no generally agreed-upon analytic framework in which to approach the task (while some historians concerned with such issues are not even aware that this is indeed the implicit thrust of their work). The aggregate findings of the economic historian or demographer serve in some ultimate sense only to structure such questions, to limit the universe of plausible interpretations.

2. Anthropologists have been accused of ignoring change and the particular history of the cultures they have studied. Historians concerned with social structure and behavior are now open to the charge of overemphasizing change and of assuming that stylized concepts such as "industrialization" and "secularization" apply uniformly to a whole society and to different societies. Conventional schemes of periodization have, of course, a similar effect. American historians, for example, feel somehow obliged to find general social meanings in the presidency of Andrew Jackson, English social historians the even more formidable task of finding some unique unity in the reign of Victoria.

3. A parallel trend has manifested itself among Marxist historians and sociologists. Both empirical and theoretical arguments have demonstrated an increasing concern with the interplay of economic organizations, social structure, and feelings of worth or identity. Alienation and anomie, for example, have become increasingly significant concepts in reevaluation of the Marxist tradition. A related interest in the work-styles of traditional and industrializing societies fits into the same pattern of concern with the existential consequences of social structural change. Eugene Genovese's recent study of slavery, *Roll, Jordan, Roll* (New York, 1974), provides a recent example of such a shift in concern.

This is not meant in criticism of quantitative methods—but simply to suggest that such methods are, for some practitioners, and in relation to most problems, means not ends. Even the most determinedly positivistic studies often point dramatically to a fundamental if elusive experiential reality beneath the forms of their aggregate conclusions. Even the most artfully contrived econometric or demographic analysis can at times only dramatize the gap between such data and the historian's own desire to understand past thought and feelings. The recent and much-discussed econometric study of American slavery by Robert Fogel and Stanley Engerman illustrates—even in its title *Time on the Cross*—the emotional (and in this case necessarily political) content often implicit in quantitative formulations.[4]

Let me suggest a tentative strategy for examining the spectrum of concerns and approaches so far discussed, and especially this emergent desire for existential understanding. Some social historians have already begun to shape such an analytical commitment; it is based logically if not always self-consciously upon the reconstruction of social options. Life can be described in terms of options, and the structure of choices— narrow though they may often be—in some ways constitutes the fabric of man's social and psychological reality. This analytic stance can be made to incorporate every aspect of human activity—and every kind of datum—in a potentially consistent framework. Every aspect of culture—patterns of socialization, adult economic activity, intrafamilial functions and responsibilities, religion and world-view generally—can be seen as constituting or helping define a particular structure of available social options. We can, that is, seek to define the particular options which faced individuals at different stages of life as they sought to internalize different kinds of roles, to impose a particular order upon their world, to express and structure basic human needs.

The preceding paragraphs may seem to imply a social history possessing a sociology but bereft of a psychology, a social history in which the intersection between individual personality and cultural realities is ingenuously avoided. I contend, however, that limitations both within contemporary psychological theory and within historical data demand that for the moment at least we content ourselves with a kind of descriptive social psychology and not impose too explicit a theoretical framework in our desire to move from particular social

4. Robert W. Fogel and Stanley L. Engerman, *Time on the Cross: The Economics of American Negro Slavery,* 2 vols. (Boston, 1974).

realities to their implications for the individual. The necessity for my position seems obvious enough; there is little in contemporary theory which we can both accept as proven and at the same time study in historical terms. This is not to say that current knowledge of individual psychological processes is no different from that available to George Bancroft or James Ford Rhodes. We have, by the 1970's, come to assume that personality develops in stages probably common to a culture, yet in its specific emotional context always individual. We believe that early childhood is particularly but not exclusively significant in determining an individual's ultimate personality and the nature of his social adjustment. We can assume the existence of certain universal human needs beyond hunger and libido. Perhaps most importantly to the historian, we have come to assume that personality development must be seen both in terms of the micro-system of the family and the macro-system of society, its norms and structured roles. Beyond these now conventional assumptions, however, there is little in the way of a useful body of theory with which to help explicate past realities.[5]

But the historian need not throw up his hands. As I have suggested, there is a tentative framework in which he can at least begin to define the knowable, the unknown, and the unknowable. The historian can seek to understand the nature of the social options available to particular individuals occupying a particular social location at particular stages of life.[6] (This would imply the study of such matters as nursing and weaning, childhood socialization, the entrance into adult economic and familial roles, and the age and form in which economic and personal autonomy is achieved or delimited.) That individuals differ in terms of inheritance, psychological need, and abilities can only be assumed. The precise emotional content of a particular individual's particular adjustment is not ordinarily within our competence.

We cannot, for example, explain why an individual may have chosen a homosexual orientation in the past; but we can study aspects of ac-

5. Historians have in the past decade turned in increasing numbers to psychiatry and Freudian and neo-Freudian developmental models in seeking to understand the texture of past emotional realities. But this is a perilous task; for these speculative psycho-genetic sequences are inevitably arbitrary—and in any case ill-suited to the historian's data. We are all familiar with contemporary ventures into a genre which has come to be called psycho-history, one in which the internal structure of particular developmental models is made to explicate the structure of past individual or group psychologies.

6. It might be argued that such an eclectic approach is misguided because some means of evaluating the psychodynamic significance of particular stages and options is necessary even to *describe* the shape and impact of particular social realities. I do not share this conviction.

cepted social behavior which might have encouraged same-sex relationships, and we can try to ascertain the then prevailing attitudes
toward such relationships. Other illustrations come to mind. Keith
Thomas' recent study of magic and religion in early modern England
concerns itself in part with witchcraft; instead of interpreting the
witches in terms of individual psychopathology —as has sometimes been
attempted—Thomas sought to suggest a context of belief and social
relationship out of which witchcraft accusations might naturally have
grown. He not only outlines the traditional belief in the ability of individuals to injure people and animals through the use of magic, but he
places it in a specific social context—that of agricultural villages in
which economic change was beginning to compromise traditional social
relationships (and, more specifically, in which dependent older women,
the customary objects of ad hoc charity, might be turned away by more
prosperous neighbors still sufficiently aware of older values to feel a cor-
responding guilt[7]).

In undertaking the analysis of past social reality, historians have customarily and casually created expository metapersons representing a
collective world-view and experience—the seventeenth-century Puritan,
the Jacksonian American, the Renaissance humanist. Historians have
always relied on such figures to explain and communicate; with
increasing understanding of past economic and social life, however, we
can begin to see the developmental history of such paradigmatic figures
as a series of structured options.[8] To accomplish this, of course, such
general constructs must be defined far more sharply, must be limited to
manageable entities—the Protestant merchant in mid-eighteenth-
century Bordeaux, let us say, not the middle class in the Enlightenment.
And we must, even while working with them, remain aware that even
such relatively well-defined aggregate figures in fact represent a myriad
of individual psyches, family configurations, and economic sub-options
within a more general pattern of viable social and economic careers.

From this point of view, the economic historian's data or the demographer's exposition of past family structure can and will be construed in

7. Keith Thomas, *Religion and the Decline of Magic* (New York, 1971). Cf. Alan
Macfarlane, *Witchcraft in Tuder and Stuart England: A Regional and Comparative
Study* (New York, 1970).

8. For many individuals in the past, options must have been few indeed; but this is in
many ways an assumption. Latitude of choice has never been systematically studied, and
until it is studied in comparative terms, a narrowness of social option should be neither
romanticized by admirers of traditional society nor bewailed by those who see this very
lack of choice as constituting the essence of exploitation.

emotional terms, and can be seen by the historian as a series of likelihoods facing individuals and small groups. There is no necessary conflict between the quantitative and the existential. Quite the contrary. Where aggregate quantitative data are available to the historian, they become a fundamental precondition to any systematic attempt to understand underlying emotional realities. Descriptions of past social structure based on aggregated data do not necessarily correspond to the reality *perceived* by individuals or groups living and working in that society. Yet, especially for the inarticulate, aggregate information is often the only information we can hope to have.

But the social historian is dependent on non-quantifiable data as well; and these entail somewhat different interpretative problems. Most frequently preserved are the materials of what I should like to term cultural ideology—the prescriptions which enforce, communicate, and legitimize social roles and cultural expectations. These include every kind of cultural artifact from sermons and theological exegeses to nursery rhymes and child-rearing manuals, engravings, and toys. As mentioned above, personal documents—letters, diaries and journals— constitute still another kind of source, frustratingly erratic in the quality of truth they convey as well as in the very accident of their survival. Social historians have, in general, utilized such documents infrequently and anecdotally; the practice of using personal documents in the elucidation of social phenomena is still in its infancy. But this must inevitably change as we become increasingly concerned with ritual and belief, with the way man throughout history has dealt with the primary social processes.

The utility of social options as an organizing concept is apparent in the work of contemporary social historians who have—consciously or by implication—sought to move from retrievable social and economic data to their emotional meaning for individuals. Philip Greven's recent study of eighteenth-century Andover, for example, may be made to demonstrate neatly a relationship between social structure and emotional predispositions.[9] Greven documents a decreased availability of land as the century progressed, a growing stricture mirrored in shifting patterns of inheritance. Connected with these new economic realities were shifts in age of marriage and, by implication, of the father's power and emotional weight within the family. The interpretative jump from

---

9. Philip J. Greven, Jr., *Four Generations: Population, Land, and Family in Colonial Andover, Massachusetts* (Ithaca, N.Y., 1970).

a demonstrably altered economic reality to changed intrafamilial role options seems obvious enough; extrapolation to the emotional meaning of such changed options is more tenuous but certainly defensible. We cannot, that is, predict how a *particular* young man in eighteenth-century Andover may have responded to such shifting patterns of economic opportunity and paternal control. We can with entire plausibility, however, assume that comparative scarcity of land meant that a changed structure of social—and thus inevitably emotional—options faced young Andover men as they grew to maturity. There are two points of significance here. The first is that such developmental patterns illustrate a kind of social reality which can be constructively seen in terms of options. The second is that we could not discuss this phenomenon, perhaps even identify it, without a basis in economic data.

Greven's work does not stand alone. Michael Anderson's study of nineteenth-century Lancashire is even more self-conscious in its analysis, yet equally dependent upon that pivotal jump from aggregate data to the personal impact of social change. To turn to another example, Stephan Thernstrom's decade-old but still influential study of social mobility in nineteenth-century Newburyport hinges formally on an attempt to trace particular heads of households through successive censuses; yet, in retrospect, the results and possible relevance to questions of ethnic mobility seem far less significant then what they—in conjunction with more impressionistic evidence—communicate of the bitter existential reality that the achievement of simple economic stability meant for those harshly enduring workers and clerks who managed to achieve it.[10] The annals of the poor may indeed be miserable and short; but we are learning more and more about the texture of that misery. In the case of workers and peasants this reality can be reconstructed only upon the basis of likelihoods defined by preliminary aggregate studies. Our sources allow us no other choice.

The family is obviously central to the emerging new social history. And it is not surprising that the past decade has seen a rapidly growing interest in family history. In the United States alone we have recently seen the establishment of a *Family History Newsletter* and a *History of Childhood Quarterly*, while the *Journal of Interdisciplinary History* has devoted a goodly number of pages to aspects of the family. The *An-*

10. Michael Anderson, *Family Structure in Nineteenth-Century Lancashire* (Cambridge, 1971); Stephan Thernstrom, *Poverty and Progress. Social Mobility in a Nineteenth-Century City* (Cambridge, Mass., 1964).

nales in France and *Past and Present* in England have been almost as hospitable. So vigorous and disparate have been these recent excursions into the history of the family that no single volume could hope to represent every approach or illustrate every substantive problem. Our present volume, however, emphasizes a significant and surprisingly little-explored comparative dimension—not so much in terms of each contributor's formal intent, but through the contrasts and comparisons implicit in the book's very structure.

All the chapters which follow emphasize that the family is a primary reality not only in terms of individual emotional development but in terms of social and economic organization as well. The family functions as a mode of structuring sexual relationships, kinship relations, and child rearing—but also as a source of labor and capital accumulation, as a mechanism for the transmission of property and the imposition of social control.

Even more strikingly, these diverse essays illustrate the historian's peculiarly strategic position within the social sciences; for we know that the family as a form changes over time. The changes inevitably alter not only the texture of intrafamiliar roles but also the functional relationship between the family's internal organization and the structural necessities of a changing society. In the essay by Stone and in the essay by Scott and Tilly, the family is seen as a framework within which adjustment to a changing economy and social relationships takes place. Hughes assumes a roughly parallel position. In the developing economy of twelfth-century Genoa, she argues, the entrepreneurial upper-class family altered its internal pattern and even its external ecological environment. In his study of two private banking firms, Landes deals with a very specialized economic role for the family in the modernization of European economic relationships. Eberhard's broadly conceived history of the upper-class Chinese family illustrates how intricately the organizational structure of the state and the infrastructure of social and economic life depended upon the cohesion and specific priorities of the family.

All of these chapters turn to a significant extent on the problem of relating beliefs and behavior; it is a problem with both substantive and methodological dimensions. The ideological formulations which explain and legitimize fundamental social roles and norms are very much a substantive question for the student of past behavior; for such prescriptions do after all constitute one dimension of perceived reality—norms to which one conforms or against which one defines one's deviance. Nevertheless, few social historians are satisfied with prescriptive materials alone; they tend to seek the behavioral flesh beneath the forms of ideology. Yet comparatively few records of behavior survive (with some exceptions such as the records of births, voting results, and the artifacts of material culture). And thus historians are all the more dependent upon prescription and casual allusion, must necessarily seek to extrapolate behavior from formal admonition. (We must presume, that is, functionally logical relationships between social needs and expressed ideas.) Formal role prescriptions are always more uniform than the behavior which may—or may not—incorporate them. Nevertheless, it would be self-defeating reductionism to contend that the materials of prescription are absolutely treacherous and best avoided.[11]

The tension between prescription and behavior is confronted again and again in the chapters which make up this book. It is, indeed, the principal burden of Zuckerman's study. Zuckerman assumes a reciprocal—and he would presumably contend inevitable—relationship between the needs of an organized, bureaucratized society and the imposition of a socialization pattern capable of fashioning personalities able to function within this society. (Thus the choice of Spock's book as a subject. The book's very popularity is proof implied of the socially functional nature of the good doctor's admonitions.) Tilly and Scott embrace another strategy entirely. They use a variety of materials to suggest the existence of social norms consistent with the necessary economic role of working women in pre-industrial and industrializing societies. Eberhard argues that ideological constraints, consciously articulated and imposed, played a significant role in shaping the Chinese family and thus society through the creation of stylized limitations in cultural choice. Though concerned ultimately with behavioral change. Stone must, like Eberhard, rely to an extent on didactic and doctrinal works of a literate upper class.

All the contributions to this volume—with the partial exception of

11. We must realize as well that society may elaborate competing and in some ways equally legitimate roles, and it is precisely the texture of such ambiguity which often constitutes the essence of a particular emotional reality. For example, I have argued elsewhere that nineteenth-century sexual options for men did not necessarily lead to repressiveness. Two diverse but equally legitimate role options were available: one of traditional male sexual prowess and the other an evangelical and repressive ethos. The particular reality of men in those generations was shaped by the availability and possible conflict between these life options. See Charles E. Rosenberg, "Sexuality, Class, and Role in Nineteenth-Century America," *American Quarterly* (May, 1973) 25: 131-53.

that by Landes—eschew concern with the sequence of particular events and concern themselves with the family as a system of values and behavioral options. Eberhard's contribution can be seen in effect as outlining the structure of plausible career options for upper-class Chinese men—of their relationship through the family to society. Tilly and Scott conclude that for young women in nineteenth-century working-class families work role and choice of marriage partners (indeed, opportunities for marriage itself) were far different from those elaborated in the categories of middle-class ideology. Hughes emphasizes not only the relatively rigid marital patterns characteristic of upper-class families in twelfth-century Genoa but also a seemingly dramatic disparity between the importance of family in the magnate class and in that of artisans at the same time and place. Landes, analyzing a peculiar kind of entrepreneurial role and how it might subsume family, emphasizes the constraints placed by class and ethno-cultural distinctions upon the real options available even to families so opulent as the Bleichröders and Rothschilds. Human beings—as commonsense tells us—live several different social roles simultaneously; to recapture any individual's emotional reality is to gain some understanding of the specific configuration and interaction of these roles.

The immanent relationship between social change and individual experience is illustrated again and again in the contributions to this volume. Stone, for example, suggests that the English woman's autonomy was necessarily altered by the development of a "patriarchal" family structure. In the "prepatriarchal" family a married woman's family of origin provided a cushion against the husband's powers within the nuclear family; she had still something of the standing granted the envoys of a foreign power. Landes, however, warns of drawing overly rigid behavioral conclusions about individuals from social location and presumed social function alone; personal and cultural constraints can shift radically the perceptions and needs of families occupying seemingly identical places in society's economic structure.

Like much contemporary work in social history, these contributions abstain from a thoroughgoing commitment to formal social science modes of analysis or exposition of data. Only Stone's essay approximates a formal sociological model in the creation of archetypal patterns of family organization and the ordering of data in terms of these categories. It is the subject matter, the questions asked, and the shift to quantitative data and statistical tests of significance which mark the new social history.

The ultimate theoretical question faced in one way or another by all these authors is the relationship between change in social structure, ideological change, and the tendency of intrafamilial roles and functions to reshape themselves in consistency with such changes. The fundamental organizing principle in Stone's essay, for example—though clearly an assumption—rests upon identifying a connection between changing family norms and a changing social structure. Zuckerman's essay, to note a disparate example, rests on the assumption of a necessary consistency between the structurally imposed demands of society and the consequent shifting of intrafamilial realities to achieve socialization patterns appropriate to the behavioral demands of a changing society. Tilly and Scott are anxious to prove the ways in which traditional attitudes toward women's work in pre-industrial society served, ironically, as a condition of social and economic adjustment to a very different kind of society. At this level of social analysis there are no simple questions—nor any final answers.

享 LAWRENCE STONE

THE RISE OF THE
NUCLEAR FAMILY IN
EARLY MODERN ENGLAND:
The Patriarchal Stage*

Introduction

Between about 1500 and 1700 the English family structure began a slow process of evolution in two related ways. Firstly, the importance of the nuclear core increased, and the influence of the surrounding kin declined; secondly, the importance of affective bonds tying the conjugal group together increased, and the economic functions of the family as a distributive mechanism for goods and services declined. These two changes were the product of three concurrent and interrelated changes: the decline of kinship as the main organizing principle of the society; the rise of the modern state, with its take-over of some of the economic and social functions previously carried out by the family or the kin, and subordination of kin loyalties to the higher obligations of patriotism and obedience to the sovereign; and the missionary success of Protestantism, especially its Puritan wing, in bringing Christian morality to a majority of homes, and in some ways making the family serve as a substitute for the parish.

At the same time, these and other forces were at work to bring about

*The preparation of this paper was assisted by a grant from the National Science Foundation (Grant No. GS 28832X). All spelling and punctuation have been modernized.

a third important development: the strengthening, for a time, of the pre-existing patriarchal aspects of internal power relationships within the family. Later, in the course of the late seventeenth and the eighteenth centuries, this patriarchal authoritarianism gave way to a more individualistic and companionate type of family structure, the causes of which are beyond the scope of this paper.

The period is, therefore, one in which three overlapping models can be seen to coexist, each slowly but imperfectly replacing the other. The first was the kin-oriented family of the Middle Ages, in which the conjugal unit of husband, wife, and unmarried children was of relatively lesser importance than the wider kinship affiliations of the cousinhood. This was an institution whose prime purpose was economic support rather than affective bonding and in which patriarchalism was the rule. The second was the more nuclear family of the sixteenth century in which loyalty became increasingly focussed inward on the conjugal core and outward on the state rather than on the kin relatives by blood or marriage. This was an institution whose function, while still primarily economic, was also beginning to be more affective and in which the authoritarian patriarchal element was very strongly reinforced. The third was the companionate nuclear family of the eighteenth century, in which affective relationships were becoming as important as economic functions and in which the authority of the husband over the wife and of the father over his children was severely reduced.

The Decline of Kinship

Between 1500 and 1750 it is clear that there was a decline in the role played in society by the kin. This was a relative and not an absolute change, for society always includes both the kin system and the nuclear family, which together share the tasks of reproduction, consumption, socialization, placement and welfare, while the state itself always has some part to play in these matters. There is rarely a clear cut alternative between the kin, the conjugal unit, and the state. What happened in Early Modern England was a slow readjustment of the previous distribution of emphasis, both in the articulation of the conjugal family to the larger kin-based structure, and in the relationship of both to the impersonal institutions of the state.

Evidence

The evidence for change can be traced in a number of areas. One indication is that claims to cousinhood ties in the subscription of letters occur far less frequently in the late seventeenth and eighteenth centuries than in the sixteenth or early seventeenth, presumably because it was no longer so useful in creating a favorable predisposition in the recipient. It would, for example, be hard to parallel in the eighteenth century the claim to cousinhood advanced in the early seventeenth century by Thomas Wentworth in a letter to Sir Henry Slingsby. The connection was indeed there, but there were no fewer than seven links in the genealogical chain which joined the two, three of them by marriage through the female line.[1]

More concrete is the very clear decline in the concept of kin responsibility for individual crimes and actions. In the sixteenth century, at any rate in the Highland Zone of the north and west, the royal writ and the royal law-courts were less important as law enforcement agencies than the blood feud and the vendetta. Under the vendetta there is collective kin responsibility for individual action, as opposed to the legal theory of individual responsibility: the law will punish the criminal but no one else; the vendetta is perfectly satisfied by the punishment of the criminal's brother, father, uncle, or nephew. By the end of the sixteenth century, this custom had virtually died out in England.[2] Henry VIII was the last English king to punish whole families, such as the De La Poles, for the treason of one member.

This erosion of the penal solidarity of the clan, by which the kin or immediate family of a fallen politician suffered punishment with him, first occurred among the patriciate of Florence in the fifteenth century, a century before it happened in England.[3] In France the custom lived on into the eighteenth century. In the late seventeenth century, Louis XIV exiled the family of Fouquet, and imprisoned that of Cartouche. Moreover, the penal solidarity of the family in the payment of taxes remained a part of French law until it was abolished in 1775 by Maupou, who denounced it as "This odious law which, from the fault of a single man, incriminates a whole family."[4] In Russia the practice

---

1. D. Parsons, *Diary of Sir Henry Slingsby* (London, 1836), p. 329.
2. L. Stone, *The Crisis of the Aristocracy, 1558-1641* (Oxford, 1965), pp. 228-29.
3. R. Goldthwaite, *Private Wealth in Renaissance Florence* (Princeton, 1968), p. 260.
4. G. Snyders, *La Pedagogie en France au XVIIe et XVIIIe Siecles* (Paris, 1965), pp. 242, 305.

only died out in the mid-twentieth century, marking the final triumph in the West of the principle of individual responsibility, first affecting the kin and later the nuclear family itself.

In national politics, there took place a slow decline in the role of kinship as the central organizing principle of political groupings. In the fifteenth century, the Wars of the Roses were almost entirely a struggle of aristocratic kinship factions and alliances for control of royal authority and patronage. In the sixteenth century, kin groupings remained powerful in politics, but slowly gave way to religious conviction and personal ambition as the state strengthened its grip on society and began to attract loyalties to itself. Even so, much of the political infighting of the century revolved around certain kinship rivalries, in particular that between the Howards and the Dudleys, until the last, illegitimate Dudley finally went into exile at the end of the century, and the Howards hitched themselves on to the court of James I. But the degree to which kinship loyalties had become subordinated to political and religious ideology became clear during the English revolution of the 1640s, when one aristocratic family in seven was divided father against child or brother against brother.[5] If the divisions within the conjugal group were so frequent, it is obvious that the cousinhood was even more hopelessly fragmented. Other loyalties now took precedence among the English political nation at the top, although how far this change penetrated down the society is at present unknown. No one knows, for example, whether yeoman or merchant families divided father against son, brother against brother in the Civil War.

At the end of the seventeenth century, the English political nation was bitterly divided into two parties going under the labels of Whigs and Tories. In binding together these political groupings, there were four main elements: dependence on a political patron, professional clientage, personal friendship and kinship. Kinship was certainly a help, and was used by politicians to increase their influence. Thus Harley carefully cultivated the remotest of cousins, and found it advantageous to find ways of signing his letters "your most faithful and humble servant and kinsman." But for every family connection which carried clear political associations, there were three or four about which nothing is known. There may have been no connection, or the kin may in fact have been split down the middle. Thus of the ten M. P.'s and

---

5. Excluding the underage, the very old, and the insane, there were 119 noblemen who could have taken sides. Eighteen of these 119 split within the conjugal family, thirteen of them on father/son lines.

candidates of the Bertie family in the reign of Queen Anne, seven were Tories, two Whigs, and one a Whiggish waverer.[6] Kinship often remained useful in the formation of the Whig factions in the eighteenth century, such as the Pelham Whigs or Rockingham Whigs, but it was no more than one element among several, and not necessarily the most important or the most durable one. The impermanence and unreliability of these connections in English eighteenth century politics, as compared with those of the early sixteenth century, suggest that in the early modern period kinship was replaced by "bastard kinship," just as in the late Middle Ages the ties of feudalism had been replaced by those of "bastard feudalism."

In local affairs, kin ties undoubtedly continued to be important well into the eighteenth century. As the English elite fissured down religious lines in the sixteenth and seventeenth centuries, religious endogamy developed among Catholics and Puritans, but in this case the lines of kinship followed and reinforced the ties of religion, not *vice versa*. (For example, Catholic priests acted as marriage brokers for Recusant families.[7]) After the middle of the seventeenth century, the amount of social mobility among the squirearchy shrank to a trickle, so that little new blood was coming in to keep the system fluid. Meanwhile in each county, for century after century, the squires were intermarrying with one another, until the web of cross-cousinhood became so dense and so universal that it lost its meaning. If everybody is everybody else's cousin, the connection does not matter any more, and the recent discovery that Charles I was a remote cousin of John Hampden does nothing to advance our understanding of the English Revolution of the seventeenth century.[8]

Another test of the declining role of kinship is the respect paid to nepotism in recruitment to state and private offices. It would, of course, be foolish to deny that this remained an important and respectable element in recruitment well into the middle of the nineteenth century. It would be very interesting to know up to what point it remained entirely

6. G. Holmes, *British Politics in the Age of Anne* (London, 1967), pp. 323, 264, 326-33, 498n., 330.

7. M. Blundell, *Cavalier* (London, 1933), p. 132; H. Aveling, "The Marriages of Catholic Recusants," *Journal of Ecclesiastical History* 14 (1963): 68-83.

8. D. Brunton and D. H. Pennington, *Members of the Long Parliament* (Manchester, 1954), p. 17. In Kent, where subdivisions of estata among brothers was unusually common and where mobility among the elite had been usually low, the situation of near-universal cousinhood was arrived at as early as 1640 (A. Everett, *The Community of Kent and the Great Rebellion, 1640-1660* [Leicester, 1966], pp. 35-36).

respectable to use nepotism to favor a close relative within the nuclear family, such as son or a brother, but not to favor a cousin from the remoter layers of the kin. This appears to have been the case by the early seventeenth century in England.[9] There is also some evidence that nepotism generally was meeting increasing competition from two alternative sets of values. In the first place, many offices, especially in the law and the army, were obtained by purchase from the incumbent or his superior, and here money was usually more important than kinship. To the extent that saleable offices increased in the seventeenth century, as they did, this undermined the importance of kinship. Secondly, here and there in the two sectors of administration where efficiency was absolutely essential for the life of the nation (the Treasury to supply and handle public funds and the Navy to protect England's shores and to blast open the sea lanes of the world for English goods and English merchants) there are signs, beginning with Samuel Pepys in the late seventeenth century, of the development of a new, impersonal, meritocratic, professional spirit.[10]

It is also noticeable that hereditary office-holding, as legally established in France by the *Paulette* in the early seventeenth century, was never officially accepted in England, although the practice of sons succeeding fathers seems to have become increasingly common in the middle ranges of offices in the seventeenth century.[11] Hereditary office was seen, rightly, as a threat to the independent authority of the state, and was always opposed by the crown. It is true that well into the nineteenth century public office in England continued to serve as a system of outdoor relief largely monopolized by the hereditary elite. Generation after generation of younger sons or illegitimate sons were found comfortable berths in the public service, either at home or in the colonies. But each time there had to be a struggle, and each time there was competition to the ties of blood or marriage from the alternative principles of money and merit.

Lower down the social scale, the ties of kinship are more difficult to determine. There can be no doubt whatever that in the seventeenth century uncles played a large part in family decisions, especially when the parents died and the children had to be found jobs and husbands. In 1637-40 the young Cambridge graduate, the Reverend Ralph Josselin, used one uncle's credit to borrow money, stayed with another when he

9. G. Aylmer, *The King's Servants* (London, 1961), p. 82.
10. For the treasury, see S. B. Baxter, *The Development of the Treasury, 1660-1702* (London, 1957).
11. Aylmer, *The King's Servants*, pp. 81-82.

was unemployed, and found his first church living by the good offices of
the first uncle, who in fact paid ten pounds of his forty-four pound a
year salary. Nearly a century later, the Reverend John Thomlinson was
lodged, launched on a clerical career, and found a variety of possible fi-
nancially attractive brides through the patronage and connections of his
two uncles, despite the fact that his father was still alive.[12]

On the other hand, Josselin's links to more distant kin relatives, such
as cousins, were very remote and casual. Of his thirty-odd first cousins,
his elaborate diary over a period of forty-two years mentions only three
of them more than five times, and only fourteen even once. "Cousins, it
seems, were not of great emotional or economic importance to
Josselin."[13] Assuming that Josselin is at all typical, one can conclude
that already by the mid-seventeenth century the cousinhood had ceased
to play a significant part in middle-class family life, if indeed it ever
had.

On the other hand, it would be a mistake to regard this development
as one of linear progression. It seems likely that kinship ties wax and
wane according to the economic stresses to which the nuclear family is
subjected. Among the commercial community, kinship ties were important in the sixteenth century, and remained important for a long
time as a source of loans, partnership investments, and agencies for job
placement. In the early seventeenth century, between one-third and
one-half of all London merchants who were active in trade to the Levant had fathers, fathers-in-law, or brothers already in the Company
when they first joined it. In the 1630s twenty-three men linked by birth
or marriage to the Elizabethan founders of the Company controlled
about half the trade of the Levant Company. Another merchant group
at this period were the new men in the American trades, who were also
linked by numerous family ties. But this was a two-way process in
which common economic interests stimulated kinship alliances, and
kinship alliances stimulated economic partnership. "Their intercon-
nected ties of business, sometimes formed on the basis of previous kinship ties, had themselves been strengthened by the establishment of new
family links."[14]

12. "The Diary of the Rev. John Tomlinson," in *Six North Country Diaries,*
Publication of the Surtees Society, vol. 118 (1910), 1:67-167 *passim.*

13. A. Macfarlane, *Family Life of Ralph Josselin* (Cambridge, 1970), pp. 17, 132,
137-39.

14. B. Winchester, *Tudor Family Portrait* (London, 1955), p. 76; R. Brenner, "The
Civil War Politics of London's Merchant Community," *Past and Present* 58 (1973): 61-
62, 71.

This use of kinship ties to develop or to cement commerical relationships was a practice which lasted throughout the eighteenth
century, although to a much diminished extent. In 1788 the biographer
of a Leeds parson reasserted the principle that men "must respect the
attachments of friendship and blood; and their attempts to draw close
these natural and artificial ties must be deemed not only innocent but
laudable. The claims of merit can, therefore, have no place where they
would interfere with the duties of prior obligation." The same principles applied among the eighteenth century merchants of Leeds and
Hull, where the family firm predominated, and Robert Pease could
explain, "we keep entirely together to help one another." Even in Hull,
however, there is clear evidence that more and more partnerships,
loans, etc., were being made outside the kin.[15] And yet for the lower
middle-class in Lancashire in the early nineteenth century, subject to
the intense stresses of both industrialization and rural-urban migration,
the kin was the main agency for job placement.[16] What we do not know
is whether or not this last was a new development, or merely the
healthy survival of an ancient practice. It seems quite possible that it
was the former.

Another area in which the principle of kinship can be shown to have
been on the decline in the seventeenth century is that of aid and welfare.
In traditional societies these problems are handled by the conjugal
family and by the kin, but in modern societies they are managed primarily by the state and various impersonal institutions, only secondarily by the conjugal family, and hardly at all by the kin. In sixteenth
century England, the prevailing demographic conditions meant that
support was needed for large numbers of orphans, many widows, many
cripples and sick, some able unemployed, and relatively few old people.
During the sixteenth century, these welfare functions were
progressively taken over by public bodies. In the early sixteenth
century, some towns began to organize their own poor relief system,
paid out of taxes, and in the second half of the century the practice
spread to the countryside, on a voluntary and emergency basis. In about
1600 a nationwide system based on local compulsory taxation and ex-
penditure was instituted, and during the seventeenth century it became

---

15. R. G. Wilson, *Gentlemen Merchants* (Manchester, 1971), p. 184; G. Jackson,
Hull in the Eighteenth Century (Oxford, 1972), pp. 108-9, 111.

16. See M. Anderson, "The Study of Family Structure," in *Nineteenth Century Society*, ed. E. A. Wrigley (Cambridge, 1972); M. Anderson, *Family Structure in
Nineteenth Century Lancashire* (London, 1971), ch. 7, 9.

a fully functioning organization which effectively relieved the kin, and also the conjugal family, of much of its responsibility for relief of the poor and sick. In addition to these public arrangements, private charity built and endowed a significant number of orphanages, hospitals, and almshouses for the old, and set up supplementary funds for poor relief in a fair number of villages.[17]

In the socialization of the child, his training for life responsibilities, the seventeenth century also saw a partial transfer of function from the kin and the family to impersonal institutions of dame schools, grammar schools, and colleges, providing literacy and piety for the many, and classics and piety for the few. While much borrowing from kin relatives continued to take place throughout the eighteenth century, the growth of country banks and joint stock companies provided increasingly important alternatives.[18] An examination of Midland wills between 1676 and 1775 shows over half of the testators making bequests to the nuclear family, and a quarter to kin relatives.[19] This suggests that by the eighteenth century kinship affiliations were weakened, but that they were still far from extinct.

Causes

This slow decline of kinship occurs both in the realm of function and that of values. As society became more dense, more complex and more organized, there developed a series of semi-public bodies, town authorities, parish overseers of the poor, schools, banks, etc., which took over many of the functions previously performed by the kin and by the family. This was a very slow and very relative process, however, and far more important at this stage were changes in the levels of social mobility, and a shift in values away from the kin towards the state.

Georgraphical Mobility. Among the poor and the artisan classes, the extraordinary geographical mobility of English society in the seventeenth century, which has now been established beyond a

17. W. K. Jordan, *Philanthropy in England, 1480-1660* (London, 1959), pp. 18, 90, 107. Professor Jordan enormously exaggerated the significance of private charity as compared with welfare supported by public taxation: see J. Hill, "A Study of Poverty and Poor Relief in Shropshire, 1550-1685" (M. A. thesis, Birmingham University, 1973), pp. 89, 99-101, 116-17, 120-21, 148-51, 271-72; and A. L. Beier, "Studies in Poverty and Poor Relief in Warwickshire, 1540-1680" (Ph.D. Diss., Princeton University, 1969), p. 178.

18. L. S. Pressnell, *Country Banking in the Industrial Revolution* (Oxford, 1956), ch. 10-12.

19. J. A. Johnston, "Probate Inventories and Wills of a Worcestershire Parish," *Midlands History* 1 (1971): 32.

reasonable doubt, made it almost impossible for kinship associations to retain their old strength. Muster rolls of male adults liable to military service and detailed census returns of two villages both suggest a population turnover in the village as high as 50 percent or more in ten years. Even if removal by death accounted for some 20 percent of those who disappeared, there are still some 30 percent or more who moved on elsewhere in a given ten-year span, which indicates that the seventeenth century English village was far from being a static or isolated unit. In one Worcestershire village, 80 percent of the seventy-five surnames disappeared from the parish records between 1666 and 1750. Village continuity was preserved by a mere five large and enduring families, which inevitably intermarried a great deal among each other. Similarly, a study of witnesses in rural court cases between 1580 and 1640, who were all men well above the poverty line, show that two-thirds had moved to a different parish during their lives, even if about half of them had only moved five miles. A 1782 census of a Bedfordshire village showed that only a third of the heads of households, of either sex, had been born in the village, although most of them came from less than ten miles away. Thus among the lower, lower-middle and middle class groups, horizontal mobility was remarkably high.[20]

These changes cannot be accounted for merely by youths and young girls going out into service or apprenticeship and moving on from master to master. What is involved is both the emigration of youth away from the parental home, and also the migration of whole nuclear families from place to place, thus breaking the bonds of kinship. Some of this flow was short-range migration for marriage or work as a servant. But a good deal of it was longer range; from the more densely populated rural areas into the forests and the underpopulated Highland Zone, and even more from the countryside into the towns. Between 1580 and 1640, three-quarters of Canterbury residents who served as

20. P. Laslett, "Clayworth and Cogenhoe," *Historical Essays, 1600-1750*, ed. H. E. Bell and R. L. Ollard (London, 1963), p. 77; S. H. Peyton, "Village Population in English Subsidy Rolls," *English Historical Review* 30 (1915): 248; E. E. Rich, "The Population of Rural England," *Economic History Review*, 2nd Series, 2 (1949): 259; P. Styles, "A Census of a Warwickshire Village in 1698," *University of Birmingham Historical Journal* 3 (1951): 45-48; Johnston, "Probate Inventories," p. 29; J. Cornwall, "Evidence of Population Mobility in the Seventeenth Century," *Bulletin of the Institute of Historical Research* 40 (1967): 143-52; P. Clark, "The Migrant in Kentish Towns, 1580-1640," in P. Clark and P. Slack, *Crisis and Order in English Towns* (London, 1972), pp. 117-63; L. Stone, Social Mobility in England." *Past and Present* 33 (1966): 29-30; R. S. Schofield, "Age-specific Mobility in an Eighteenth Century Rural English Parish," *Annales de Démographie Historique* (1970): 261, 264.

witnesses in court cases were immigrants into the city from elsewhere. But the truly massive influx was into London. The population of London and its suburbs increased from about 60,000 in 1500 to about 550,000 in 1700, despite the fact that the urban death rate was so high that the city was far from reproducing itself. This staggering growth was, therefore, caused by a constant and massive flow of immigrants from the countryside. Once entered into the anonymity of the city, these immigrants often tended to remain transients without deep roots. A London parson in the days of Elizabeth remarked that every twelve years or so "the most part of the parish changeth, ... some going and some coming." A sample of deponents in lawsuits in Stepney between 1580 and 1639 shows that less than 8 percent had been born in that parish or neighboring Whitechapel. Moreover, the evidence of apprenticeship records suggest that artisan immigration in the sixteenth century was of a very long-range variety, with nearly half the immigrants coming from the North of England. Only at the end of the seventeenth century did immigrants begin to come predominantly from the surrounding areas.[21]

This very high rate of mobility from place to place, much of it over long distances and sustained for over a century, must have done more than anything else to weaken the ties of kinship among the lower levels of society. Travel was both slow and expensive, and correspondence among illiterates difficult if not impossible. Many of these movements must have permanently detached the nuclear family from its parents and kin in the village, and permanently detached the adolescent children from their parents. For these large numbers who were mobile, the web of kin relations that enveloped them in the home village was now cut, which necessarily threw them back on the isolated conjugal family type. Some migrants no doubt found temporary shelter with a kin relative, but before long, the nuclear pair, or the lonely adolescent, were on their own in alien corn, and only a minority could hope to marry into a wider kin which could offer support in the new surroundings.

Shifts in Values. As well as these material reasons for the decline of kinship, there were shifts in values, which among the upper classes were probably the more significant. The ideal of kinship as the highest focus of loyalty found itself increasingly challenged by two alternative

---

21. Clark, "The Migrant in Kentish Towns," p. 122; E. A. Wrigley, "London's Importance, 1650-1750," *Past and Present* 37 (1967): 46; D. Cressy, "Occupations, Migration and Literacy in East London, 1580-1640," *Local Population Studies* 5 (1970): 58; Stone, "Social Mobility," pp. 30-32.

ideals: that of the state and that of the conjugal family, while at a later stage both were to come under challenge in their turn by a third, that of individual freedom of choice.

The modern state is a natural enemy to the values of kinship, especially among the upper classes, for kinship is a direct threat to the state's own claim to prior loyalty.[21] Kinship leads to aristocratic faction and rebellion, such as the Wars of the Roses or the Fronde, to the independence of entrenched local potentates using kin loyalties to create powerful local connections, and to making the working of the jury system of justice impossible by the subordination of objective judgment to ties of blood. In the sixteenth century, the State in England increasingly assumed monopoly powers of justice and punishment, military protection, welfare, and the regulation of property. This takeover was accompanied by a massive propaganda campaign for loyalty, inculcating the view that the first duty of every citizen is obedience to the sovereign, that man's highest obligation is to his country, involving the subordination of all other considerations and loyalties, even life itself. Medieval society had been held together by vague claims of obedience to the most powerful kinship network of all, headed by the king. Soon this royal network began seeking to exploit and to extend the powers of the central government for its own benefit. Later, however, it developed a new desire for impersonal and efficient service, and a new demand for prior obedience to the sovereign it had created. It also developed a new sense of responsibility for the welfare of those it ruled over. Early modern society was thus transformed from an association of cousins in the kin into an association of subjects to the sovereign monarch, and of citizens of the commonwealth. Rebellion against the divinely-ordained sovereign became not merely dangerous, but impious and immoral, and failed conspirators now invariably confessed the sinfulness of their actions just before their execution.[23]

The Rise of the Nuclear Family

The second major change was the rise of the nuclear family, not as a unit of cohabitation, which it had always been, but as a focus for

22. See P. Petot, "La Famille en France sous l'Ancien Regime," in *Sociologie Comparée de la Famille Contemporaine* (Paris, 1955), pp. 9-14.

23. Stone, *Crisis*, pp. 267-68.

psychological loyalty and devotion. The decline of kinship was a major cause, and also a consequence, of the rise of the nuclear family. Their movements were linked like a pair of scales. But as loyalty to kinship declined, it shifted not only inward towards the nuclear core, but also outward towards the state, whose policies and actions were to no small extent responsible for the decline of the kin. The chief instrument for forging loyalty to the new nation state of the sixteenth century was the flood of official propaganda placing greater emphasis on the need for authority and obedience. Two very important methods used to strengthen the power of the state were first the destruction of the political power of aristocratic kinship; and secondly, a deliberately fostered increase in the power of the husband and father within the conjugal unit, that is to say, a strengthening of patriarchy. As Wilhelm Reich has pointed out, "in the figure of the father, the authoritarian state has its representative in every family, so that the family becomes the most important instrument of power."[24] The rise of patriarchy in the sixteenth century also met certain functional needs of the family at that time, and conformed to certain cultural patterns peculiar to the period.

The first task is to demonstrate and explain the growth of the nuclear family as a social and psychological unit. The strengthening of family responsibilities finds ideal expression in Thomas More's *Utopia,* where family firms, family trades, family political units, and family military units are the rule, and community controls are virtually nonexistent. Whereas Plato's ideal had involved the destruction of the family, that of More involved the destruction of all other social units.[25] Among the upper landed classes, the country gentry and nobility, this growing concentration on the nuclear family is reflected in the formulation of lengthy genealogies which pay only cursory attention to collateral branches, and are mainly concerned with tracing the male line backward in time. Similarly the growing complexity of coats of arms recorded primogenitural alliances of the nuclear family, not kin connections, while the same emphasis is reflected in the increasing stress laid upon ever larger and more elaborate family tombs in the sixteenth century. It is noticeable that the family mausoleums of the period housed members of the primogenitural nuclear family from generation to generation, but only rarely adult younger children or kin relatives.

24. W. Reich, *Mass Psychology of Fascism* (New York, 1971), p. 53.
25. T. More, *Utopia,* ed. E. Surtz and J. H. Hexter (New Haven, 1965), pp. xli-xlv.

Religious Causes

This shift towards the nuclear family was given powerful support by Reformation theology and practice. The medieval Catholic ideal of chastity, as a legal obligation for priests, monks, and nuns and as an ideal for all members of the community to aspire to, was replaced by the ideal of conjugal affection. The married state now became the ethical norm for the virtuous Christian.

The demand for married love was a constant theme of Protestant sermons of the sixteenth century, which were directed to all classes in the society; it was reflected in Puritan literature of the early seventeenth century and Anglican literature of the mid-seventeenth century; and it reached a new moral level in the writings of John Milton about marriage and divorce in the 1640s.[26] Both Robert Cleaver and William Gouge, authors of two of the most popular family handbooks of their day, emphasized that the purpose of marriage was spiritual intimacy in addition to the ancient reasons of the avoidance of fornication and the procreation of children.[27] Calvin's Geneva was certainly a male-dominated society, but the ideal of the companionate marriage was stressed, women participated with their husbands in the singing of psalms, and wife-beating was discouraged. It was Archbishop Cranmer who in 1549 first added a third to the two basic reasons for marriage in the Prayer Book: "mutual society, help and comfort, that the one ought to have of the other, both in prosperity and adversity."[28]

Having repelled efforts to legalize divorce for the adultery or desertion of the wife, which was recognized by most Reformed churches abroad, the English Protestants had no alternative but to urge the importance of affective ties as a necessity for marriage, in addition to the old Pauline arguments. Although as respectful as ever of the need for social equality and economic security as prime factors in mate selection, they were nonetheless obliged to oppose the strongly commercial at-

26. W. and M. Haller, "The Puritan Art of Love," *Huntington Library Quarterly* 5 (1941-42): 235-36; L. L. Schüking, *The Puritan Family* (New York, 1970), pp. 40-50; W. Perkins, "Of Christian Oeconomie or Household Government," in *Works* (London, 1631), p. 689; J. Halkett, *Milton and the Idea of Matrimony* (New Haven, 1970), pp. 3-30.

27. R. Cleaver, *A Godly Form of Household Government* (London, 1598; imprinted by T. Creede for T. Mann), pp. 143-59; W. Gouge, *Of Domesticall Duties*, 3rd ed. (London, 1634), pp. 222-24.

28. N. Z. Davis, "City Women and Religious Change in Sixteenth Century France," in *A Sampler of Women's Studies*, ed. D. G. McGuiar (Ann Arbor, 1973), pp. 33-36; Schüking, *The Puritan Family*, p. 22.

titude to marriage which had been prevalent in the late Middle Ages and the early sixteenth century, by which bride and groom had been bought and sold without their consent. They still believed that love could and should grow only after marriage, but an important new criterion was that the couple should be able to envision such a development.[29]

In the seventeenth century this new attitude to married love found less guarded expression in secular literature, with the romantic novels of Mlle. De Scuderi, and was raised to a new plane of idealistic hyberbole by the preachers: Daniel Rogers thought that "husbands and wives should be as two sweet friends" and Jeremy Taylor declared that "the marital love is a thing pure as light, sacred as a temple, lasting as the world."[30] It is no accident that Charles I and Henrietta Maria were "the first English royal couple to be glorified as husband and wife in the domestic sense," even if this development owed as much to the rarefied cult of Neoplatonic love in Court circles as it did to the attitude of the contemporary moral theologians.[31]

It should be noted that none of these Protestant or Puritan writers were willing to carry their ideas about the spiritual nature of the marital union to the point of giving it priority over all other considerations. The nearest they came to putting the main stress on married love for its own sake, rather than as a means to the other ends of the procreation and socialization of children and the channeling of sexual appetite, was when they took their cue from the early Continental Reformers. It was Bullinger who described marriage as a union "with the good consent of them both, to the intent that they two may dwell together in friendship and honesty, one helping and comforting the other, eschewing uncleanness, and bringing up children in the fear of God." It was left to Milton to remove all other ends to marriage—children, sexual control, the state, the church—and to focus it exclusively upon the end of mutual comfort. The logical conclusion to this step was to advocate, as Milton did three hundred years ahead of his time, divorce in cases of hopeless temperamental incompatibility.[32]

In the context of the shift from a kin-oriented to a nuclear family, in which these intellectual developments are being discussed, it is essential

29. Stone, *Crisis*, pp. 594-95. See also E. Morgan, *The Puritan Family* (New York, 1966), pp. 42-54.

30. Quoted in Haller, "Puritan Art of Love," p. 269, and in Schüking, *The Puritan Family*, p. 48.

31. R. Strong, *Van Dyke: Charles I on Horseback* (London, 1972), p. 70.

32. Halkett, *Milton*, pp. 10-11, 50-55.

to note that married love has an important social function: it detaches the conjugal pair psychologically from their parents and their kin, and strengthens their independence against the latter. It helps them to form a solid alliance against parents, relatives and in-laws of all kinds, and replaces the kin as the principal support for the new marriage. This major shift in moral allegiances, well understood by the preachers who advocated married love, was frankly conceded by Cleaver: "it is a less offence [for a man] to forsake father and mother and to leave them succourless . . . than it is [for him] to do the like towards his lawful married wife." As reformulated by a modern sociologist, "the degree to which love is a usual, expected prelude to marriage is correlated with (1) the degree of free choice of mate permitted in the society, and (2) the degree to which husband-wife solidarity is the strategic solidarity of the kinship structure."[33]

The new pressures brought to bear on the English family system by Protestant preachers were not merely confined to very slowly trying to wean the propertied classes from regarding marriage as a business transaction best handled by the parents. They were also directed downward, into the lower classes, to persuade them to abandon altogether the traditional habit of consensual unions unblessed by the church. There was an earnest effort not only to ensure that upper-class marriages took place with the consent of both parties but also that all sexual unions, whether of clergy and their pre-Reformation "housekeepers" or of the poor, should now be recognized and sanctified by a formal Christian sacrament. Some tentative evidence of the success of this pressure upon the lower classes is the apparent decline in illegitimacy rates in the backward north and northwest from about 4 percent in the 1590s, before educated Protestant ministers first became available in large numbers in these areas, and about 1 1/2 percent in the mid-seventeenth century when the Puritan supremacy was at its height. Since the registered rural illegitimacy rate in the whole country was on the average only about 3 percent even in the Elizabethan period, it is clear that the practice either of consensual unions or of casual fornication followed by abandonment was relatively rare and not a common practice.[34] But the decline over the next fifty years is eloquent evidence of the success of the Protestant, and especially Puritan, ministers in

33. Ibid., p. 12; Cleaver, *Household Government,* p. 94; J. Goode, "The Theoretical Importance of Love," in R. L. Coser, *The Family: its Structure and Function* (New York, 1964), p. 217.

34. P. Laslett and K. Oosterveen, "Long-term Trends in Bastardy in England," *Population Studies* 27 (1973): 260, 274.

Christianizing the marriage practices of the poor, as well as in introducing an element of consent into those of the rich. For all members of
society—clergy, men of property, and the poor—the ideal state was
now that of marriage. But this marriage had to be arranged with the
knowledge and approval of parents, accompanied by the willing consent
of the bride and groom, and sanctified and legitimized by the church.

There were also perhaps more profound, although less easily
demonstrable, effects on the family of the change from pre-Reformation
Catholicism to Anglican Protestantism. In post-Tridentine Catholicism, the power of the priest was enhanced and his moral control over
the parishioners was reinforced by greater stress laid upon the catechism, the confession box, and the sacraments. Other Catholic organizations, apart from the parish, were the youth groups and the religious
confraternities, which persisted in urban areas for a very long time.
These were often restricted to specialized social or craft membership;
they had a high degree of social integration; and they attracted a great
deal of loyalty. For example, they offered prayers for the dead members
of the confraternity, not for the kin, as had the medieval chantry priest
or hired mass priest.[35]   )

Thus in post-Tridentine Catholic Europe, the parish, the youth
groups and the confraternity were serious competitors for loyalty with
the state, the kin, and the conjugal household. In Protestnat England,
however, the confraternities all disappeared, and there is no evidence of
organized youth groups. Furthermore, the parish tended to be replaced
by the household as the main agent for piety, prayer, and moral indoc-
trination, in part because of the failure of the Anglican Church under
Elizabeth to fulfill this urgent need, and in part because of the Puritan
stress on the household for these purposes. Even traditional parochial
festival and carnival organizations died away under the withering blast
of Puritan disapproval of such pagan relics as maypoles and churchales. The secular administrative functions of the post-Reformation
English parish increased, as a unit of taxation and of organized poor-
relief. But its social, festive, psychological, and religious functions
tended to be replaced by the household as it ceased to be the main focus
for communal activities. Similarly, the parish church ceased to be used
as the main building for a wide range of group functions. The church in

35. R. Trexler, "Ritual in Florence," *The Pursuit of Holiness in Late Medieval and
Renaissance Religion*, ed. C. Trinkhaus (Leiden, 1974), pp. 200-64; A. N. Galpern,
"Late Medieval Piety in Sixteenth Century Champagne," Ibid., pp. 141-76; N. Z. Davis,
"Some Tasks and Themes in the Study of Popular Religion," Ibid., pp. 307-36.

the past had acted as the library, the central news agency, the place for whipping unruly servants or disobedient schoolchildren, the site of political elections, and the arena for cockfighting or drinking parties for the benefit of the clergyman. All these activities were now either transferred to the home, to the inn, or to specialized buildings, or else were suppressed altogether. It was primarily the household, and secondarily the inn, which were the main beneficiaries of this transfer of functions.[36]

In terms of religious and moral functions, the transfer is very clear. Attendance on service in church remained a formal Sunday obligation, but devotional piety shifted to the daily attendance at family prayers; moral control by the priest was partially replaced by moral direction by the head of the household; church catechisms were partially replaced by catechisms for the household, about a hundred of which were published between 1550 and 1600 alone. Edward Dering's popular *Catechism* was described by its author as "very needful to be known to all householders whereby they may better teach and instruct their families in such points of Christian religion as is most meet."[37] In the more pious households, husbands and wives would mutually confess their own or their partner's sins to each other at home, rather than to a priest in church.[38] In many other cases the private diary was the substitute for the confession box, although the forgiveness of the latter is much easier on human frailty than the self-torture of the former. The Protestant ideal, as described by Robert Cawdrey in 1600, was that each family head should have "a church in his house."[39] In towns in southern England, the Bible was now available in most upper and middle and even lower-middle class homes, and public readings from it by the head of the household replaced the ritual of the Sacrament in the church as the main vehicle of religious expression.[40] At the risk of oversimplification,

36. N. Z. Davis, "The Reasons of Misrule: Youth Groups and Charivaris in Sixteenth Century France," *Past and Present* 50 (1971): 42-43; T. Barnes, "County Politics and a Puritan Cause Célèbre: Somerset Churchales," *Transactions of the Royal Historical Society*, 5th Series, vol. 9 (London, 1959), p. 103-22; C. Hill, "The Secularization of the Parish," in his *Society and Puritanism in Pre-Revolutionary England* (London, 1964), ch. 12.

37. C. Hill, "The Spiritualization of the Household," *Society and Puritanism*, ch. 13; H. S. Bennett, *English Books and Readers, 1558-1603* (Cambridge, 1965), pp. 147-48.

38. Schüking, *The Puritan Family*, p. 41.

39. Quoted by C. Russell, "Arguments for Religious Unity in England 1530-1650," *Journal of Ecclesiastical History* 18 (1967): 208.

40. I owe the information about bible ownership to a study of inventories of Kentish townsfolk by Mr. Peter Clark.

it could be said that Reformation Protestantism was a religion of literacy, domestic prayer, and the family book in the family home, whereas Counter-Reformation Catholicism was a religion of visual display, public ritual, and the sacred image or relic in the holy place.

Sir George Sondes certainly made his family and servants attend church services twice on Sundays. But "all the week after, it was my constant course to pray with my family, once if not twice every day; and if I had not a [chaplain] in my house, I performed the office myself." As for Sir Nathaniel Barnardiston, "towards his children he executed the office of an heavenly father to their souls . . . and many times he would take them into his closet and there pray over them and for them."[41] In the high Anglican household of Sir Christopher Wandesford, apparently in the 1630s when he was master of the Rolls in Ireland, there were family prayers three times a day, at 6 A.M., 10 A.M., and 9 P.M. After his death, the widow would assemble her children every day before breakfast to pray together and read or repeat psalms and chapters of the Bible, after which the children knelt to receive their parent's blessing.[42] In this all-enveloping atmosphere of domestic piety, in many gentry homes and probably also bourgeois homes, the household had clearly replaced the parish, and the father the priest.

This general tendency was carried a stage further by the Puritans, who tended to elevate a select few chosen for their godliness. This selectivity thrust the burden of maintaining piety back onto the household, and the end product might well be a separated church constructed from the voluntary association of a group of godly families. Although this outcome was not visible at first, the essence of Puritanism was a family church, and this implication of its drive for purity is clear to us today.[43] Since all could not aspire to these heights of godliness, the religious unit would inevitably tend to cease to be the parish, embracing all who lived in a geographical area, whether saints or sinners, and would become a collection of private, self-selected families, drawn from any level of social class, but in practice mostly at the yeoman, husbandman, artisan, and tradesman level, with some gentry leadership at the top.

Whether in Anglican or Puritan households, there was, in varying

41. Quoted by A. Everett, "The County Community," in *The English Revolution, 1600-1660,* ed., E. W. Ives (London, 1968), pp. 55-56.

42. *Autobiography of Mrs. Alice Thornton,* Publication of the Surtees Society, vol. 62, (1875), p. vii.

43. Morgan, *The Puritan Family,* pp. 135-39.

degrees, a new emphasis on the home and on domestic virtues, and this was perhaps the most far-reaching consequence of the Reformation in England. The household was the inheritor of much of the responsibilities of the parish and the church, the family head was the inheritor of much of the authority and powers of the priest. The transubstantiated Host, carefully preserved at the east end of the church, was replaced by the Holy Bible on a lectern in the hall or kept in a bible-box. It was a book which also, significantly enough, often served at all levels of society to record the family genealogy.[44] Thus the Word of God was removed from the parish church and transferred to the private home; the Holy Spirit was domesticated.

Economic Causes

The second level of explanation for the rise of the nuclear family is that there was a significant erosion of community controls over the economic activities of the family unit. There took place a general shift of control of private property to the patriarchal family, consequent upon the decline of the influence of village custom, kin advice, and aristocratic patronage pressure via clientage. As enclosure of the open fields and common lands developed, and as English rural society increasingly became a three-tiered structure of landlords, wealthy leasehold farmers with a fair degree of security of tenure, and landless laborers, so manorial courts and the custom of the manor which they had administered withered away. The result was the transfer from the village community to the individual farmer of a whole range of economic decisions which had hitherto been decided collectively. The family could now determine when and what to plant, when to harvest, and how to rotate the crops. At the same time the putting-out system in cloth manufacture and the development of home industry, particularly spinning, actually strengthened the family as an economic unit of production by making the home the place of work and by providing employment there for wives and children.

Finally, the slow rise of a force of landless laborers and cottagers, which developed throughout the sixteenth, seventeenth and eighteenth centuries, meant the growth of a group of persons whose only ties to their employer were the strictly economic ones of the wage earner to the man who pays him. These new poor lacked the paternal ties of the land-

---

44. In Kentish towns in the early seventeenth century, four out of five males who left inventories owned a Bible, usually kept in the hall, study, or parlor. (I owe this information to Mr. Peter Clark).

lord to his tenants or the farmer to his living-in servants. Once again, the bonds tying the individual to intermediate institutions or patrons were weakened, and those to his family consequently increased.

Another important cause of the decline of community controls over property was the very high level of geographical mobility that existed even at the village level in the sixteenth and seventeenth centuries. The spirit of *gemeinschaft,* a sense of collective responsibility for individual actions and behavior, inevitably declined as the village increasingly became a collection of transients, with only a central core of stable families remaining to provide some continuity.[45]

Thirdly, the rise of literacy, perhaps to as high as 30 to 40 percent for adult males by 1640, was opening men's eyes to a wider world beyond the confines of the village.[46] Meanwhile aristocratic clientage, both political and social, was on the decline, although it certainly remained as a key factor in English politics in the sixteenth century and as an important one well into the nineteenth century. But the increasing cost of elections after 1660 meant that voters had more and more to be wooed or bribed rather than merely told what to do, as they had been before, while the astonishing expansion of the electorate in the seventeenth century was evidence of a wide extension of political participation. The fierce party struggles in the late seventeenth and early eighteenth centuries stimulated independent thought and created a politically very sophisticated electorate.[47] At the same time, kin control over marriage, which was so critical a determinant of the movement of property, was on the decline.

In the towns the same process was at work as the craft guilds and religious confraternities, which had played so important a part in urban life in the Middle Ages, progressively withered away. Later on in the seventeenth century, the urban electors established their political independence from noble or gentry clients—if only in order to be able to sell their votes to the highest bidder. Increasingly, therefore, decisions first about the disposal of private property and then about political power fell under the more or less exclusive control of the patriarchal nuclear family as the ancient controls of custom, community, kin, and the pa-

45. See above, fn. 20.

46. L. Stone, "Social Mobility in England, 1550-1700," *Past and Present* 33 (1966): 29-36. L. Stone, "Literacy and Education in England, 1640-1900," *Past and Present* 42 (1969): 98-112.

47. J. H. Plumb, "The Growth of the Electorate in England from 1600 to 1715," *Past and Present* 45 (1969): 90-116.

tron fell away. The first beneficiary of this shift of power was the head of the household, and only later did the individuals who composed the family assert their rights to share this new authority for their own benefit.

Reinforcement of Patriarchy

Parallel to, and part consequence of, this enhancement of the importance of the conjugal family and the household, was an increase in authoritarianism in internal power relationships: an increase, that is to say, in patriarchy. Before discussing this development, it should be noted that patriarchy in its ideal type, which flourished on the southern and eastern shores of the Mediterranean, was never present in England in more than a much attenuated form. If one defines patriarchy as a Weberian ideal type, it has the following characteristics. In terms of power relationships, the man rides to work on a donkey or mule—if he goes to work at all—while the wife follows behind on foot with the heavy tools. The husband is legally and morally free to beat his wife, although not to the point of maiming or murder. A wife has no right whatever to dispose of her own property, and all she owns passes to her husband on marriage. A wife serves the husband and eldest son at the table, but rarely sits down with them. In terms of sex, male adultery is a venial sin, female adultery an unpardonable crime. Female premarital chastity is a matter of family honor, unmarried girls are always chaperoned, and seducers are killed. Marriages are arranged by the fathers without consulting the wishes of the bride or groom. A wife provides the sexual services demanded by her husband, but is not herself expected to achieve orgasm in sexual intercourse. In religion, the Virgin Mary is the most venerable symbol of worship, and women create a female church culture of their own, being the main supporters of and attenders at church. Priests are celibate and visit the homes by day.[48]

It is obvious from this description that at no time, so far as we know, did England conform fully to this ideal, which was present only in a very modified form. In the sixteenth century, however, there are clear signs of a strengthening of paternal authority in the family. For a time,

48. E. P. Thompson, "Rough Music: 'Le Charivari Anglais'," *Annales* 27 (1972): 302.

49. Stone, *Crisis,* pp. 178-80.

the powers of fathers over children and of husbands over wives were both strengthened.

A legal change, which probably had little to do with this trend, nonetheless powerfully reinforced it. During the Middle Ages control over landed property through entail meant that the head of the family was no more than a life tenant of the estates, with little freedom to dispose of them at his pleasure. In the late fifteenth century, the lawyers found a way to break entails without too much difficulty, and some confusing legislation of the 1530s had the result of still further widening the breach. This greatly strengthened the ability of the current head of the family to dispose of the property as he chose, although it also greatly weakened his capacity to prevent his heir from doing the same thing.[49] He could now quite easily either sell land to meet current needs or split it up amongst his children as he thought fit. The increase in this freedom of action of the current owner meant an increase in his capacity to punish or reward his children or siblings. Thus it meant the further subordination of the children, including the heir, to the father, and of younger sons and daughters to their elder brother if he inherited the estate before they were married.

It would be wrong to assume that this major transformation in the disposal of property within the family flowed from specific feats of ingenuity performed by certain lawyers. After all, lawyers strive to please their clients, and the root cause of the changes must therefore lie in changing attitudes towards family responsibility held by different generations of landed proprietors. To account for these changes, one is compelled to enter into the realm of speculation. There can be little doubt that the landed classes of the late fifteenth and early sixteenth centuries underwent a severe crisis of confidence: their medieval military functions were eroded, but nothing else was available to take the place of these functions as a justification for the landowners' enormous wealth and power. They first threw themselves into a romantic revival of the ancient chivalric ideal, but that was too brittle to sustain the weight placed upon it, and it soon collapsed.[50]

The reckless alienation of property by the great old families at this period can be explained in part as a reaction to the takeover of many of their functions by state-appointed lesser men, and to the frustration and sense of despair this loss of power engendered. Many other late

50. See A. B. Ferguson, *The Indian Summer of English Chivalry* (Durham, N. C., 1960), *passim*.

sixteenth century landowners were new men, recently risen upon the
ruins of church property, who had not had time to develop a mystique
about the sanctity of the family estates, and who therefore felt free to
alienate them, either to provide for their younger children or to support
current consumption. There can be no doubt that these generations
faced severe problems about the disposition of younger sons, since so
few job openings were available. The military career was very insecure,
since there were long intervals of peace and no standing army. The law
was mostly occupied by elder sons, positions in the post-Reformation
church were now despised, and the state bureaucracy was very small
with hardly any local offices at all. Since openings in the professions
were so scarce, the best—indeed in many cases the only—way to
provide for surplus sons seemed to be to settle upon them a portion of
the family estates, so that they could continue to support the life style of
minor gentry. All these explanations are plausible, but all that we know
is the fact that the more flexible legal arrangements considerably
increased the power of the head of the household over his children, and
to a lesser extent over his wife. He could now not only bribe them with
promises of more; he could threaten them with total exclusion from the
inheritance.

Parents and Children

During the period from 1500 to 1660 there is overwhelming evidence
of a fierce determination to break the will of the child, and to enforce his
utter subjection to the authority of his elders and superiors, and most
noticeably of his parents. The first pastor of Plymouth, Massachusetts,
was only reflecting current ideas when he observed that "there is in all
children . . . a stubbornness and stoutness of mind, arising from
natural pride, which must in the first place be broken and beaten
down." "Children should not know, if it could be kept from them, that
they have a will of their own."[51] In other words, in the seventeenth
century the early training of children was directly equated with the
breaking in of young horses or hunting dogs.

In the Middle Ages, schools had used physical punishment to enforce
discipline, and the characteristic equipment of a schoolmaster was not
so much a book as a rod or a bundle of birch twigs. The emblem of
Grammar on Chartres cathedral porch is is a master threatening two
children with a scourge; at Oxford University the conferral of the
degree of Master of Grammar was accompanied by presentation of a

51. S. Katz, *Colonial America* (Boston, 1971), p. 130n.

birch as symbol of office and by the ceremonial flogging of a whipping boy by the new Master.[52] But only an infinitesimal minority was subjected to such discipline in the Middle Ages, since so few undertook the study of Latin grammar, and those who did were presumably highly motivated to learn. Moreover, even in the schools, at any rate in France, there is a good deal of evidence to show that many punishments took the form of fines. It was only in the fifteenth century that flogging began normally to be substituted for fines, and then it was confined to the poor who could not pay the fines (and who were thought socially suitable for physical punishment) and to the very young boys.[53]

In the early sixteenth century, three things happened. The first is that flogging became the standard routine method of punishment for all schoolchildren, regardless of rank or age; the second was that a far larger proportion of the population began to go to school, and therefore became liable to this discipline; thirdly, since education became more widespread, many were now poorly motivated to learn, and therefore more liable to be beaten to force them to do it. Moreover, in the sixteenth century severe physical punishment was practiced in the home, the school, and even the University as a matter of principle and practice. To what extent the greater evidence of this brutality in the sixteenth century school is a reflection of a harsher reality, or merely of a larger and more revealing body of written records, is very hard to say. For the moment the evidence suggests that both played their part, that conditions were certainly extremely brutal and authoritarian in the sixteenth and seventeenth century home and school, but that the deterioration from the late medieval period may be exaggerated by the differences in the amount and nature of the evidence. All that can be said is that whipping was now so normal a part of a child's experience that when a late seventeenth century moral theologian wished to convey to children some idea of Hell, the best way he could think of describing it was as "a terrible place, that is worse a thousand times than whipping. God's anger is worse than your father's anger."[54]

Scholastic punishments normally took two forms. The first and most common was to lay the child over a bench, or alternatively to horse him on the back of a companion, and to flog his naked buttocks with a

52. H. A. Rashdall, *The Universities of Europe in the Middle Ages,* ed. F. M. Powicke and A. B. Emden (Oxford, 1936), 3: 347, 358.

53. P. Ariès, *Centuries of Childhood* (New York, 1965), pp. 257-58.

54. J. Janeway, *A Token for Children: being an Exact Account of the Conversion, Holy and Exemplary Lives and Joyfull Deaths of Several Young Children* (London, 1671; reprint ed., Boston, 1781), p. ii.

bundle of birches until the blood flowed. The second was to strike his hand with a ferule, a flat piece of wood which expanded at the end into a pear shape with a hole in the middle. One blow with this instrument was enough to raise a most painful blister.

There can be no doubt whatever that severe flogging was a normal and daily occurrence in the sixteenth and seventeenth century grammar school, and some of the most famous headmasters of their day, like Dr. Busby of Westminster School or Dr. Gill of St. Paul's, were notorious for their savagery. Indeed, some of them seem to have been pathological sadists, and John Aubrey's account of Dr. Gill's "whipping-fits" suggests a man who had become the slave to an irrational obsession. But what is significant is that society was willing to give him a free hand without censure or restraint, since flogging was then regarded as the only reliable method of controlling both children and adults.[55]

It seems likely that institutionalized brutality was standard in public schools and grammar schools, but varied from master to master in the countless small private schools run by clergymen for a handful of local children and boarders in the seventeenth century. Some were virtual prison camps run by sadists, while others were models of compassion and understanding. But these latter cases, when they are mentioned in the records, are always described as exceptions to the rule. Thus Simonds D'Ewes records that he was never flogged by his London schoolmaster Henry Reynolds, explaining that,

> *he had a pleasing way of teaching, contrary to all others of that kind. For the rod and the ferula stood in his school rather as ensigns of his power than as instruments of his anger, and were rarely made use of for the punishment of delinquents. For he usually rewarded those who deserved well . . . . and he accounted the primitive punishment of not rewarding the remiss and negligent equipolent to the severest correction.*[56]

Despite this kindly treatment, D'Ewes asked to be removed to Bury Grammar School, since he did not think that Reynolds' learning was sufficiently deep for him. But D'Ewes was an exceptionally diligent and able student, always one of the best in the class, and as such was presumably normally free of the ferocious punishments meted out to his more dim-witted or idle companions.

The extension of flogging even reached into university education. During the late sixteenth century the colleges of Oxford and Cambridge

55. J. Aubrey, *Brief Lives*, ed. A. Powell (London, 1949), pp. 277-82.

56. *Autobiography and Correspondence of Sir Simonds D'Ewes* (London, 1845), 1:63-64.

had received for the first time a huge influx of sons of the wealthy laity, for whom the accomodations had been greatly enlarged. The key feature of the sixteenth century college was the application to lay children of the strict, prison-like conditions previously applied to regular clergy in monasteries and colleges. This was the time when the college assumed its now familiar function of acting *in loco parentis,* with all the aids of high walls, gates closed at 9 P.M., and strict internal surveillance by the tutors. This was also the time, between 1450 and 1660, when colleges freely used physical punishments on their younger students, normally, but not always, under the age of eighteen, either by public whippings in the hall or over a barrel in the buttery, or else by putting them in stocks in the hall. By the medieval statutes of Balliol and Lincoln colleges, the college head had powers of physical punishment, but in the sixteenth century this authority was greatly extended, and delegated to deans and even tutors.[57] Aubrey, who entered Oxford in 1642, noted that there "the rod was frequently used by the tutors and deans on his pupils, till Bachelors of Arts."[58]

It should be emphasized that this widespread and constant use of flogging as the prime method of spreading a knowledge of the classics was the last thing that the Humanist educational reformers had in mind when they pressed for a classical training of the European elite. From Guarino to Vives to Erasmus they were, without exceptions, opposed to the use of severe physical punishments. They believed that children could and should be enticed into the classics, not driven like cattle. But what happened in practice was that hard-pressed schoolmasters continued and extended the medieval tradition of flogging on an ever increasing scale as classical education spread, since it was the easiest and least troublesome means of drilling Latin grammar into thick or resistant skulls. Renaissance school practice thus bore no relation whatever to Renaissance educational theory: the subject matter was identical, but the method of instruction was in substantial contradiction.

This extension of the use of physical punishment throughout the

57. G. M. Edward, *Sidney Sussex College, Cambridge* (London, 1899), pp. 29, 67; A. Gray, *Jesus College, Cambridge* (London, 1902), p. 93; H. P. Stokes, *Corpus Christi College, Cambridge* (London, 1898), pp. 95, 108; A. Clark, *Lincoln College, Oxford* (London, 1898), pp. 69, 208; C. H. Cooper, *Annals of Cambridge* (Cambridge, 1842-53), 2: 277; H. L. Thompson, *Christ Church, Oxford* (London, 1900), pp. 75, 133; H. W. C. Davis, *Balliol College, Oxford* (London, 1899), pp. 36, 58; W. C. Coston, *St. John's College Oxford,* Oxford Historical Society, new series, vol. 12 (Oxford, 1958), pp. 4, 130; C. Wordsworth, *Social Life and the English Universities in the Eighteenth Century* (Cambridge, 1874), p. 441.

58. J. Aubrey, *Brief Lives,* ed. A. L. Dick (Ann Arbor, 1962), pp. xxiii-iv.

whole educational system merely reflected a growing use of this method of social control throughout the society. A late sixteenth century Dutchman—appropriately enough called Batty—who was rapidly translated into English, developed the theory that the providence and wisdom of God had especially formed the human buttocks so that they could be severely beaten without incurring serious bodily injury.[59] The late sixteenth and early seventeenth centuries was for England the great flogging age: every town and every village had its whipping post, which was in constant use as a means of preserving social order.

Children were particularly singled out for harsh treatment, and John Aubrey in the late seventeenth century could reflect that in his youth, parents "were as severe to their children as their schoolmasters; and their schoolmasters as masters of the House of Correction. . . . . Fathers and mothers slashed their daughters in time of their besom discipline when they were perfect women." As a result, "the child perfectly loathed the sight of his parents as the slave his torturer."[60] Aubrey was clearly exaggerating, but his remarks are significant since he is contrasting this period in the past to the more amiable relations that he thought prevailed when he was writing in the late seventeenth century. In France, Pierre Charron also spoke of the "almost universal" custom of "beating, whipping, abusing and scolding children, and holding them in great fear and subjection."[61]

One case in which this disciplinary process in the home can be followed in great detail is that of the young son and heir of King Henri IV of France, the future Louis XIII. The child was first whipped at the age of two, and the punishments continued (usually for obstinancy) after he became king at the age of nine. He was whipped on the buttocks with a birch or a switch, administered first by his nurse immediately upon waking on the morning after the transgression. The whippings increased in frequency when he was three, and on one occasion his father whipped him himself when in a rage with his son. As he grew older, his nurse could not control him, and the child was held down by soldiers while she beat him. At the age of ten he still had nightmares of being whipped, and the threats to whip him only stopped in 1614, not long before his marriage.[62] If this was the treatment meted out to a

---

59. B. Batty, *The Christian Man's Closet* (London, 1581), p. 26 (quoted by Schüking, *The Puritan Family*, p. 75).

60. J. Aubrey, *Brief Lives*, ed. A. Powell, p. 11.

61. D. Hunt, *Parents and Children in History* (New York, 1970), p. 134.

62. Ibid., pp. 133-35, 147-49, 156.

future and even reigning king in the early seventeenth century, on the instructions of his father, it is clear that Aubrey and Charron were describing a harsh reality about late sixteenth and early seventeenth century domestic relations between parents and children in the home.

This stress on domestic discipline and the utter subordination of the child found expression in extraordinary outward marks of deference which English children were expected to pay to their parents. They had to kneel before their parents to ask their blessing, perhaps one or two times a day, a practice John Donne believed to be unique in Europe. The children of the widowed Lady Alice Wandesford in the 1640s knelt daily to ask her blessing, and in 1651 her twenty-eight-year-old eldest son knelt for her blessing before leaving on a journey. Even as adults, children were expected to keep their hats off in their parents' presence, while daughters were expected to remain standing in their mother's presence. "Gentlemen of thirty and forty years old," recalled Aubrey, "were to stand like mutes and fools bareheaded before their parents; and the daughters (grown women) were to stand at the cupboard-side during the whole time of their proud mother's visit, unless (as the fashion was) leave was desired, forsooth, that a cushion should be given to them to kneel upon, . . . after they had done sufficient penance by standing." Well into his middle age Sir Dudley North "would never put on his hat or sit down before his father unless enjoined to it." Elizabeth Countess of Falkland always knelt in her mother's presence, despite the fact that she had married above her parents into the peerage.[63] In the early seventeenth century, a son, even when grown up, would commonly address his father in a letter as "sir," and sign himself "your humble obedient son," "your son in continuance of all obedience" or your most obedient and loving son."[64] As late as the 1680s, Edmund Verney as an undergraduate at Oxford cautiously began his letters home with "Most honoured father . . ." while those he received began with the peremptory word "Child."[65]

63. E.g., letters of Thomas Legh to his father Sir Peter Legh in 1619 (Brasenose College MSS, Legh transcripts). Schüking, *The Puritan Family*, p. 73; Stone, *Crisis*, pp. 591-92; *Autobiography of Mrs. Alice Thornton*, pp. vii, 64; Aubrey, *Brief Lives*, ed. A. Powell, p. 11; Stone, *Crisis*, p. 592; I. Pinchbeck and M. Hewitt, *Children in English Society* (London, 1969), 1: 18-19.

64. E.g., Brasenose College MSS, Legh transcripts; *Wentworth Papers, 1597-1628*, ed. J. P. Cooper, Publication of the Surtees Society, 4th Series, vol. 12 (1973), pp. 48-51, 57.

65. *Memoirs of the Verney Family in the Seventeenth Century*, ed. F. P. and M. M. Verney (London, 1907), 2: 417.

A New England book of etiquette of 1715, which copied English works of the previous century, had the following advice to offer to children in the home:

1. *Make a bow always when you come home, and be immediately uncovered.*
2. *Be never covered at home, especially before thy parents or strangers.*
3. *Never sit in the presence of thy parents without bidding, tho' no stranger be present.*
4. *If thou passest by thy parents and any place where thou seest them, . . . bow towards them.*
   . . . . . .
6. *Never speak to thy parents without some title of respect, viz.: Sir, Madam, etc.*
7. *Approach near thy parents at no time without a bow.*
8. *Dispute not nor delay to obey thy parent's commands.*[66]

The evidence suggests an increased subordination of children to parents and a greater degree of severity adopted in their upbringing in the sixteenth century. Paradoxically enough, this was the first result of a greater interest in children. So long as no one cared about them very much, they could be left to run wild, or in the hands of nurse, servants and tutors. But the Protestant drive for moral reformation brought with it an increasing concern for the sinfulness of children. A movement which had begun a century earlier with the Italian renaissance, as a glorification of the purity and innocence of the child, was twisted in its northern transplantation into a deadly fear of the liability of children to corruption and sin, particularly those cardinal sins of pride and disobedience. Richard Allestree was merely repeating the conventional wisdom of a century of Calvinist moral theology when he wrote in 1676 that "the new-born babe is full of the stains and pollutions of sin, which it inherits from our first parents through our loins."[67]

This being the case, the solution was clear, and as early as the 1520s William Tyndale gave children forewarning of what was in store for them: "if thou wilt not obey, as at His commandment, then are we charged to correct thee, yea and if thou repent not and amend thyself, God shall slay thee by his officers and punish thee everlastingly." Calvin had decreed the death penalty as the punishment for disobedience to parents, and in the 1640's both Connecticut and Massachusetts turned the precept into legislation, although so far as is known

---

66. R. H. Bremner, *Children and Youth in America* (Cambridge, Mass., 1970), 1: 33.
67. R. Allestree, *The Whole Duty of Man* (London, 1676). p. 20.

no child was ever executed for this crime. In Connecticut, the magistrates were authorized in 1647 to commit a child to the House of Correction on complaint from his parents about "any stubborn or rebellious carriage," while Massachussetts imposed the death penalty for any child over sixteen who "shall curse or smite their natural father or mother," or refuse to obey their orders.[68]

Parents were advised that the only way for them to enforce their authority was to avoid any hint of friendliness towards the child. "Bow down his neck while he is young," recommended Thomas Becon in his catechism of 1560, "and beat him on his sides while he is a child, lest he wax stubborn and be disobedient unto thee, and so bring sorrow to thy heart." In the newly sanctified conjugal marriage, the duty of the wife and mother was to assist her husband in the task of the repression of their children. She "holds not his hand from due strokes, but bares their skins with delight to his fatherly stripes."[69] One theory has it that this obsession with childish "stubbornness" or "obstinacy" was caused by the personal insecurity of the parents in a hierarchical society; that there existed in all pre-modern societies a constant tension between the insubordination of the will of the individual and the pressing need for social order. According to this theory, parents were determined to break the wills of their children since their own wills were constantly being subordinated to those of others.[70] It is perfectly true that in the hierarchical, deferential society of early modern Europe, men and women were constantly obliged to emphasize their subordination to superiors by overt marks of respect, particularly the removing of their hats in their presence. Conversely, they constantly asserted their superiority over inferiors by insisting on identical marks of respect and obedience from those below them. It was indeed an authoritarian society in which the free expression of the will was not to be tolerated. Since all authoritarian societies depend on authoritarian child-rearing practices, early modern England was no exception to the rule.

The cause of this passion for crushing the will of the child went deeper than this, however, since it was applied with particular emphasis to the social elite, including kings. It was at the most elite public schools like Eton and Westminster that flogging was at its most fe-

68. Schüking, *The Puritan Family*, p. 73; Bremner, *Youth in America*, 1: 37-38; A. W. Calhoun, *Social History of the American Family* (New York, 1945), 1: 47, 120-21.

69. Batty, *The Christian Man's Closet*, p. 209. Quoted in Schüking, *The Puritan Family*, p. 75.

70. Hunt, *Parents and Children*, pp. 153-58.

rocious—and where it has lasted longest, even into our own day. The instructions given by Henri IV about the treatment of his son and heir were clear and explicit:

> *I wish and command you to whip him every time that he is obstinate or mis-behaves, knowing well for myself that there is nothing in the world which will be better for him than that. I know it from experience, having myself profited, for when I was his age I was often whipped. That is why I want you to whip him and to make him understand why.*[71]

The motivation in whipping a future king was clearly not to teach deference in a deferential society, since he was destined to become the apex of the pyramid.

Another theory has it that the process was a cyclical one related to in-dividual psychology. "Fathers whipped their sons for their own good because they themselves were whipped as children. These fathers had been thwarted in their own infantile efforts to be autonomous," leaving them with "a pervasive sense of shame and doubt."[72] But there is absolutely no evidence that Henri IV himself suffered from any such feelings; he seems to have been the very epitome of the well-adjusted, dynamic and commanding extrovert personality. Moreover, such an explanation blocks off any possibility of change, since each successive generation is automatically obliged, by the very fact of its own child-hood experience, to impose the same experience on its children. And yet there were to be very significant changes over time in the eighteenth century in this very area of the enforcement on the young child of obedience to superiors.

There is undoubtedly some little truth in these explanations of highly repressive child-rearing practices, based on modern theories of ego-psychology, but it is essential for a fuller understanding to dig deeper into the particular values of the specific historical culture. The first of these was the firm belief in the innate sinfulness of children, which has already been discussed; and the second was the particular need for filial obedience dictated by the social aspirations of the propertied classes in the early modern period. The whole story of the dauphin's relations with Henri IV show that what the latter was particularly determined to enforce was obedience to the will of himself, the father. It was this that he was so anxious should be forcibly impressed upon his son. It was an obedience which began in little things, but was planned to lead to

71. Ibid., p. 135.
72. Ibid., p. 157.

obedience in big ones. In the case of Louis, this obedience concerned one critical decision only, but in the cases of most children who were not heirs to great titles and estates, it concerned not one but two.

The principal justification for these extraordinary measures taken to break the child's will at an early stage was that he would accept with passive resignation later on the decisions of his parents in the two most important choices of any man's life, that of an occupation and more especially that of a marriage partner. It was the parents who decided, with the interests of the family primarily in mind, who a child was to marry and whether he was to be trained for the church, the law, trade, or some other occupation. When Sir Peter Legh forced his younger son Thomas to adopt a clerical career in 1619-22, against repeated objections and declarations of a total lack of vocational interest, all the young man could do was to write acidly to his father that "I . . . . trust you have begged of God, together with my consent unto your will, his acceptance of my weak endeavors and performances."[73]

This was not an exceptional case, for in upper-class circles it was the father who decided while they were still children which of the younger sons should be educated at the university to enter the church, which should learn Latin and go on to the Inns of Court to become a lawyer, and which should be apprenticed in London to become a merchant. Each case involved long planning ahead and a heavy financial investment, and once begun there was no turning back. The only children of this class who were free were those who were trained for nothing in particular, and were left to make their own way in the world as best they could.

The choice of marriage partner was even more critical than the choice of a career, especially in a society where divorce was unknown. In the early sixteenth century, marriages among the landed classes were normally strictly controlled by the parents, with little or no freedom of choice allowed to the children, especially the daughters. Noblemen and gentlemen made arrangements for the marriages of their children in their wills, and contracts by which children were bartered like cattle were still being made by squires in the more backward North right up to the end of the sixteenth century. Thus in 1558 Michael Wentworth specified in his will that "if any of my daughters will not be advised by

73. Brasenose College MSS, Legh transcripts; *History of Northumberland,* issued under the direction of the Northumberland County history committees, 15 vols. (Newcastle, 1893-1940 in progress), 4: 415.

my executors, but of their own fantastical brain bestow themselves
lightly upon a light person," then that daughter was to have only sixty-
six pounds instead of the one hundred pounds which was promised to
the obedient. This was powerful posthumous economic blackmail.
Further down the social scale, even more dictatorial terms were being
set at an even later date. In his will of 1599, William Shaftoe curtly decreed: "To my daughter Margery, 60 sheep, and I bestow her in marriage upon Edward, son of Reynold Shaftoe of Thockerington." When
high politics were at stake, extreme measures were sometimes resorted
to; and it is alleged that in the early seventeenth century, Sir Edward
Coke, the ex-Chief Justice, not only abducted his daughter by force from
her mother, but also had her "tied to a bed-post and severely whipped,"
in order to force her consent to marriage with the mentally unstable
brother of the Duke of Buckingham, a maneuver that was designed to
restore her father's lost favor at Court.[74]

It is significant that up to 1640 the landed classes continued to
endure, although with increasing discontent, the practice of wardship,
by which the marriages of young fatherless heirs of landed property
were put up for sale by the crown. The Court of Wards was tolerated as
long as the society upon which it preyed had itself little respect for individual freedom of choice, and its own children with as little
consideration for personal feelings as did the Court itself. Thus in 1567
the first Lord Rich made provision in his will for his illegitimate son
Richard. He directed his executors to purchase from the crown "one
woman ward or some other woman" with an estate of two hundred
pounds a year clear "for a marriage . . . to the said Richard." If
Richard were to refuse the girl, he lost all inheritance, for the executors
were then "to sell the said ward . . . to the uttermost advantage." The
possibility that the girl ward might refuse Richard clearly did not cross
Lord Rich's mind. It was not until a century later that the Court of
Wards was finally abolished, due in part at least to a growth of the
sentiment expressed by the political radical James Harrington:
"whereas it is a mischief beyond any that we can do to our enemies, we
make nothing of breaking the affections of our children." He thought
that the time had come to have the same "care of our own breed, in
which we have been curious, as to our dogs and horses."[75]

74. *North Country Wills,* Publication of the Surtees Society, vol. 116 (1908), 1: 246;
Stone, *Crisis,* p. 595, 596. For a late sixteenth-century restatement of absolute parental
authority, see J. Stockwood, *A. Bartholomew Fairing for Parentes . . . . shewing that
Children are not to marrie without consent of their Parentes* (London, 1589).

75. Prerogative Court of Canterbury, 12 Babington. See also, Stone, *Crisis,* pp. 600-4.
J. Harrington, *Oceana,* ed. H. Morley (London, 1887), p. 115.

In the sixteenth and early seventeenth centuries, there must have been many cases like that of Henry Martin, the son of a prominent and wealthy judge—but few with such shattering incidental consequences. "His father found out a rich wife for him, whom he married something unwillingly. He was a great lover of pretty girls, to whom he was so liberal that he spent the greatest part of his estate . . . . He lived from his wife a long time." Aubrey, who tells the story, attributed Martin's deep hatred of Charles I to an encounter with the prudish king in Hyde Park one day, when Charles said loudly, " 'Let that ugly rascal be gone out of the park, that whoremaster.' . . . . So Henry went away patiently, but it lay stored up deep in his heart." During the Civil War, Martin became a radical opponent of the king and was one of the judges who signed Charles' death warrant, for which act he later paid with a sentence of life imprisonment.[76]

In the seventeenth century, the control of marriage extended beyond that of parents over children to that of patrons over clients. Thus when in 1678 the Rev. William Butterfield asked Sir Ralph Verney for his dead father's living of Middle Claydon, Sir Ralph temporized, "desiring first to see him married." Having no one particularly in mind, the young man consulted his patron, who recommended a Miss Sarah Lovett. William obediently "goes a-wooing might and main to Mrs. Lovett," and in the end won both the wife and the living.[77] In a society where premarital love was both dangerous and unnecessary, such authoritarian dispositions often met with remarkably little opposition. Marriage was a business matter, like most other acts in life, in which the wishes of the powerful were naturally to be obeyed, and in many cases were neither resisted nor even resented.

The one escape from the control of parents was on the not infrequent occasions when the father died before his son had married. If he was an heir to the estate, the son was then more or less free to suit himself. Thus in 1624, long after his father's death, Sir Thomas Wentworth decided to court Arabella, the sixteen-year-old daughter of the Earl of Clare. "He grew passionately in love with her after his first acquaintance, insomuch that for 3 or 4 months before they were married, he missed not 3 days from being most part of the afternoons in her company."[78] Even girls were freed by the death of both their parents. When the nineteen-year-old orphan Mary Abell was being wooed by the enighboring Verneys for their son Edmund, mainly with a view to

76. Aubrey, *Brief Lives*, ed. A. L. Dick, pp. 213-14.
77. *Memoirs of the Verney Family in the Seventeenth Century*, 2: 307.
78. *Wentworth Papers, 1597-1628*, p. 324.

uniting the two estates, it was reported that she "is resolved to marry where she thinks she may live happy, and if there be a liking between the young folk, it may be a match."[79]

Filial obedience in the sixteenth and seventeenth centuries was not limited to the choice of career and marriage partner, but extended into all spheres of life, including education. In 1685 Edmund Verney wrote furiously to his nineteen-year-old eldest son Ralph: "I hear you hate learning and your mind hankers after travelling. I will not be taught by my cradle how to breed it up; it is insolence and impudence in any child to presume so much as to offer it." The memory of this mild act of insubordination still rankled some months later, when young Ralph died suddenly of a fever. His father saw the hand of God in the tragedy and hastened to press the moral home to his second, and now only, son: "I . . . exhort you to be wholly ruled and guided by me, and to be perfectly obedient to me in all things according to your bounden duty . . . . . For should you do otherwise and contrary in the least, ... I am afraid that you will be in that evil circumstance snatched away by death in your youth, as your poor brother was last week.

Because the key to the system of controlled marriage was the exchange of property, it theoretically follows that children lower down the economic scale would be left with greater freedom of choice. Whether this is so or not is not at present known for certain. Harrington thought that the arranged marriage system did not press "so heavy on the lower sort, being better able to shift for themselves, as upon the nobility and gentry." On the other hand, a large proportion of the population owned some property, and there is plenty of evidence for arranged marriages among the yeomanry in the sixteenth century. Napier's casebooks suggest that the choice of marriage partner was the principal issue which divided parents and children at all social levels above that of the poor in the early seventeenth century.[81]

Among the bottom third of society, however, conditions were probably very much freer, as they certainly were in the eighteenth century. In the first place, their parents had little economic leverage over their children since they had little or nothing to give or bequeath them. In the second place, most of their children left home at the age of ten to fourteen in order to become an apprentice, a domestic servant, or

79. *Memoirs of the Verney Family in the Seventeenth Century,* 2: 175.

80. Ibid., 2: 420, 422.

81. Harrington, *Oceana,* p. 114. I owe this information about Napier to Mr. Michael Macdonald.

a live-in laborer in other people's houses. This very large floating population of adolescents living away from home were thus free from parental supervision and could, therefore, make their own choice of marriage partners. The only thing that held them back was the need to accumulate sufficient capital to set up house and to start a shop or trade, which was the principal cause for the long delay in marriage into the middle twenties.

Apart from the need to break the child's will, a secondary cause of the widespread brutality towards children was the enormous extension of elementary and secondary education, much of it still conducted in the home. This fundamental shift in the upbringing of children forced them to do such unnatural things as to sit still and to concentrate their minds on rote book learning. When the subject was as boring and irrelevant as Latin grammar, this could only be achieved by relentless physical punishment. Renaissance education, because of its insufferably tedious content, demanded effective repression of the will. In part, at least, the increased use of physical punishment was a natural accompaniment of the spread of the Classics as a subject of study in school and home. This connection was clearly seen by Locke, who asked, "Why . . . does the learning of Latin and Greek need the rod, when French and Italian needs it not? Children learn to dance and fence without whipping; nay arithmetic, drawing, etc. they apply themselves well enough to without beating."[82]

Husband and Wife

There is evidence to suggest that a similar trend towards authoritarianism in husband-wife relations was developing in the sixteenth century. But powerful countervailing forces began to operate towards the end of the century and in the seventeenth century, so that the picture is by no means clear. For a considerable period, two conflicting trends were operating at the same time, and the thrust towards authoritarianism can only be seen in a relatively pure form for the first half of the sixteenth century.

At this time a woman's legal right to hold and dispose of her own property was limited to what she could specifically lay claim to in a marriage contract. A husband always had full rights over his wife's real estate during his lifetime, and by an act of 1540 he was empowered to

82. *The Educational Writings of John Locke,* ed. J. Axtell (Cambridge, 1968), p. 185. H. A. Rashdall (*Universities of Europe,* p. 359) also refers to "some peculiar and mysterious connection between the rod and classical scholarship."

make long leases for three lives or twenty-one years. By a judicial interpretation, a husband's debts were ruled as a prior charge on his wife's jewels and other personal property. As Widow Blackacre put it in Wycherley's *Plain Dealer* (1666), "matrimony to a woman is worse than excommunication in depriving her of the benefit of the law." Defoe's *Roxana* was even more critical of the legal impotence of a wife: "the very nature of the marriage contract was . . . nothing but giving up liberty, estate, authority and everything to a man, and the woman was indeed a mere woman ever after—that is to say a slave."[83] This legal subjection of women to husbands or fathers was the reason why the franchise was always restricted to male householders, a position which even the radical Levellers in the late 1640s never questioned. Women were evidently not free persons, and therefore were not any more eligible for the vote than children or live-in servants.

In the sixteenth century a widow's rights over real estate were in practice weakened by the rise of the use to feoffees, a legal device which could effectively bar her from her dower; moreover, her medieval common law right to a share of the personal estate was now effective only in Wales, the province of York, and the city of London.[84] If women entered the agricultural and servicing labor market, as they did increasingly in the sixteenth and seventeenth centuries, they were everywhere paid at a rate which was only one-quarter that of men.[85]

In some ways the status of women also seems to have been on the decline in the sixteenth century, despite the "monstrous regiment of women" who by genealogical accident became queens at that period. Thomas More's *Utopia* is remarkable in that the subjection of wives to husbands is the one authoritarian feature in an otherwise egalitarian society. Some Elizabethans revived the Platonic doubts as to whether a woman could be regarded as a reasoning creature; others questioned whether she had a soul.[86]

Despite a century-long trickle of books in praise of women, many lay

83. W. Wycherley, *The Plain Dealer,* act 5, sc. 3; D. Defoe, *Roxana* (London, 1724; reprint ed., London, 1964), p. 148.

84. C. S. Kenny, *The History of the Law of Married Women's Property* (London, 1879), pp. 72, 88, 52, 67. For the arguments, see Gouge, *Of Domesticall Duties,* pp. 298-306. In seventeenth-century New England, the law was significantly more liberal in this matter than it was in England. See R. B. Morris, "Women's Rights in Early American Law," *Studies in the History of American Law* (New York, 1930), p. 126-200.

85. N. Z. Davis, "City Women," p, 38. See A. Clark, *The Working Life of Women in the Seventeenth Century* (London, 1919).

86. C. Camden, *Elizabethan Women* (New York, 1952), pp. 23-24.

commentators in the late sixteenth and seventeenth centuries remained thoroughly ambivalent in their attitude towards them. In a sermon before Queen Elizabeth, Bishop Aylmer trod cautiously between the two poles of opinion:

Women are of two sorts: some of them are wiser, better learned, discreeter, and more constant than a number of men; but another and worse sort of them are fond, foolish, wanton, flibbergibs, tattlers, triflers, wavering, witless, without council, feeble, careless, rash, proud, dainty, tale-bearers, eavesdroppers, rumour-raisers, evil-tongued, worse-minded, and in everyway doltified with the dregs of the devil's dunghill.[87]

From the baroque richness of the vocabulary in the latter section, there can be little doubt about what the bishop really thought of women, despite his care to mollify his highly sensitive Queen. Others were less tactful in expressing their feelings. Thomas Fuller thought that they were "of a servile nature such as may be bettered by beating," but nevertheless advised against it. John Smith of Nibley recorded a local Gloucestershire saying, "a woman, a spaniel and a walnut tree, the more they are beaten, the better they be" but added doubtfully "sed quaere de hoc." Others relapsed into total cynicism. George Wilkins thought that "women are the purgatory of men's purses, the paradise of their bodies, and the hell of their mind." The ninth Earl of Northumberland was even more severe: "toys and vanities in their youths are the subjects they are bent to; miserableness and psalms in their latter days." It is highly significant of popular attitudes towards women in the early seventeenth century that Joseph Swetnam's *The Araignment of Lewd, Idle, Froward and Unconstant Women,* a savage anti-feminist piece of polemic, went through no less than ten editions between its first publication in 1616 and 1634, even if it did give rise to four angry rebuttals.[88]

The Protestant preachers and moral theologians were as zealous as the laity in advocating the total subordination of women. In Calvin's

87. C. L. Powell, *English Domestic Relations, 1487-1653* (New York, 1917), p. 161. See L. B. Wright, *Middle Class Culture in Elizabethan England* (Chapel Hill, 1935), ch. 13.

88. T. Fuller, *Holy State* (London, 1642), p. 9; J. Smyth, *History of the Hundred of Berkeley* ed. J. MacLean (Gloucester, 1885), p. 32; G. Wilkins, *The Miseries of Inforst Marriage* (London, 1607), act 1, sc. 1; G. B. Harrison, *Instructions to his son by Henry Percy, 9th Earl of Northumberland* (London, 1930), p. 55: E. Sowernam, *Esther hath hanged Haman,* (London, 1617), C. Munda, *The Wormeing of a Mad Dog,* (London, 1617), R. Speght, *A Mouzell for Melastomus,* (London, 1617), *J. Swetnam, the Womanhater arraigned by Women,* (London, 1620).

Geneva, which formed so important a model for much of Protestant Europe, women's legal rights declined, while their inferior position was emphasized by their exclusion from the priesthood and from the consistory.[89] William Gouge, in his popular manual *Of Domesticall Duties* of 1622 and 1634, flatly declared that "the extent of wives' subjection doth stretch itself very far, even to all things." He even argued that "though an husband in regard of evil qualities may carry the image of the devil, yet in regard to his place and office, he beareth the image of God." The old arguments from the Bible were dredged up and repeated to support this position. "We cannot but think that the woman was made before the Fall that the man might rule over her." There was, Gouge thought, good reason "that she that first drew man into sin should now be subject to him, lest by womanish weakness she fall again." The only concession that he was prepared to make was that a husband may not beat his wife. In the same vein, the Geneva Bible advised that "masters in their houses ought to be preachers to their families, that from the highest to the lowest they may obey the will of God." "God chargeth the master of the family with all the family," warned Robert Cawdrey. Even when advocating married love, Cawdrey never forgot the need for male mastery: "we would that the man when he loveth should remember his majesty."[90]

Of greatest impact, in the sense that it must have reached the widest audience, over the longest period of time, was the Homily on Marriage, which was the eighteenth of many from which all parsons were ordered by the Crown to read in church every Sunday from 1562 onward. It left the audience in no doubt about the inferior status, rights and character of a wife: "the woman is a weak creature not endued with like strength and constancy of mind; therefore, they be the sooner disquieted, and they be the more prone to all weak affections and dispositions of mind, more than men be; and lighter they be, and more vain in their fantasies and opinions." For the sake of domestic peace, however, the husband is advised not to beat her, as is his right, but to take account of the psychological fact that a woman is "the weaker vessell, of a frail heart, inconstant, and with a word soon stirred to wrath." On the other hand, women were bluntly reminded of the traditional view that "ye wives be in subjection to obey your husbands . . . . for the husband is the head

---

89. Davis, "City Women," pp. 31, 36, 38.
90. Gouge, *Of Domesticall Duties*, pp. 270-71, 394-97, 275; Cleaver, *Household Government*, p. 171.

of the woman, as Christ is the head of the Church." Obedience was, therefore, the first necessity for a happy and Christian marriage.[91]

The ideal woman in the sixteenth and seventeenth centuries was in character docile and submissive, like the wife of the Massachusetts minister whom he publicly praised for her "incomparable meekness of spirit, towards myself especially." Her function was housekeeping, and the breeding and rearing of children. In her behavior she was silent in church and in the home, and at all times submissive to men. Wives signed their letters to their husbands "Your faithful and obedient wife," and sisters to their brothers "Your sister to command."[92]

It would, of course, be absurd to claim that the reality matched the rhetoric, and there are plenty of examples of Elizabethan women who dominated their husbands. All that is claimed here is that the theoretical and legal doctrines of the time were especially reflective of the subordination of women to men in general, and their husbands in particular.

The reasons for this decline in the status and rights of wives in the sixteenth and early seventeenth centuries are not at all clear. One obvious cause was the decline of kinship, which left wives exposed to exploitation by their husbands, since they lost the continuing protection of their own kin. The destruction of Catholicism involved the destruction of the female religious cult of the Virgin Mary, and the disappearance of celibate priests and the confession box, which had hitherto been so very supportive of women in their domestic sufferings. Puritanism was unable to fill the same role for more than a tiny majority of female zealots who attached themselves to charismatic preachers. [93]

Finally it could be argued that the Protestant sanctification of marriage and the demand for married love itself facilitated the subordination of wives. Women were now expected to love and cherish their husbands after marriage and were taught that it was their sacred duty to do so. This love, in those cases where it in fact became internalized and real, made it easier for wives to accept that position of subordination and submission to the will of their husbands which the preachers were also insisting upon. By a paradoxical twist, one of the first results of married love was a strengthening of the authority of the husband over

91. *Certain Sermons or Homilies appointed to be read in Churches* (Oxford, 1844), pp. 446-58.

92. L. Koehler, "The Case of the American Jezebels," *William and Mary Quarterly* 31 (1974): 58, 57.

93. *Letters of Thomas Wood*, ed. P. Collinson, Special Supplement no. 5 to *Bulletin of the Institute for Historical Research* (London, 1960), *passim*.

the wife, and an increased readiness of the latter to submit herself to the dictates of the former. This is similar to the paradox by which the first result of an increased concern for children was a greater determination to crush their wills by whipping them.

Underlying the growing authoritarianism and the emphasis placed on obedience both of wives to husbands and of children to parents, lay more fundamental considerations. The first was the importance attached by Protestantism to the household, which also enhanced the role of its head, who took over many of the leadership functions from the priest.[94] When husbands were encouraged to become more active as heads of households, they also tended to displace and subordinate their wives. Secondly, the growth of paternalism was deliberately encouraged by the new Renaissance state on the traditional grounds that the subordination of the family to its head is analogous to, and also a direct contributory cause of, subordination of subjects to the sovereign. In 1609, James I informed his somewhat dubious subjects that "the state of monarchy is the supremest thing upon earth; for kings are not only God's lieutenants and sit upon God's throne, but even by God himself they are called Gods." One of the arguments James advanced was that "kings are compared to fathers in families: for a King is truly *parens patriae*, the politic father of his people."[95] When some 30 years later Robert Filmer again argued the case for absolute monarchy, he used the same logic, but more coherently expressed: "It is found in the Decalogue that the law which enjoins obedience to Kings is declared in the terms of: 'Honor thy Father' "(as a strong anti-feminist, he discreetly omits "and Mother!")[96]

In New England the standard catechism, by John Cotton, ran as follows:

Question: *What is the fifth Commandment?*

Answer: *Honor thy Father and mother that thy days may be long . . . .*

Question: *Who are here meant by father and mother?*

Answer: *All our superiors, whether in family, school, church and commonwealth.*

94. See above, *passim.*

95. *Political Works of King James I,* ed. C. H. McIlwain (Cambridge, Mass., 1918), p. 307.

96. R. Filmer, *Patriarcha,* ed. P. Laslett (Oxford, 1949), p. 62. See also (C. Russell, "Arguments for Religious Unity in England 1530-1650," *Journal of Ecclesiastical History* 18 (1967): 205-6.

Question: What is the honor due to them?

Answer: Reverence, obedience, and (when I am able) recompense.[97]

In France the old lines of argument were, if possible, made even more explicit. In 1639 a royal declaration stated that "the natural respect of children towards their parents is the bond of the legitimate obedience of subjects towards their sovereigns." Conservatives like Bossuet believed that "one makes Kings on the model of fathers," and liberals like Montesquieu believed that there was a clear relationship between "the servitude of women" and "despotic government."[98]

In the early modern period, as indeed in the Middle Ages, it was generally agreed that there was a clear causal relationship between authority patterns and habits of deference within the family and authority patterns and habits of deference in society at large and towards the state in particular. The state, therefore, had a direct interest in reinforcing patriarchy in the home, and the result was a flood of propaganda put out under official auspices, and given wide circulation thanks to the newly invented printing press and to the increased subordination of clerical homilies to State directives. The powers of Kings and of heads of households grew in parallel with one another in the sixteenth century. The State was as supportive of the patriarchal nuclear family as it was hostile to the kin-oriented family; the one was a buttress and the other a threat to its own increasing power.

There are reasons to think that this support given by the State to the principle of patriarchy paid off in generating an internalized sense of obligation to obedience to the absolute sovereign, as well as obedience to the absolute husband and father. In 1616 Richard Mocket published a book, *God and the King,* in which he made the connection even more clear: "the evidence of reason teacheth that there is a stronger and higher bond of duty between children and the father of their country than the fathers of private families."[99] All subjects were the children of the King, and bound by the Fifth Commandment to honor and obey him. James I was so delighted with this book that he ordered it to be studied in schools and universities and bought by all householders, thus ensuring a very wide sale. It can plausibly be argued that the otherwise astonishing rallying of large numbers of gentry and poor peasants

97. Bremner, *Youth in America,* 1: 32.
98. Snyders, *La Pedagogie,* pp. 259-61. Montesquieu, *De L'Esprit des Lois,* ed. A. Masson (Paris, 1950), 1: 357. See also, Ariès, *Centuries of Childhood,* p, 351.
99. R. Mocket, *God and the King* (London, 1616), pp. 1-2.

around the King at the outbreak of civil war in 1642 was due in considerable measure to a deep ingrained sense that both honor and duty called for obedience and support to the King as the father of his people. Despite Charles' long record of duplicity and illegal actions, very many individuals were in the last resort unable to shake off the ideological chains with which they had so long been bound. They were exasperated enough to destroy the machinery of royal government in 1640-41, but not enough to take up arms against the King in 1642. It smacked of parricide, which was why the execution of King Charles in 1649 was greeted with such horror. When in the same year Arthur Lord Capel was tried and executed for leading an unsuccessful royal re-bellion, he defended himself on the grounds of obedience to the Fifth Commandment: he was rallying in defense of the nation's father. This same patriarchal theory, reinforcing the traditional habits of deference and authority which were basic to the social structure and value system of seventeenth century England, undoubtedly helped to smooth the path to the Restoration of Charles II in 1660.[100]

Conclusion

It seems clear that during the sixteenth and seventeenth centuries there took place a series of important changes in the structure of the English family and in affective relationships within it and to groups out-side it. Under pressure from the State and from Protestant moral theology, it shifted from a predominantly kin-oriented structure to a predominantly nuclear one. Within this nuclear core power flowed increasingly to the husband over the wife and to the father over the children. At first the nuclear family thus became more patriarchal and more authoritarian than it had been before. And yet this was only a temporary phase, which had hardly become established, before it was undermined by a new set of values, inculcated partly by political thinkers, such as Lilburne or Locke; partly by certain built-in tendencies to reliance on the private conscience that existed within Pu-ritan moral theology; and partly to basic economic developments which led to a more capitalist society based on the ideals of possessive indi-vidualism and private enterprise rather than those of collective responsi-

100. G. J. Schochet, "Patriarchalism, Politics and Mass Attitudes in Stuart England," *Historical Journal*, 12 (1969): 413-41; J. G. Marston, "Gentry Honor and Royalism in Early Stuart England," *Journal of British Studies* 13 (1973): 21-43.

bility and the evils of social mobility.[101] What this essay has tried to describe is, therefore, no more than one stage in the very complex process of the evolution of the English family over the last five centuries. One key aspect of this stage of development of the nuclear family, the reinforcement of patriarchal authoritarianism, was already under challenge by the middle of the seventeenth century; while another, the growth of affective bonds between husband and wife and parents and children within the family, was about to undergo a very rapid development. The situation which has been described was, therefore, characteristic of a transitional stage, squeezed in between the more kin-oriented family of the late Middle Ages and the more companionate and egalitarian nuclear family of the eighteenth century.

101. J. Demos (*A Little Commonwealth* [New York, 1970], pp. 88-99) argues that in seventeenth-century New England both theory and practice became more companionate. Among the middle class in England in the early seventeenth century there was also a significantly greater sense of freedom and equality (Wright, *Middle Class Culture*, ch. 7).

ᐁᐃ WOLFRAM EBERHARD

THE UPPER-CLASS FAMILY IN TRADITIONAL CHINA

Most sociologists during the last forty years have been reluctant to work with historical materials. This reluctance is understandable, particularly in the case of the history of social institutions. The difficulty lies in the fact that institutions can and must be studied in more than one way and that the usual survey methods cannot be used in most historical research. One of the ways is to study the actual behavior of individuals or groups in certain repetitive situations and to establish the normal pattern of that institution. The second way is to study, in literate societies, the written rules of behavior as they are laid down in law books, philosophical works, and other documents. While the first approach brings out what people do, the second tells us the ideals of the intellectual leadership in the same society or, in other words, the ideology. Non-sociologists have often not clearly distinguished between these two approaches, so that in many studies of the Chinese family, actual behavior is confused with ideal behavior, or ideal behavior is described as if it were the actual behavior of some or all people. In this study, which deals with both levels, *actual* behavior and ideology concerning the Chinese family, the clear distinction between the two is essential. The reason for choosing the upper-class family is the very practical one that only for this class are the historical data relatively rich and easily accessible.

A sociologist beginning to study the social structure of a society normally looks at its social institutions to find their function. To the degree that he is a functionalist, he assumes that each institution fulfills a basic need of man and that all needs of man are fulfilled by the sum of all institutions, representing the structure of that society. Although the

59

generally accepted list of the basic needs of man is not long, recently there has been much discussion about them, and we have come to understand that most of them are inferred by scholars and are not consciously felt by every or any member of a given society. Nevertheless, different societies have made different decisions about one important social need: the need for family structure. Such decisions, which one may call ideological, may depend on a-priori assumptions concerning the nature of man and the universe, and it seems that it is a difference in a-priori assumptions, rather than anything else, that causes differences between some societies which otherwise are similarly structured. For instance, the Chinese family is patriarchal, patrilinear, and patrilocal; but so is the family in many other historical and contemporary societies. Yet, the traditional Chinese family is unlike many other families with the same structure. We shall look at the Chinese upper-class family system not only as a need-fulfilling institution, but also as an institution that was constantly influenced by specific a-priori assumptions. The way in which the resulting family system changed and became stable again, and how it operated in the political reality in the course of history, including the main developments up to the present time, will be examined. We shall leave undiscussed many other aspects of the Chinese upper-class family system, such as its important psychological implications.

The history of China, many historians agree, has three main periods which, for the sake of convenience, may be called ancient, medieval, and modern—although there is no general agreement concerning the characteristics and the duration of each period. My preference would be to call ancient China the period between roughly 1500 and 200 B.C.; medieval China, the period between 200 B.C. and 960 A.D.; and modern China, the period between 960 and 1911 A.D. One can see each of these periods as characterized by specific cultural traits or social institutions, and one of them is the structure of the society, including the organization of its upper-class whose development fell roughly into the same three historical periods.[1] We may, therefore, say that ancient China was the period of *clan* society; medieval China, the period of *great-gentry* society; and modern China, the period of *small-gentry* society. Let it be understood that these terms describe only the family structure of the upper class, not of the other social classes of the population.

1. See my *A History of China*, 2nd edition (Berkeley, 1966).

According to the new chronology, the Shang dynasty may have begun around 1500 B.C., not earlier. Rulers calling themselves "King of Hsia" may well have existed before Shang time, but the Hsia time has left no documents. What the Chinese texts—all of much later date—report about the Hsia is meager and seems to be legend rather than history. In agreement with many Chinese historians, my assumption is that all reports on rulers of pre-Shang time are historicized myths and legends, and I think one can speak of "Chinese" society only for the time after 1500 B.C.—an opinion which forces me to conclude that "Chinese" culture is not the spontaneous work of one ethnic group, but the result of the confluence of many, probably around twenty more or less complex ethnic units, all of which contributed to the formation of what we later admire as the great "Chinese" culture.[2] These early cultures, which I have called Local Cultures, differed from each other in many ways, especially in the structure of the family. Some of them were patriarchal, patrilinear, and patrilocal, but others were matrilinear[3] and matrilocal;[4] and some even seem to have had matriarchal traits.[5] In some of these Local Cultures many taboos surrounded courtship and marriage; in others there was considerable freedom in the relations between the sexes before marriage, and sometimes even extra-marital sexual freedom during early years of matrimony.

The process of amalgamation of the Local Cultures into a "Chinese" culture was a gradual one. At first, only parts of the Local Cultures melted together, while other parts continued independently and developed along their own lines, some of them until the present time, as testified by the existence of millions of non-Chinese tribal people within China's borders today. Many a scholar has failed to recognize the existence and importance of the Local Cultures in China and therefore thought he had discovered, for example, a survival of an early matrilinear "stage" of Chinese society, when in reality he had discovered a custom of a non-Chinese Local Culture.[6] Today we can say that in all three historical periods after 1500 B.C., the Chinese upper-class family

2. See my *The Local Cultures of South and East China* (Leiden, 1968), pp. 21-31.

3. Ibid., pp. 113-15.

4. Ibid., pp. 108-9; for a modern case, see Francis L. K. Hsu, *Under the Ancestors' Shadows* (New York, 1948), p. 99f.

5. Cases mentioned in my *Kultur und Siedlung der Randvölker Chinas* (Leiden, 1942), sections g57, h8, i57, v31.

6. See for instance W. Koppers, "Die Frage des Mutterrechts und des Totemismus im alten China," *Anthropos* 25 (1931): 981-1002, or F. Gräbner, *Ethnologie* (Hinneberg, *Kultur der Gegenwart* [Berlin, 1905], part 3, section 5), p. 520.

was patrilocal, patriarchal, and patrilinear, never matriarchal or matrilinear. While this principle of structure had not changed over the millenia, there were many changes within its framework. Some of them were caused by developments in the general material culture, others by ideas of individuals—leaders or philosophers who succeeded in impressing their thoughts on the ruling elites. Thus, the changes in Chinese society moved, often simultaneously, in two directions: from "below" to the "top" through cumulative shifts in the material and social conditions of the lower classes; and from the top downward as a result of upper-class attempts to change the lower classes by spreading the more and more elaborate system of upper-class rules of behavior.

When China emerged into the light of history during the Shang dynasty, it was already a highly stratified society with a royal house surrounded by noblemen, roughly comparable to European knights because they were warriors rather than administrators. There is good reason to believe that this elite ruled not only over their own people, who lived mainly in cities, but also over many others who lived in the countryside and adhered to their own culture, at least to a large extent. The Shang have left no systematic statement concerning their ideas about the world and society, and the tens of thousands of texts surviving from that period (almost all oracles) tell us little about their families. Recent research has shown that the royal family was patrilinear, but the rules of succession stipulated that the king's brothers, one after the other, ascended to the throne before members of the next generation had their turn.[7] This indicates a principle that has been important throughout Chinese social history: each generation forms a unit, and no mixing of the generations is allowed. In all genealogies the generations are numbered, and in the relations between people the "generational rank" of an individual is more important than his rank by age. In large families it is not unusual, for instance, that a man have an uncle who is still a baby. The baby uncle ranks higher than the adult nephew. A study of the marriages of the Shang rulers came to the conclusion that the Shang abided by very elaborate marriage rules based on a division of

7. Chang Kwang-chih, "Posthumous Names of the Shang Kings and the Royal Genealogy of the Shang Dynasty," *Bulletin of the Institute of Ethnology, Academia Sinica*, no. 15 (1963):65-95, and "Further Remarks," *Bulletin of the Institute of Ethnology, Academia Sinica*, no. 19 (1965):53-70; Ting, William S., "The System of the Posthumous Names of the Shang Kings and Queens," *Bulletin of the Institute of Ethnology, Academia Sinica*, no. 19 (1965): 71-79.

society into two segments, and into a number of marriage classes within the segments, a system which has parallels in other societies, for example, the Australian aborigines.[8] This reconstruction of the Shang marriage system is still controversial, and we do not know whether other noble families followed the same rules.

We are more certain for the next dynasty, the Chou, which seems to have begun around 1050 B.C. after the Chou's military conquest of the Shang state. The unit of the upper class of the Chou was not the nuclear family but the clan, that is, the descendants of a common, supposedly historical ancestor in the paternal line. The main clan, that of the royal house of Chou, was the clan Chi. After the Shang were defeated and their last ruler was killed, the first Chou king administered the country by sending into the different parts of the Shang territory members of his own family, members of branches of his family, and less closely related members of his entire clan, all accompanied by soldier-settlers. Where there already existed a town, they occupied it and ruled as feudal lords, tied to the Chou king by clan ties as well as ties of personal loyalty.[9] Where there was no town, they created new urban settlements much like the castle-towns of early Europe. The attack against the Shang was made not by the Chi clan alone, since the Chi were at the head of a coalition of clans, apparently of different ethnic origin. The leaders of these allied clans were also rewarded with fiefs, but not the most important ones.[10] Finally, some of the Shang's neighbors, who had been in loose subordination to them, went over to the Chou, their rights to local rule were reaffirmed, and they were made vassals of the Chou. The developments during the next centuries were again similar to those in European feudal societies. Those vassals who were related to the king-lord by family or clan remained loyal to their lord only as long as the family ties were close. Soon one vassal fought the other, until their

8. Liu Pin-hsiung, "An Interpretation of the Kinship System of the Roayl House of the Shang Dynasty," *Bulletin of the Institute of Ethnology, Academia Sinica* 19 (1965): 89-114.

9. There is an extensive discussion on feudalism in China, which depends mainly upon the definition which is adopted. For our purposes, the narrow definition is used. See D. Bodde, "Feudalism in China," *Feudalism in History*, ed., Rushton Coulborn (Princeton, 1956), pp. 49-92.

10. This discussion is based upon the research on clans by G. Haloun, "Beiträge zur Siedlungsgeschichte chinesischer Clans," *Fr. Hirth Festschrift* (Leipzig, 1922); and "Contributions to the History of Clan Settlement," *Asia Major* (Leipzig, 1924), 1: 76-111.

number was reduced from about one thousand to seven. The lord could not rely on his vassals' military assistance and soon found himself without power. The loosely structured "feudal" state in fact disappeared, giving way to a number of independent states, and at the end of their internecine battles there remained one state which then unified China under a new type of political organization.[11]

This lord-vassal system was an aristocracy, and the vassals faced the same problems that have occurred in many other aristocracies. At the time of the establishment of the Chou dynasty the lineage, as a sub-unit of the clan, was without a doubt the all-important unit for this upper class. Marriage partners had to be persons belonging to different clans and/or different lineages, and strict rules against endogamy were set up. In fact, marriages were concluded preferably between members of allied lineages, since only these were considered socially equal. As soon as the branches of a lineage had spread over a wide area, marriages became a political tool, used in familiar ways, for example, to solidify alliances with neighboring vassals or to solemnify treaties between two fief holders. In many cases not only one daughter was given in marriage to the son of another vassal, but also a whole set of girls (up to nine) consisting of sisters and cousins and accompanied by a staff of female servants.[12] In these cases the girl-receiving party could be fairly confident that the allied vassal and his clan would remain loyal, particularly if that clan had no other girls left to cement another alliance with another vassal. M. Granet thought that this marriage custom was the survival of an ancient group marriage, at a time when presumably a man had sexual rights to the sisters of his wife. It is universally true that the relations between a man and his wife's sisters are precarious, and many societies have set up taboos to prevent sexual relations between them. On the other hand, women used to die young, and if a man's bride died early in life, could he not rightly expect a replacement? This would be the argument of a man who had spent much wealth for the bridal price, and also of a man who had married in order to seal a political pact. A family that received for its son more than one girl from the same family avoided the danger of total loss of investment; there is

11. See Richard L. Walker, *The Multi-State System of Ancient China* (Hamden, 1953).

12. The first intensive discussion of this custom was by M. Granet, *Lapolygynie sororale et le sororat dans la Chine féodale* (Paris, 1920). See also Eberhard, *The Local Cultures*, p. 181.

no need for the hypothesis of an institutionalized group marriage in prehistorical China.[13]

The concept of marriage as a political tie between two families, and not as a union of two loving persons, developed among this upper class of vassals aspiring to power at the same time that the common people in the territory of China allowed individuals considerable freedom in the choice of their partners.[14] However, it was this politically oriented, aristocratic model of marriage that the Chinese thinkers used when they went about constructing the norms for Chinese society.

The immediate consequence of the concept of political marriage was the requirement of the bride's virginity, presumably because the high status of the groom's family would make it an insult to offer "secondhand merchandize." Bridal virginity remained extremely important far beyond the ancient period and was stressed increasingly up to modern times.[15] The modern rationalization is that a daughter is raised

13. Some authors believe that China also went through a period of promiscuity. See Kuo Mo-jo, *Chia-ku wen-tse yen-chiu* (Study of Oracle Bone Texts) (Peking 1931), section Shih-tsu-pi, p. 2b. There is evidence for "hospitable promiscuity" in ancient China (texts collected by M. Granet, *Danses et legendes de la Chine ancienne* [Paris, 1926], pp. 584-85), in medieval China (*Wei-shu* 32; K'ai-ming edition, p. 1976d; and *Pei-meng so yen* as quoted in commentary to *Chiu Wu-tai-shih* 51: 4266ca), and in parts of modern South China (*Min-su* no. 74, p. 21 and *Chung-hua ch 'üan-kuo feng-su chih*, part 1, chapt. 4, p. 29). There are also reports on ritual promiscuity in medieval China (G. Maspero in *Journal Asiatique* [1937]: 402) and modern China (J. Needham, *Science and Civilization*, [Cambridge, 1956] 429), and in Vietnam (*France-Asie*, no. 92/3 [1954]: 374-75).

14. In the *Book of Rites (Li-chi)*, marriage is defined as "the union of two clans in friendship and love" (Ai-kung wen 10; *Couvreur*, 2: 368; see also Hun-i 1; *Couvreur*, 2: 641). Fen Yo-lan (in *Ku-shih pien*, 2: 227) comments upon this and states that the meaning of marriage is the production of children, and love is only a secondary element.

15. Thus, we find in China customs which were also formerly practiced in other societies. In some parts of China, until very recently, the bride brought a piece of cloth with her to be put on the bridal bed. On the next morning, the cloth was exhibited at the door of the bridal room (*Hun-ch 'ien, hun-hou* [Taipei, 1964], 2: 19). In Hopei, Yung-p'ing district, the mother examines her daughter before the wedding. If she is not a virgin, the parents-in-law return her; if she is, this is celebrated the day after the wedding (*Erh-ku* 3, 3b; nineteenth century). The exhibition of the cloth and public announcement of virginity is also reported from Peking (*Ch 'i Ju-shan ch 'üan-chi* 7, Pei-p'ing huai-ku, p. 39). See also R. van Gulik, *Sexual Life in Ancient China* (Leiden, 1961), p. 207. Several classical plays mention court proceedings in which the virginity of a girl was examined by a specially appointed woman (so *Wang hu t'ing*). On the other hand, ritual defloration just before the wedding is reported widely from Central Asia, Northeast China (see D. Schröder in *Anthropos* 51 [1956]: 1091), southern and southwestern neighbors of China and South China (Eberhard, *Local Cultures*, p. 134). General discussion by Hirosato Iwai in *Tōyō Bunko* no. 7, p. 105f, and P. Pelliot, *Memoire sur les coutumes de Cambodge* (Paris, 1951), p. 17.

as a "trust" for her future husband. The groom repays the parents for all the cost they have incurred in raising the girl. If another man has already enjoyed the girl, he should have been responsible for at least a part of the investment. Only when, under the impact of Western ideas, political marriages began to give way to love marriage, i.e., when the woman was regarded as an individual with rights of her own, did virginity lose its importance as a marriage requirement.[16]

There were further consequences of the aristocratic system. In human sexual life, physical attraction is an indisputable factor, and as it cannot always be taken into consideration where marriage is a political act, the society may make provisions for sexual relations that are based on physical attraction. This was achieved, from the male upper-class point of view, already in ancient China by permitting concubinage, that is, allowing men to cohabitate within the family with a woman, or women, from below the social level of the main wife, not for political reasons, but as a result of physical desire.[17] Polygyny is usually beset with the problem of competition between wives for the husband. The Chinese attempted to solve it by defining the role of the main wife as the ruler of the house, with the concubines subordinated to her. Peace in the family can be achieved more safely if the main wife herself pre-selects the girls among whom the husband then makes a choice, than if the husband brings home a woman with whom he has already fallen in love.[18]

16. In a modern collection of "Letters to the Editor," dealing with questions of marriage, a woman states that her husband did not want to have relations with her, when he found that she was not a virgin. The editor says that she had bad luck to get one of the few husbands who are so backward (*Hun-yin hsüeh hsin-hsiang* [Taichung, 1967], p. 155-59). Similarly, the editor defends a woman who was pregnant when she married the father of her child despite criticism by neighbors (p. 168-74), though he finds a boy of eighteen too young to have premarital relations with his girl friend (p. 83-89). Discussions of this kind are now quite common.

17. Public bordellos existed in China certainly since the Han period, but perhaps already in ancient China (van Gulik, *Sexual Life*, p. 65), but men of the upper classes, especially government officials, were not allowed to visit them, though they could ask a girl to come to their house.

18. Wu Ching-chao in *Nanking Journal* 1, no. 1 (Nanking, 1931), pp. 47-49, discussed the position and treatment of imperial concubines in Han times. The ritualists set up detailed rules for them, such as, the right to spend one night in every five with the husband up to their fiftieth year (*Li-chi, Nei-tsê* 2: 15; *Couvreur* 1: 661). This statement is open to question: Chinese handbooks of sex, old and recent, state that men, even between the ages of twenty to twenty-nine should have intercourse not more than once every three days, and after age forty once every seven days (*Hsing-i ta-ch 'üan* 2: 30, and other sources, some with slight variations). Also, one should not have intercourse with a woman over forty *(Yu-fang pi-chüeh)*. A folk rule states that a couple should stop having intercourse when their son married, so as to prevent having a son who is younger than the grandson. The

The bridesmaids,[19] whom the aristocratic bride in Chou time brought with her into her husband's household to serve as her maids, were in fact pre-selected concubines for the husband, although they continued being the bride's servants.[20]

This solution naturally created another problem common to many aristocracies: What about the children of the different wives? As long as they were children in the paternal family, no distinctions were made, since all children could be considered children of the main wife.[21] But difficulties arose at the time a concubine's child was to be married. The other side's negotiator would again talk of second-class merchandise, and there would be objections to a son-in-law or daughter-in-law with only one parent of noble descent, so that in case of need, support could be expected from only one parental lineage, the father's, because the lineage of the mother, the concubine, was nonexistent or not part of the power structure. As to inheritance, the fief went to the main wife's sons and not to the son of a concubine. A concubine's son would receive some other piece of land whose income he could use for himself and his new family, thus starting a branch family whose relations with the main house were soon severed.[22] The tie of the concubine's sons to their father's lineage waned from the beginning. They and their descendants kept a record of their noble descent but they lived as independent

---

hierarchical structure of polygymous families existed among Chinese in Taiwan down to the recent period. The modern form is to set up separate households and to abolish hierarchy (Yang Ch'ing-yu, "T'ai-wan-ti min-su," *Hsin-shê-hui* 12, no. 4 [1960]: 15-16). For modern times, see also O. Lang, *Chinese Family and Society* (New York, 1946), p. 218f, and H. Lamson, *Social Pathology in China* (Shanghai, 1935), p. 513f.

19. See M. Granet, *Danses*, p. 96f. *Han Fei-tzu* (chapt. 11) mentions one case in which the princess was accompanied by seventy girls. The custom of bridesmaids is found even among the Miao tribes in Yunnan (*Chung-hua ch'üan-kuo feng-su chih*, part 2, chapt. 8, pp. 24-25).

20. During a period of medieval China, a man who had married a princess was not allowed to take a concubine. In the opinion of Yuan Hsiao-yo, this made women jealous; therefore, he recommended that this custom be abolished (*Wei-shu* 18, p. 1943c). In some areas of Central China during the medieval period, the concubine could become the principal wife after the death of the wife; in northern China, this never occurred. The widower always married another main wife (*Yen-shih chia hsün* 4; 1: 9a; and Yeh-k'o ts'ung-shu 15, 2b).

21. However, in recent times the concubine was mentioned in the family genealogy only if she became the mother of a son. Otherwise, her name was not entered (T. Makino, *Studies on Modern Chinese Clans* [Tokyo, 1949], p. 102).

22. When Chinese families in later periods developed a special coding system for the personal names, sons of concubines in some families received a name which deviated from the code, so that within the family, everybody could know who was a son of the main wife and who was a son of the concubine(s).

families whose members worked in various occupations, as landowners, or as teachers or clerks at the courts of large ruling families.

In an aristocratic society where marriage is a political affair, the position of women in relatively strong, even if the family is patriarchal, because a noblewoman represents her family and if she is mistreated, her family will interfere in her behalf. In fact, at that time women often played a considerable political and public role, and we even hear of court scandals. When this aristocracy disappeared from the Chinese scene after 250 B.C., the patriarchal structure remained and the role of the husband grew. One consequence was that all children by any mother were recognized as legitimate children of their father and considered equal or almost equal in rank, eliminating any problem of illegitimate children. We have reasons to believe that children who were not recognized by their father were aborted, while children of prostitutes, if female, were raised by them to sustain their mother when she was too old to continue working. The second consequence was that the status of the wife, whether main or secondary, declined.

When the feudal system and its aristocratic concepts broke down, when it became clear that China was no longer a political unit under a king, but was instead a group of independent states, when technological changes led to changes in the economy, and when more and more non-Chinese tribes and states were sucked into the influence zones of Chinese kinglets, the men of letters began to reflect on man and society. This is the age of China's famous philosophers, and Confucius, in the late sixth century B.C., was not only the greatest, but probably one of the earliest. He and many others between 500 and 250 B.C. developed an ideological system which unified nature, political rule, and the individual. Though changing in details, it has continued to influence all Chinese up to the present day and been responsible to a large degree for subsequent changes in Chinese society. The thinkers were members of noble families or of branch families established by sons of concubines. They were worried about the breakdown of their society and wanted to stop this deterioration. With the possible exception of a few who may have known and thought about the social structure and the family system of the lower classes, all of them based their philosophies on the same assumptions that underlie the social concepts and practices of the upper class.

Every philosophy, every idealogy depends on certain assumptions from which conclusions are drawn and rules derived. The forms of society are influenced, of course, by material conditions, but man has usually, if not always, a choice between several approaches to his problems. However, once a choice has been made, certain consequences may follow automatically, leaving no place for further free choice. The Chinese thinkers in the period under discussion made their choice by accepting a number of a priori assumptions. They were surely conscious of some of them and perhaps not conscious about others. Let us discuss only those that were decisive for the development of the Chinese upper-class family and for the society in general.

The first of these assumptions is the Chinese version of Kluckhohn's principle, "nature over man"—in other words, it is assumed that in a logically constructed, unified universe man is a part, not a master.[23] He must fit into the universe which is governed by its own rules, and therefore man's behavior must be governed by rules, too. The aim of laws is not to codify what is, but what should be.[24] Laws and rules set forth the prescripts of behavior and aim at improvement, so that society may eventually be perfect, i.e., in complete harmony with the universe. This concept stands in contrast to the Anglo-Saxon concept of law whose codified rules aim to reflect the prevailing mores of a given time. Chinese law wants to improve mankind, Anglo-Saxon law wants to protect citizens.

The second assumption is that man can be improved, that humans are educable. An individual may be a stupid fellow, yet he can be taught at least some things. He can be changed. When one reads later philosophers, one may sometimes feel that this belief was not shared by everyone. On closer inspection one will find that it was generally ac-

---

23. To my knowledge, this principle has not yet been extensively studied in relation to China. For modern Japan, see W. Caudill and H. Sears, "Japanese Value Orientations," *Ethnology* 1 (1962): 53-91. It is used as one of the elements by which achievement can be measured (Paul E. Breer and E. A. Locke, *Task Experience as a Source of Attitudes* [Homewood, 1965], p. 197). For the general question of man in nature see D. J. Munroe, *The Concept of Man in Early China* (Stanford, 1969).

24. The first codified laws in China seem to be from the sixth century B.C. (A. Hulsewé, *Remnants of Han Law* [Leiden, 1955], p. 317); the first actual texts which we have are fragments from the Han period (Lo Chen-yü, *Liu-sha sui-chien* [Peking, 1914], 2: 12a and *Asia Major*, N.S. 1, p. 211). The Confucianist classics, however, could also be used as if they were law codes (Hulsewé, *loc. cit.*, p. 51). This could still be done in the nineteenth century (Hu Hsien-chin, *The Common Descent Group in China* [New York, 1948], p. 105).

cepted, but that the terms "human" and "human society" did not always mean the same as today. Thus, some authors denied educability for slaves and the so-called "mean people" because they were considered not a part of human society but somewhat like domestic animals. Other authors excluded the non-Chinese tribes, comparing them to wild animals. At the opposite end of the social scale, some authors excluded persons like Confucius, whom they regarded as supermen, and ordinary men, who therefore did not need education. Applied to life, the assumption of man's educability means that it is the duty of those who know, the elite, to educate and uplift the rest of the population. Government is legitimate as long as it fulfills this duty to educate and as long as it enforces the laws designed to improve people. The laws should outline and teach moral principles, and in a morally good society of properly educated people, punitive laws need not be applied.

The third assumption is the intrinsic inequality of people. Any two persons differ from one another at least in one way, usually in more than one way, with the older person ranking above the younger one, the male above the female, and the person of higher status in society above the one of lower status.

The fourth assumption refers directly to the family system. While certain rights and the worth of the individual were not denied, the unit of society was not the individual but the family. Individual activities were therefore subordinate to the concerns of the family, and society was seen as a network of families.

All four assumptions were interrelated, and they determined individual behavior within the family. There could be no unlimited individualism—the Chinese did not even have a term for "individual" or "individualism" before their contact with the West—because the family, including each individual, must fit into a universe which no individual can obstruct or fight, as an individualist might want to do. Since the universe operates under recognizable, logical rules, mankind must observe the same rules, and there can be no human being who is by nature in opposition to the universe. Hence, each human being has a "correct" place in relation to all other humans. In contrast, in egalitarian societies, including societies where everyone is assumed to have the same rights, no one has a definite, let alone "correct" place in society, because theoretically every place can be taken by any contender. Competition and achievement are one result, but social unrest and hostility are the negative concomitants.

These four main assumptions have never changed in the course of Chinese history. They have given to the social institutions of the Chinese their particular shape and continuity, though externally certain Chinese and non-Chinese institutions have similarities.

The philosophers in later periods have developed detailed rules of "correct" behavior, laid down in the various books of etiquette, where almost every conceiveable action and movement of a person was prescribed. Confucianist thinkers have clearly stated that they did not expect every citizen to be able to follow these rules which, in their totality, constituted an ideal ultimately to be achieved by society.[25] But it was expected that the present and future leaders of society know and obey all, or at least most of the rules, and that they make them known and enforced them among the lower classes. The local officialdom was familiar, for example, with the premarital freedom of many local cultures. Again and again one reads that an administrator stopped these customs and forcibly introduced the Chinese marriage rule which stipulates that marriage must be initiated by parents and that sexual relations can begin only after the couple was formally married.[26] Or, one reads that an administrator proudly reports to his superiors that the "uncivilized" in his district have taken to wearing "correct" clothing, that is, Chinese clothing which covers the body completely. This percolation process concerning Chinese rules has happened in all fields of activity to the eve of modernity.

In recent centuries this process was accelerated by technological inventions. For example, the invention of printing opened up new possibilities, and by the eleventh century the ability to read was no longer a monopoly of the upper class.[27] Large sectors of the middle classes began to read, and inexpensive books were printed for them with the money of philanthropists or by profit-seeking entrepreneurs.[28] But whether published by a donor or a business man, all books propagated the values

25. The classical text is in *Li-chi*, Ch'ü-li part 1, ch. 4, section 50; *Couvreur*, 1: 53. Concerning the role of the rites see N.B. Fehl, *Rites and Propriety in Literature and Life* (Hong Kong, 1971).

26. The classical text is in *Li-chi*, Sang-chi 33; *Couvreur*, 2: 422.

27. According to the definition which one uses, printing may have been invented in China very early. The oldest presently known print from a Chinese settlement is a slip which warns of a dog (*Asia Major*, N.S. vol. 1, p. 239), but the earliest existing fragments of reprinted books are a Buddhist text of 868 and a calendar of 877 (*Bulletin of the School of Oriental Studies* 9 [1937]: 1030-31 and 1033-34).

28. As early as the twelfth century an author complained that books were now cheap, but full of printing mistakes (*Shih-lin yen-yü* 8, 2b-3a).

and rules of the upper class.[29] With the introduction of the modern school system in the late nineteenth and twentieth centuries, these ideas reached a whole generation of young people of all social classes.

This "percolation" process can be better understood through two examples. The concept of marriage as a political pact between two families was accompanied in this patriarchal society by the idea that the wife belongs to the family of her husband, even after the husband's death. Therefore, theoretically and ideally, a widow was not supposed to remarry. She should continue to live with her husband's family, raising his children and serving his parents. Some non-Chinese societies allow a widow to marry the dead husband's brother or, if he is already married, to become his secondary wife. This custom of levirate has existed also in China since antiquity, judging from the repeatedly recorded interdictions.[30] From early times to about the eleventh century there *were* remarried widows; some of them became the wives of famous men.[31] In other words, at this time the non-remarriage of widows remained largely an ideal, even in the upper class. But from the eleventh century on there was more and more pressure against remarriage of widows,[32] and at the same time the government rewarded

29. A man in Sung time printed the works of two T'ang period essayists and poets at his own expense and sold them on the market at any price, because he wanted people to read these books (Ch'ü-yo chiu-wen 4, 4b). *Ying-shih* 13, 3b mentions that the collected essays of a scholar were available on the market, i.e., in a commercial edition. At about that time, the government prohibited the private printing of books about astronomy and astrology, examination essays and law books (*Bulletin of Chinese Studies* 5 [1945]: 95-99).

30. Texts in W. Eberhard, *Local Cultures*, p. 112, and *Lokalkulturen im alten China* (Leiden, 1942), pp. 72 and 275.

The Mongol rulers of China prohibited levirate for Muslims and Jews in 1340 (*Yuan-shih* 40, 7b; see also H. Serruys, *The Mongols in China* [New York, 1959], pp. 174-75). Chu'u T'ung-tsu (*Chung-kuo* fa-lü yü Chung-kuo she-hui [Shanghai, 1947], p. 74f) states that since the Manchu dynasty (1644-1911) levirate was allowed. N. Niida (*Chinese Rural Families* [Tokyo, 1952], p. 194) and others (O. Osgood, *Village Life in Old China* [New York, 1963], p. 286; Yeh Te-chün in *Min-chien*, vol. 2, no. 5 [Hang-Chon, 1934], p. 62; and *T'ai-wan feng-t'u*, no. 37 [1948]) state that it still occurs occasionally in rural areas.

31. The *Li-yüan ts'ung-hua* (chapt. 23, 6a) enumerates twenty-six cases of remarrying princesses and other cases down to the eleventh century. The *Ch'ui-kang lu* (3, 10b) mentions further cases from T'ang and early Sung times. Fan Chung-yen, the great moralist of the eleventh century, in whose family two remarriages occurred, even gave a stipend to a remarrying widow. Fan lived 989-1052.

32. Szu-ma Kuang (1019-1086) prohibited remarriage (*Tzŭ-chih t'ung-chien* 291). In 1017 remarriage of a widow of a high official was prohibited (*Liao-shih* 15, see K. A. Wittfogel, *Liao* [New York, 1949], p. 262, and also p. 201). But the first text against remarriage of widows is already in *Li-chi*, Chiao-t'e-sheng 3,7; *Couvreur*, 1: 607, a Confucianist text.

chastity of widows by allowing her family to erect a monument in her honor.[33] Public ostracism of remarriage together with rewards for chastity of widows were the reasons for the gradual upper class acceptance of this rule. It began to spread also into the lower classes, although a widow was a financial burden and, being normally unwanted, did not have an enviable position in the family.[34] In the following centuries, until the onset of new ideas from the West, fewer and fewer upper-class widows married again, and the rule was even extended to girls who had merely been engaged to be married before the death of a fiancé.[35] Since engagements were often concluded when the future partners were still children, occasionally before they were born, and since life expectancy was low, the number of virgin widows must have been quite high. In spite of the ideal, most of them probably got married to someone else after the fiancé's death; but the fact remains that there are more reports of chaste virgin widows for the time after the eleventh century than there are for earlier times.[36] At the same time, pressures against the levirate were mounting. In this period the role of the individual in daily life became more important and the brother of a woman's husband became like any other man in relation to her. Up to modern times it has been the rule that a woman should marry only once. This could and did mean for a long time that a woman should marry only into one family, but gradually it was taken to mean that a woman should marry only one *man*. Consequently, in the course of Chinese history the levirate disappeared. We find laws prohibiting the levirate from the fourteenth century on.

The second example of "percolation" concerns the rules of mourning. According to the Confucianist ideology, the most important social relationship is the bond between father and son. Therefore, a man's public expression of grief should be greatest at his father's death. Ideally, a man who lost his father was supposed to leave his family and

33. See J. J. M. deGroot, *Religious System of China* (Leiden, 1892), 2: 744-61 and Wang Hui-chen in D. Nivison, *Confucianism in Action* (Stamford, 1959), p. 93.

34. In early twentieth century Kuangtung province, commoners did not like to marry widows (*Chung-hua ch 'üan-kuo feng-su chih*, part 2, chapt. 7, p. 9), while it was still common in Shansi (ibid, part 2, chapt. 2, p. 30) and Fukien (part 1, chapt. 4, p. 13). Cases of suicide and self-immolation of widows are not rare (deGroot, *Religious System*, 2: 737; 741f).

35. As an example, see H. Wilhelm in *Sinica* 6 (1931): 232-33. The procedure and cost of having a widow honored are described by Huang Tien-ch'üan in *T'ai-wan shih-shih yen-chiu* 2: 48-50.

36. See the general discussion in W. Eberhard, *Social Mobility in Traditional China* (Leiden, 1962), p. 135f.

wife, move into a hut near the father's tomb, and stay there for three years of mourning.[37] Clearly, only very well-to-do families could observe this severe rule, and even the upper class did not follow it religiously. The three years were whittled down to twenty-five months, and the mourner did not really live in a hut near the tomb.[38] But the rule that a man who lost his father must give up his position in the government and stay at home for the period of mourning, was more and more strictly enforced.[39] No attempt was made to force the lower classes to obey the rule, since obviously a peasant family would starve to death if it did. But some parts of the mourning rules were impressed on the lower classes. For instance, the prohibition of weddings in the family during the mourning period became generally accepted in time, and to some extent also prohibition of sexual intercourse.[40]

These two examples of "percolation" illustrate the following two points. First, once a society or rather, its leaders, have made their decisions concerning certain basic values, the society's thinkers begin developing practical rules that follow from these values. This process is characterized by a proliferation of regulations, as they are applied to many areas of social life. The second point is that the rules remained essentially unchanged, with only occasional minor adjustments, and that they were made obligatory for one social class after the other, although some allowance was made for special life conditions, especially in the lower classes. Material, and particularly economic progress, was apparently regarded as a necessary condition for the development of high morality, but certainly fewer and fewer people were exempted from the rules. Each new rule and each new application of an old rule put a new limit to the freedom of individuals and groups. It is signifi-

37. *Meng-tse* 3a, 2; R. Wilhelm, p. 50; *Mê Ti* 25; A. Forke, p. 301-2; *Hsun-tzu* 19; H. H. Dubs, p. 239; *Lun-yü* 17, 21; R. Wilhelm, p. 198; J. J. M. deGroot, *Religious System* 2: 500f. Data on the hut in deGroot, *loc cit* 2: 369 and 480f. Men were supposed to live in the hut for a year (*Li-chi,* Sang-chi, 2: 20; *Couvreur,* 2: 241).

38. Already in the *Li-chi* (San-nien wen 3 and 6; *Couvreur,* 2: 581 and 583) says that three years really meant only twenty-five months. Early writers mention that in Han time few mourned for three years, some only for thirty-six days (*Yeh-k'o ts'ung-shu* 13, 4b). *Meng-tse* (7a, 46; Wilhelm, p. 170) deplores the abbreviation.

39. Hsün Shuang (128-190) criticized the court for obliging high officials to reduce the period of mourning (Ch'en Ch'i-yün, "A Confucian Magnate's Idea of Political Violence," *T'oung Pao* 54 [1968]: 83).

40. J. J. M. deGroot, *Religious System,* 2: 608f. An interesting modern exception is the custom that a widower remarries within the first hundred days after the death of his wife (Hung Hsiu-kui in *Newsletter of Chinese Ethnology,* no. 7 (Oct. 1967): 22). In T'ang time, a person to whom a child was born during the mourning period was punishable (*Ta T'ang lü-li,* section 156).

cant that in the Chinese language there was no word for "freedom" before the impact of the West. Because of the principle of harmony between society and nature, which every government claiming legitimacy must bring about through educating the people, there can be no freedom. On the other hand, this ideology was a stabilizing factor, since its ultimate aim and, therefore, the direction of the development remained the same—as long as the reins were in the hands of the same upper class, that is, until the twentieth century.

Against the background of this conservative ideology there was the reality of life, ever changing in all areas of culture, and especially in technology. The interplay between this ideology and actual life is, or was, Chinese social development, of which the development of the upper-class family was a part. This has been true since the end of China's feudal period, the period of clan society.

Returning to social reality at the beginning of the medieval period we see that, as a result of marriages with concubines and other women of common origin, there were now families whose bonds with the old lineages were weak. Political developments had also favored the breakdown of lineage unity, because already at Confucius' time every noble home considered itself independent, often showing signs of splitting into smaller units, namely individual families. Eventually these noble families, and also the families descended from sons of concubines, began to take on family names which they selected according to principles similar to those used for naming in European countries; some families chose the name of the place where they lived; others named themselves after the office held by an ancestor; still others after physical traits, and so on.[41] By the end of the feudal period, around 250 B.C., apparently every upper-class family had its own family name which was passed on from father to son and, with very few exceptions, was never changed down to the present time.[42] Persons with different family names were allowed to marry, on the assumption that there was no blood relation-

41. A comprehensive study of the principles actually used is still lacking, but valuable remarks are found in *Bulletin of the Institute of History and Philology, Academia Sinica* 26 (1955): 189-226 and 28 (1957): 713-716. Modern lists of Chinese family names have a total of 1181 different family names (*Hsin-sheng pao*, Taipei, March 12, 1965).

42. There are cases where a family or a branch of a family changed its family name in order to escape political persecution. In later generations, intermarriage between the original family and the newly named branch family were forbidden, because both families were still regarded as related. Other cases of forbidden intermarriage between families with different names are explained as caused by a bond of "blood-brotherhood" created by ancestors of both families at some time in history. Cases of this type are more common in South than in North China.

ship between any two families of different name for at least the last five generations. Persons with the same family name were not permitted to marry, even if it could be proved that there was no blood relationship at all.[43] This rule, too, has been observed up to the present time, with very few exceptions.

As one fief after the other disappeared, one noble family after the other lost its rank. But, as in feudal Europe, when a feudal family lost its fief in a war against another vassal, its members were not degraded to the status of "commoners." The victor gave the loser a piece of land, large enough to feed the family and its household retainers. Thus, like the descendents of concubines—sons who had already become families of landowners—the deposed families also became landowners. Land, formerly the property of the fiefholder—although ultimately, at least in theory, the property of the king—now became the property of individual families. Again, this development is not very different from what happened in Europe, where former feudal families also became families of landlords. Thus, at the beginning of the new period of medieval China shortly before 200 B.C., when the successors of the feudal system, the various local states, were replaced by a centralized absolute monarchy with a bureaucracy, we find a class of landlords who lived off the income of their land. The farm work was done by their retainers whom we now call "tenants." But the traditions and the glory of the feudal period were not forgotten in these families. As best they could, they emulated the customs and manners of the old time and had their sons instructed in the ways of gentlemanly behavior by hired teachers. They developed into the class we now call "gentry."[44]

Any aristocratic society is based on the principle of "ascriptive status," that is, one belongs to an elite through birth, and does not achieve membership through merit. But even in a feudal system some services are so important that aptitude not status is decisive. A feudal lord has always needed persons not related to him by family ties, if only to control and spy on his relatives and sub-vassals. He needed special people for the tedious job of keeping records and files, for his personal service, and for those questionable jobs that rulers often feel they must

43. Therefore, masters gave their slaves—and in later periods, their servants—the same family name which they themselves had. Slaves often were foreigners who had no family names, or their ancestry was unknown.

44. Definition and description of the gentry and a discussion of the problem is given in my *Conquerors and Rulers*, second edition (Leiden, 1965), p. 22ff.

get done. In all feudal societies there were certain "ideal" persons for these jobs, among them foreigners and other people from outside the ruler's jurisdiction, people without a family to back them up, and people who, for one reason or another, could not return to their families. Persons of this kind became the nucleus of the new bureaucracy and, as in every bureaucracy, it was achievement that counted most, not ascribed status. Careers in the government administration came to be determined by the two principles of merit and seniority. Already at the end of ancient China, the kings of the various local states had began to rely heavily on officials rather than their own vassals.

The centralized monarchy of medieval China, needing a large army of administrative officials, was necessarily faced with a problem of recruitment. At the beginning of this period, some forms of examinations were already being developed as a means of selecting the best men for administrative work. Over the next two thousand years, the system of examinations was repeatedly revised and refined, until it was abolished in 1904. Examinations, of course, imply the existence of certain standards and requirements. For instance, it was required that all officials speak the same language and write the same script. As China had many dialects and as the script had developed differently in the various local states, the first steps of the centralized government were unification of the language, through the compilation of dictionaries and encyclopedias, and unification of the script, through the compilation of word lists. Those who wished to enter the bureaucracy naturally needed teachers. The first such tutors were the men who had left their home and had entered the service of a lord to work as his clerk or, at best, as his political advisor. When these men were old, or tired of life at the court, they retired and became tutors of upper-class youth. Confucius was one of the first of these teachers—after a lifetime of trying in vain to find a ruler in whose services he could prove his wisdom. The frustrated man who never quite made good, but always claimed respect as the mental father of his pupils, remained, until the recent past, the typical figure of a teacher in Chinese society. People respected and yet belittled him. He was full of knowledge and yet full of resentment.

Any bureaucracy can choose between two principles in the selection of its officials. Either it fills the positions with men especially trained for each kind of job, or it trains a personality whose cultivated behavior enables him to do well in any job under all circumstances. The Chinese, like the pre-modern Europeans, decided to apply the second principle and administered their government with a special type of person, the educated upper-class gentleman. In Europe and in China, this type was fashioned after the model of the nobleman. Confucius, who has described the traits that make a gentleman, was perhaps the first to emphasize that nobility is not caused by blood alone, but that those are noble who think and behave like noblemen. The newly developing gentry, claiming descent from noble families and cherishing family traditions, tried in addition to become "noble" by learning "noble" behavior, and it was convinced that a state could be run only by "noble" persons, not by technicians or specialists. All later Chinese governments agreed that a "noble" man with a proper education, which emphasized moral values, is able to do well in every leading position, because he understands the moral principles that must guide his actions. If technical advice is needed, a craftsman or other specialist can be called to help out. Thus, the state used its system of examinations to find men of superior character, not men of knowledge, so that the gentry of medieval China continued in a modified way the ideals of the ancient aristocracy. The difference was in theory: everybody able to learn to behave like a gentleman could enter the government and rise up to the highest posts.

Of course, "everybody" did not exactly mean every citizen. As previously mentioned, at times slaves were not considered members of human society, and members of the so-called "mean classes" (chien-min), which included artisans and merchants during much of the medieval period, were not full citizens. "Everybody" therefore, meant essentially the families of landlords and free farmers. (And few small farmers could afford to hire a teacher). Besides, the Chinese bureaucratic governments did not let more candidates pass the qualifying examinations than there were job openings. Those who failed were considered, and had to consider themselves, unqualified for government service, and they filled the ranks of teachers. Thus, competition in the examinations was always fierce. In the Han period (206 B.C. to 220 A.D.), the candidates had to come to the capital for the examinations, and in order to have a pre-selected group, the local administrators in the provinces had to recommend candidates from their own districts and were held responsible for their quality. If a candidate was excellent, the recommending administrator could be sure to benefit officially, while at the same time the successful candidate became obliged to the man who had recommended him. If a candidate failed, or at any time committed acts regarded as immoral, the administrator might lose his job and receive additional punishment. Administrators were therefore cautious with their recommendations. Understandably, every administrator was under pressure from his own family to recommend relatives. As a result of these circumstances, the circle of persons with access to the examinations and to governmental positions soon became smaller, especially if we keep in mind that the sons of high court officials were given special privileges and special schooling, so that they had better chances to begin with than a boy from the provinces. Exceptions always occurred, but in general we can say that in the medieval period of gentry society, the political power was in the hands of the so-called "hundred families." Throughout many centuries, and in some cases throughout a thousand year period, members of the same families occupied the leading governmental positions.[45]

What was the emperor in such a system? Essentially there were two types of dynasties in medieval China.[46] Some dynasties came into power by acts of violence, either by conquest (foreigners conquering parts of China) or by rebellion (men of lower-class origin overthrowing the existing ruler). Naturally they put their own relatives and supporters in the key positions of power. But not a single new dynasty of this type had enough capable and trustworthy people of its own to staff the existing bureaucracy. Also, after one generation, the supporters' sons as well as the new ruler's own relatives were not more, but often less reliable than the conquered gentry. Thus, a new dynasty of this type was soon forced to select its officials again from the ranks of the gentry and often, after a generation or two, most of the newly "arrived" families faded out again, so that the circle supplying administrators and other leaders was hardly larger than before. The second type of dynasty is the dynasty created by the victor in a fight between cliques within the circle of gentry families. A ruler who did not want to become a tool of his clique had to try balancing clique power by appointing men belonging to competing cliques and playing them against each other. Some emperors were incapable of playing this game and were used by one clique which ultimately pushed the hostile clique out of the power positions, deposed the emperor, and replaced him with a man from its own ranks. This

45. Their claim to belong to such a famous family may not in all cases have been based upon genealogical facts, but sometimes on belief or make-believe.

46. These problems are discussed in my *Conquerors and Rulers*, p. 98f.

type of dynastic change changed nothing in the circle of gentry families, except the relative power of the individual families.

The only other typical means of access to power, besides dynastic change and a few exceptional cases, was through relation to the emperor himself. Gentry China no longer had an aristocracy. There was the emperor, an absolute ruler, who ranked above all other families. He could not have an equal wife. Only occasionally was a medieval or modern Chinese emperor forced to recognize the ruler of a foreign country as quasi-equal (which Chinese historians have always tried to avoid admitting). Occasionally a Chinese emperor was obliged to conclude a political marriage with a foreign ruling house. But as all societies around China were polygamous, a Chinese princess given in marriage to a foreign ruler did not become the foreigner's main wife, nor did a foreign princess become empress of China—in stark contrast to monogamous Europe.[47] The Chinese emperors took their empresses from the circle of the gentry families, those families that not only exercised the actual power of government but also had the desirable background and education. In addition to the empress, the emperor could have as many concubines as he wished. Concubines were maidens of special beauty, selected from all over the country by local administrators who, in return for such a valuable gift, gained not only the emperor's recognition, but also the gratitude of the concubine on whose support they could count if they needed help. These concubines often brought their brothers and cousins into positions of power, and some concubines even became empresses when the empress died or had no son. In this case the concubine's whole family suddenly rose to power and joined the circle of the "hundred families." This dynastic system provided, on the one hand, continuity of gentry power and, on the other hand, some chance for outsiders to enter the gentry ranks. Cases of rapid social mobility, where an emperor took an interest or found pleasure at the sight of a man and raised him from nothing to a high rank, were very rare in China.[48]

The structure of the gentry, the upper class, then appears to be the secret of the stability and continuity of medieval China. In contrast to

47. The Chinese apparently rarely gave real daughters of the emperor to foreign rulers, and the "morganatic" marriages of the medieval European upper class were concessions to the principle of monogamy.

48. In all this we must keep in mind that the picture given here is an attempt at establishing the rule—to which exceptions can always be found. In our sociological approach the goal is generalization; the unique is the subject for the historian.

despotic systems, where any individual might make a career or find sudden death, an individual in gentry China could play a role only because of his membership in an important family.[49] The family had its home seat in the countryside, on the land that constituted the base of its economic security. Those of its members who were interested and capable of playing the political game would move into the capital, where they would join their relatives by blood or marriage (members of the same clique) who saw to it that the newcomer was classified among the privileged and found his place in the administration. Once in a power position, he could protect his own and related families and their properties; and by virtue of his power he could acquire more wealth and more land. He could promote other family members and bring them into positions of influence. He could fall into disgrace and be executed, and his whole family might be executed with him. But even in this worst of all cases, some member of his family was sure to get notice early enough to go into hiding, often with the help of related families, so that eventually the survivors could rebuild the family's position of power and wealth, particularly if some or all of the land was still intact. On the other hand, a gentry man who was not interested in power could remain in the family home as the manager of the family property, at the same time playing the role of mediator in village conflicts. A gentry man who was not willing to be either an official or a farm manager, but was interested in science, poetry, or painting could devote his time to learning the skills in these fields and spend his life in leisure and meditation, either in the city or in a house in the mountains. The family could afford to support him adequately.[50]

The rules of Chinese ancestral worship required, as Chinese society was patrilinear, that every man should have a son, as only he could perform the rituals which guaranteed an acceptable continuation of existence after death. But the political importance of a large family, which we have just mentioned, also made it imperative that each family have at least one son, and with the relatively high infant mortality and low life expectancy (by some calculated as somewhere around thirty years), a family needed more than one son. As some men, in spite of having concubines, did not beget sons or even children, adoptions were

49. The exception is the military career which in periods of general unrest made it possible for persons with no background to rise to the top of the society. The typical example for this is the period between 906 and 960, in which so many military leaders moved into the leadership that the whole structure of Chinese society was changed.

50. These problems are discussed in my *Social Mobility*.

always common. The rule was, until the present, to adopt only a child of one's own family, preferably a son of a brother or a cousin. As a family tried not to give away their first son, it was often the second or third son who may have been given away, a situation which caused psychological difficulties for second or third sons. Only in coastal South China, were non-related children sometimes adopted; the reasons for this lie in the special conditions of that area. In many periods of Chinese history, adoption of non-related sons was forbidden by law.[51]

It is obvious that the gentry families, like the feudal families, could not let their children marry indiscriminately. The status of a gentry family depended on the security of its power, and this security could be achieved only by building up a network of relations, including mutually binding marriage ties, with other gentry families so that together they could form a clique. Daughters were needed for these ties; sons were needed even more, not only to manage the rural properties, but most of all to occupy as many posts as possible in the government. Therefore, considering also the chances of early death, gentry families always hoped for a large number of sons. So it happened that, on the average, Chinese upper-class families had more children than lower-class families, and more of their children lived to adulthood because of better living conditions. For a lower-class family a daughter was a net loss: she had to be fed until she was old enough to work, and then she had to be given in marriage at the cost of a dowry. Both expenses together were not offset by the bride price received from the groom's family. One or two sons were good for use on the farm, but small farms could not feed many people, and if there were many sons, who brought in wives and had more children, there was hunger, starvation, and sickness. Here again we have a difference between China and the West: because of the principle of primogeniture governing inheritance in the European feudal system, the European aristocracy considered too many sons as well as too many daughters a burden. Second, third, and fourth

---

51. See Sh. Kato, *Studies in Chinese Economic History* (Tokyo, 1953), 2: 766-67, and N. Niida, *Legal Documents* (Tokyo, 1937), p. 513 and 516. Niida (p. 517) mentions special exceptions during periods of famine. The adoption of non-related sons is reported in *Ch'iu-yü-wan sui-pi*, ch. 5, p. 17b for South China; for Taiwan see Lin Heng-tao in *T'ai-wan feng-t'u*, no. 62 (1949), and Yang Ch'ing-yü in *Hsin shê-hui* 12, no. 4 (1960): 15. "Kan-erk" (dry son) is not an adopted son, but comparable to a god-child. This custom is not often mentioned in historical sources (e.g., in *Chu-ching-shue-shê ling-mo*, ch. 3, p. 10b). For the regular adoption during the Han period see now Ch'ü T'ung-tsu, *Han Social Structure* (Seattle, 1972), pp. 18-20.

sons could at best enter the army or become settlers in colonial lands; too many daughters meant that some of them were likely to remain un- married and could only be sent into convents or be kept at home as useless spinsters. Later, the European upper-bourgeois families also wanted few children in order to be able to provide their sons with the best education and starting capital, and their daughters with education and dowry. In gentry China inheritance had nothing to do with pri- mogeniture, although the oldest son had ritual responsibilities or pri- mogeniture. (Because he had to represent the family in the ancestral rituals, he did receive some extra land to defray the cost of rites.)[52] The limited number of positions in the government, even if large, ensured that gentry families could not expect, even under favorable conditions, to get all their sons into power positions. This resulted in a considerable amount of downward social mobility. While one son was successful in government service and created a high status for his nuclear family, his brothers might have remained on the land, living a life of leisure, and not infrequently wasting property and capital until their descendants ended up as small farmers. Because they were still related to the affluent branch of the family, they might receive its help, but never enough to restore their upper-class status. The old "rule of five generations" continued to be applied: after five generations, a branch family could, by an act of law, be declared independent, and its domicile could be registered as a new family's home. For the wealthy branches this had the advantage of absolving their responsibility for the fate of the new branch; and for the new family, of securing its safety in case a powerful branch, or the main branch fell into disgrace. In medieval China many separating branches migrated to one of the less developed parts of the country, usually in the south.

52. A Ming text (*Ming-chai tsa-chi*, reprinted in *Li-tai hsiao-shuo pi-chi hsüan, Ming*, p. 244) states that in those high-ranking families in which a son had a right to get a position after the death of the father, attempts were made to put the oldest son into the job of the father and to have the youngest get the rank of the father. I do not know whether this was a general custom at that time. The aborigines of Taiwan which have a feudal social structure, have primogeniture (for the Bunun tribes see *Shè-ch'ü yen-chiu shih-hsi pao-kao* [Taipei, 1959], p. 40b; for the Paiwan, Wei Hwei-lin, "Ambilateral Lineage and Class System of the Paiwan," *Bulletin of the Institute of Ethnology, Academia Sinica* 9 [1960]: 98-99). In matri-clan societies, such as among the Ami on Taiwan (Wei Hwei-lin, "Matri-clan and Lineage System of the Ami," *Bulletin of the Institute of Ethnology, Academia Sinica* 12 [1961]: 29) and among the inhabitants of Amami in the Liu-ch'iu is- lands (D. G. Haring, "Selected Aspects of Chinese and Japanese Cultural Influences on the Northern Ryūkyū Islands," *Sociologus* 13 [1963]: 63) the eldest daughter can become head of the family.

Wolfram Eberhard

In a way, this downward mobility contributed to the stability of the gentry system by eliminating from its ranks those who did not fit the system. On the other hand, one must not think that gentry continuity and stability were achieved at the price of cultural stagnation. Anyone acquainted with the history of medieval China knows that great progress was made in all areas of human thought and activity, even in technology. Not many gentry men built instruments or made measurements with their own hands, but neither did the European scientists as long as they had trained craftsmen to do it for them. Like the great scholars of early Europe, and like the modern Chinese upper middle class, a gentry man shied away from physical labor. But in spite of this attitude, inventions were made in medieval China, and there was no lack of cultural development.

The history of medieval China can be subdivided into two periods. During the first, from about 250 B.C. to 300 A.D., the gentry developed to its full bloom. During part of the second period, from 300 A.D. to around 580 A.D., at least half of China—the highly developed northern area—was under foreign rule. Some of the conquering groups, especially the Turkish tribes, were representatives of aristocratic societies of their own.[53] In spite of their contempt for the "barbarians," the Chinese gentry families who cooperated with the foreign rulers were impressed by their aristocratic manners and attitudes and began to imitate them. Gentry families started working on their genealogies, trying to prove that they had descended from kings or lords, and that other families who claimed the same were not of noble Chinese descent. These other families were accused of being orginally either foreigners who had adopted a Chinese name in order to be regarded as gentry, or descendants of slaves who had received their master's family name. In the period of foreign rule, many foreigners had actually taken Chinese names, because their own names were awkward to write or pronounce in Chinese. As to the slaves, it was indeed customary that the master give his family name to the slaves when he granted them freedom. This practice served to prevent any member of the master's family from ever getting married to a descendant of the former slave's family, since marriages of persons with the same family name were prohibited. The interest in genealogies resulted in long lists of gentry families, with information on the family home and other details similar to the European

53. These problems are discussed in my *Das Toba-Reich Nord-Chinese* (Leiden, 1949).

"Gotha" handbook of the aristocracy. These were the "good" families into which a gentry member could marry. Some extremely exclusive families considered only four or five families socially equal and eligible for marriage arrangements. The Ts'ui family in the seventh century refused to intermarry even with the imperial house, the Li house of the T'ang, because they suspected the Li's of being upstarts from a non-Chinese frontier family. As a consequence of these exclusive tendencies, during the second part of the medieval period the gentry began to split into "top" gentry and "ordinary" gentry—a factor which, however, had more influence on marriage and clique combinations than on politics. On the other hand, in this period a fair number of foreign families who had belonged to the tribal aristocracy were accepted into the ranks of the gentry because these families had been nobility in their own societies and could be said to be of equal status. These upper-class foreigners were more than willing to give up their own values and customs, including even language and clothing, and become fully Chinese. This assimilation occurred at the same time that the descendants of the commoners among the foreign invaders rejected Chinese values and finally left China to return to the steppes whence their fathers had come.

Profound changes in the political as well as economic sphere set in around 800 A.D., initiating the next historical period, which I call "modern China," and putting an end to the medieval gentry society, discussed above. In the realm of politics, the most important event was the breakdown of the unified empire, first into more or less independent satrapies, and then, during the period of the Five Dynasties (906 to 960) into a number of independent states. In the numerous new, small states in south China, relatively unimportant provincial cities suddenly became centers of cultural activities, sustained by the wealth which was produced by trade and by the production of products such as silk, paper, tea, metal. The rulers in these southern states were often former generals from the North who created their own domain with the help of armies they had brought with them. Masses of people had moved from the North to the South in search of security and peace when and after the North was lost, in the tenth century, to various foreign rulers, including the Mongols (Ch'i-tan). Once before there had been a mass exodus to the South, when foreigners overran the North between 300 and 580 A.D., but at that time "South" meant mainly the lower Yangtse area. For the tenth century, "South" meant the area between the

Yangtse and the southern coast. There were cities and towns in this deep south, but in general the area was underdeveloped, thinly settled with Chinese, and inhabited by non-Chinese tribes.[54]

With the establishment, first, of the small states, and then with the re-establishment of the Sung dynasty south of the Yangtse river after its defeat in the North (1127), a new era of colonization began. Apparently whole families left their homes in central and north China and settled on new land in the South. The constant wars and the foreign conquests of the northern area, which was the home of the gentry, had destroyed the old gentry almost completely. Besides, there no longer existed a large empire with a central government in need of many officials. The ever-changing rulers, some former bandits or soldiers, others foreign military leaders, had preferred their own men and had rarely succeeded in setting up a government that could pay salaries. Often the gentry family's land was conquered by one military leader and the capital by another, which destroyed the necessary unity of the family's two essential parts. When, from 960 on, the Sung dynasty succeeded in annexing the southern small states and uniting parts of China, important parts of the North remained under foreign rule. Besides, the Hsi/-hsia, the Kitan (Ch'i-tan), and the Sung contended for a large nothern area which consequently became economically depressed. Some of the old gentry families reconstituted themselves and continued to play a role when the Sung had their capital in K'ai-feng, not too far from the homes of many gentry families; but others never recovered from the devastations. The tenth century is perhaps the period of the greatest social shift experienced by China before the twentieth century. One of the results was that the capital no longer served as the only place of political importance. Even after the unification of the southern small states, many cities in central and south China remained important economic centers with a potential for political as well as cultural activities. To be transferred to a southern province as governor, or to a district as a magistrate, was no longer equivalent to exile. On the contrary, life there would be gayer and more exciting than in the captial. Thus, the medieval gentry was transformed into a kind of "small gentry"— families with a structure similar to that of the medieval gentry, but not so much interested in the power game at the imperial court as in political and cultural activities on the provincial level. The population grew, especially in the South, so that the government needed more

54. For details see my *Social Mobility*.

administrators and created new positions. The Sung rulers, more than their predecessors, paid attention to economic questions, and even in decisions concerning foreign relations they were often guided by economic rather than purely political considerations. This resulted in more personnel being employed in the financial and economic sector of administration. In the new South, as in every colonial area, the chances for amassing wealth in a short time were great and often more tempting than a career in government service. Thus, while some medieval gentry families disappeared from the scene, many new families attained prosperity and power, some from very modest origins. The examination system began to function more truly as a selective method because the court was no longer dominated by those "hundred families" which, in spite of examinations, had prevented persons from outside their own group from getting into power positions. Now there were many more positions than the "hundred families" could control, and the government appointed new people who had no family traditions. These men were surely interested in securing a place for their sons, but they were not part of a system of political alliances based on ties of intermarriage. Important among the new economic factors was, first, the shift toward rice as a staple food which made the South, the main rice producer, increasingly important. Secondly, the country shifted to a full money economy, accompanied by the development of banks and credit institutions. Thirdly, since the invention of printing, studying for participation in the examinations had become less expensive, so that even relatively poor people were enabled to compete.

The growth of this local "small gentry" is one characteristic of the period of modern China. By being "small" it never achieved the centuries-long stability of the medieval big-gentry families. The second characteristic is the emergence of landlord families in the South. They acquired great wealth and often saw to it that at least one son went into business, such as wholesale trading in rice and salt, silk, cotton, and silver. These sons would settle in the commerical centers but, unlike the city dwellers of the medieval gentry, they were not normally interested in government positions. Many of these families established their own intermarriage rules, but they were not the same as those of the "big" gentry in medieval China. For example, in one area in the South there were two lineages that had exchanged their sons and daughters among each other, whenever at all possible, for over eight hundred years—the reason being that both families were the first Chinese settlers in a non-

Chinese area, so that, from their point of view, no other marriages were possible. There were other cases in which groups of ten or more families had married exclusively among themselves, apparently because they all came from the same home country and migrated into the colonial area as a group.

An extremely important development in the modern period was the emergence of the individual. This does not mean to say that there were no individuals in medieval China, but not until the Sung period did literary works begin to speak of people as individuals. Instead of people being labelled with sterotypes—"good" or "bad", loyal or disloyal—people appear in the literature as real persons with their own weaknesses and strengths. For the first time, human tragedies are described; for example, there exist examples of persons caught in a dilemma where any action would violate one of the basic rules, leaving suicide as the only way out. The novel and the theatre play, new forms developed in early modern China, became the media of dealing with the individual. The topic might be individual heroism, or individual opposition to the government, which is praised where the government is depicted as corrupt.[55] In historical texts, rulers with despotic desires were described as individual personalities with passions and moods, not just good or bad representatives of a supreme order.

In many western societies, the breakdown of family units based on blood relationship was accompanied by the growth of an anonymous unit, the state, which then tried to tie unattached individuals directly to itself. At first this led to absolute monarchy or despotism, but afterwards to government by the rule of a multitude of replaceable individuals over masses of individuals. In China, the modern period contains the beginnings of similar trends. From the fourteenth to seventeeth centuries, during the Ming, there were emperors who tried to establish themselves as despots. In order to safeguard their power, they surrounded themselves not with regular officials, that is not with educated gentlemen representing the moral principles of gentry society, but with eunuchs who were individuals without education, without family, without any ties.

Another trend toward individualism in modern China can be seen in the changing status of women. Novelists created the type of heroic female, the beautiful fighter for righteousness, who defeats bandits and

---

55. A very perceptive analysis of the hero East and West is found in James Liu, *Chinese Knight-Errants* (London, 1967), p. 196f.

protects frail scholars.[56] Genealogists, who formerly recorded full names only for fathers and sons, began to give the names of mothers, the personal names of daughters, and often even the names of the daughter's husbands. More and more one reads of fathers who saw to it that their daughters received an education, not only in the female arts, but in reading and writing literature, attainments formerly limited to sons. A famous Chinese novel (*Ching-hua-yüan*), written before Western ideas about the rights of women could have been known to China, asks its male readers to imagine that they were women and proceeds to outline a society in which women are equal to men in every respect.[57] It is true that another century had to pass until these ideas became law, but at the

56. The typical heroine of this type is in the novel *Erh-yü ying-hsiung chuan*. Figures of this kind are common from Ming time on. They still play a great role in modern plays and movies.

57. It is an interesting question to ask whether in this period women of the upper class got more freedom in the selection of their husbands. As far as we can see, this was not the case in the majority of marriages, but we find in numerous plays and stories the motif of a girl asking potential grooms to come to the front of a balcony or window of her house. She then throws a ball into the crowd, promising to marry the one who catches the ball. This is well-known Chinese tale motif (W. Eberhard, *Typen chinesischer Volksmärchen* [Helsinki, 1937], no. 193) which has very close parallels in the Near East (W. Eberhard and P. N. Boratav, *Typen türkischer Volksmärchen* [Wiesbaden, 1953], Index under "Ballwurf"). In the Chinese drama, it is most prominent in the cycle of plays around Hsüeh P'ing-kui (also called *Wang Pao-ch'uan* cycle), such as *P'ing-kui pich yao* in *Ti-fang shi-ch'ü chi-ch'eng*, (Canton), pp. 327-37; *Pieh-yao* in *Hsi-ch'ü hsüan* 5: 119-35; *P'ao-ts'ai chu'hsü*, in W. Grube, *Chinesische Schattenspiele* (München, 1915), p. 146; and even in the *Wang-Pao-ch'uan* and the movie based upon it. It also occurs in the cycle of the plays around Lü Meng-cheng, such as *Hsi-pao* in W. Grube, *loc. cit.*, p. 182; a folk ballad in Min-nan dialect, *Ts'ai-lou p'ei*, also has this story. The motif also occurs in a Buddhist play, *Hsiang-shan chi* (*Ch'u-hai*, pp. 856-59) and in the famous Fukienese play *Li-ching chi* (about this motif in the play see *T'ai-wan feng-wu* 1960, no. 2, p.16). It is found in the classical novel *Hsi yo chi* (chapt. 93-95) and occurs in the legendary genealogy of the T'ang emperors as it is told presently (L. Schram, *The Monguors* [Philadelphia, 1956], p. 27a). The ceremony of throwing the ball is in this case connected with the festival of the second day of the second month; the Lü Meng-cheng plays connect it with the fifteenth day of the eighth month (T'ai-wan feng-t'u, no. 114). A full study of the motif still has to be done. At the present, the earliest clear reference is in the *Li-ching-chi*, which is the recent form of the *Li-ching chuan*, the tale of Ch'en San and Wu-niang. The earliest known version of this work is from 1566 (Wu Shou-li in *T'ai-wan feng-wu* 10, no. 2 [1960]: 6) and comes from Southern Fukien. Now we have reports that the throwing of the ball, connected with the festival on the fifteenth day of the seventh month, was an actual custom in Fukien (W. Eberhard, *Local Cultures*, pp. 126-27). Thus, we may be faced with a local Fukienese custom and not with a motif which points towards a tendency to give women more rights. The *Yeh-yü ch'iu-teng lu*, part 1, chapt. 4, p. 4a, reports as an actual happening in Peking that a girl selected as a husband the man who got the highest points in dice throwing. Each throw cost ten silver tael. The story comes from a mid-nineteenth century book and the girl was not from a high-ranking family.

time when this novel was published, few Europeans were as progressive as its author.

It is not easy to explain the reasons for the trend toward individualism in China. One may point to the diversity of cultural centers, to the broadening base of the upper class, and to the emergence of an urban quasi-patriciate.[58] The development of numerous urban centers inhabited by rich businessmen—who, incidentally, soon engaged in industrial enterprises—gradually led to a new type of city life. These *nouveau riches* could afford to have artists decorate their houses with paintings; they could hire theater companies and specify the plays they wished to see; they could employ geishas for their parties and visit geisha houses. These diversions were "for men only" and took place outside the home, away from the family. Wealth counted more than family status in these commercial entertainments. We know of cases where wealthy businessmen boasted that they had invited impoverished scholars and had them compose poems in return for food and money. Although officially condemned by the upper class, this pleasurable life must have had an attraction also for upper-class men. Without a doubt, personality and originality were assets in such an environment.

While the *actual* development of the society went toward greater individual freedom, more specialization, broadening of the upper class, and greater social mobility, the *ideological* development went in the opposite direction, not without having its own factual consequences. The ideology of the early modern period has been called Neo-Confucianism. Confucius, in his time, had been worried about the breakdown of the feudal traditions around him and therefore developed his ideas about the ideal society. Similarly, the Sung philosophers in the eleventh and twelfth centuries worried about the decay of gentry society and its traditions and tried to re-establish a good society by solidifying its family basis. It seems that they considered Buddhism their main enemy.

Ever since Buddhism came to China around the beginning of our era, if not earlier, the Confucian thinkers have rejected Buddhism, charging that it disparaged family and marriage and thus undermined the basis of Chinese society. For centuries the Buddhists tried to defend themselves against the accusation of being individualistic and selfish. As long as Buddhism was a religion of the lower classes, which it was at first, and as long as Buddhism was of interest to the upper classes only because of the science it had brought to China or because of the fasci-

58. Details in my *Social Mobility*, p. 259.

nation of meditation, the danger for the Confucian society was negligible. But the later years of the gentry period brought forth whole communities of Buddhists, comparable to Christian church communities. People of all classes and of both sexes came together for common worship; they became organized; they created welfare institutions for their members, such as orphanages, cemeteries, hospitals, pharmacies and schools. All these institutions were immensely important in a period of internal unrest and war, when every family might come to grief. In other words, the Buddhists began to take into their hands what, in the eyes of Confucianists, had heretofore been the domain of family and state. The Neo-Confucian thinkers in the early modern period reacted by reformulating parts of the Confucian philosophy. They incorporated certain Buddhist elements which they expressed in purely Chinese terminology without using the foreign terms that the Buddhists had introduced. Also, new family institutions were created to take over the functions of the Buddhist welfare institutions. The most important step in this direction was what we might call the family or lineage "foundation," which was an income-producing piece of land or other property whose profits could be made available for special or unexpected family or individual needs, such as the education of impoverished lineage members, funerals, weddings, and food in case of famine. From here on there were lineage schools all over the country, and some of them admitted also non-lineage children, if they showed promise. On the higher level, state welfare institutions were created or improved to protect the rest of the population in cases of famine or flood, and to instruct the public in morals and ethics through free lectures. The clear result of these measures was the Buddhism lost its appeal and never regained it, especially not in the upper classes whose literary men were now attracted by the intellectual stimulation provided by the Neo-Confucian teachings. Buddhism fell back to being a religion of the lower classes.[59]

If one wanted to describe briefly the social goal of the new ideology, one might say that Neo-Confucianism proposed to build a "good" society by avoiding social change. If everybody had his place, in the family and in the state, the society would run smoothly and would never be out

59. There were always exceptions: men and women emotionally attracted to Buddhist thinking. There were always monasteries for men who did not fit into society and nunneries for women who, usually after the death of their husband, could not or would not live in their own or their husband's families. In modern folk religion, Buddhism also has other social functions.

of gear. Chu Hsi (who died in 1200), the most important exponent of the new system of thought, wrote his *Family Instructions* which tightened the old rules and condemned "modern" misuses. In the *Family Instructions*, which were promulgated not only in the whole empire but also in Korea, Japan and Annam, remarriage of widows was forbidden, the husband's power in the family was enlarged, and the freedom of women was diminished. It was Chu Hsi who was shocked about the freedom of women in the province of Fukien, where he was a magistrate, and who introduced the veil there.[60] Also, it was he who proposed the banishment of women into the harem, which soon became fact for the upper class and eventually also for the middle and lower classes. This development was accompanied by the custom of foot-binding, first observed in court circles around the turn of the tenth century, and soon to became general practice in class after class, from the top down.[61] On their tiny bound feet these women were physically unable to walk freely or to move around normally outside the house. It is not surprising, then, that the ideal of the robust, strong woman of T'ang time gave way to the ideal of the slender, frail, and helpless plaything of the Sung period. Chu Hsi and his predecessors recognized that the upper class was broadening and that a new middle class was emerging; so he was all the more intent on imposing his rules not only on the upper, but also on the middle and possibly lower classes. His intention was to improve the life of the lower classes, but they may have suffered more than they gained.

This, then, was the situation in the middle of the nineteenth century, when Western military and civilian techniques, as well as Western religious and political ideas really began to penetrate China. These ideas met with Neo-Confucianism, the ideology requiring an unchanging society ruled by moral codes through an elite, but they also met with a considerably different social reality. A new middle class had developed

60. This is a local tradition in Chang-chou (*K'ang-yu chi-hsing* 14, 3a); in nearby Ch'ao-chou (Kuangtung) the Confucianist Han Yu is regarded as responsible (*Ch'iu-yü-wan sui-pi* 6, 23b). How far this custom was accepted, is not clear; in En-p'ing (Kuangtung) it was supposedly common (*Chung-hua ch'üan-kuo feng-su chih*, part 1, chapt. 8, p. 48), while in Yang-chiang (Kuangtung) only upper class women practised it (*Yang-chiang hsien-chih* 1, p. 63b). The custom was prescribed for the upper class in the ancient ritual texts (*Li-chi*, Nei-tsê 1, 12; *Couvreur* 1: 630) and is often reported for upper class women in medieval China.

61. See detailed discussion in H. S. Levy, *Chinese Foot-binding* (New York, 1966).

with its own standards, and many upper-class people felt closer to these standards than to the official code of ethics. The middle class began learning from the Westerners through their business contacts and soon became wealthier than before. This new middle class was particularly open to new ideas, especially those involving more freedom for the individual. At the same time the upper class began to lose faith in its own mission; it began to doubt the validity of its ideology and drifted around in a multitude of values, without unifying principles. Perhaps one can say that these are the ultimate reasons for the loss by China's old upper class of its mandate to rule.

This process was accentuated by the fact that since the Manchu conquest (1644), the ruling class had been a mixture of Manchu officials whose main qualification was their ethnic status, and Chinese gentry, who held government jobs mainly on the basis of merit. The tensions between these two groups had decreased in the eighteenth century, so that ethnic problems played no important role. But when Western ideas equality and democracy, of individual freedom and nationalism became known, the tensions reappeared, splitting and demoralizing the upper class. Loss of unity and loss of belief in itself made the upper class incapable of dealing with the problems created by the assault of the West. Here, I believe, lies the true difference between China and Japan in the nineteenth century. Both were faced with the same problems, but their own situations were different and led to different decisions. In Japan, the aristocracy continued to believe in its mission and was willing to sacrifice first some, then all of its rights and privileges, in order to save the nation. Thus, the Meiji reformation was not disruptive, and under the leadership of its old upper class Japan grew into the industrial age. In China, the elite was split, had lost its faith, and made no or only token adjustments to the requirements of a new era. These failures precipitated the revolution of 1911, which swept the whole upper class out of power and was not followed by consolidation or formation of a new upper class. After a period of disintegration and decay, much of China was overrun and occupied by Japan and came close to losing its independence altogether.

The two Chinese societies of the recent past after World War II have both come from a common root originating in the 1920s. Each has its own new upper class. In Taiwan, the individual has been accepted as the theoretical basic unit of society, but Confucian ethics are being reexamined in the attempt to find a new definition for the family and to

adapt it to Western aspects of life.[62] In Communist China on the main-
land, the state, or society as a whole, ranks so much above the individual that the individual cannot be considered the basic unit of society,
even though it may be so in certain laws. As to the family, the situation
is clear: Communist China has stripped the family of its economic,
social, and educational functions in order to destroy it as a unit. With
the help of the new marriage law, the wish of either marriage partner
can dissolve the family. The mobilization of the young against the old,
of women against men, and the ridiculing and abolishing of family
status differences were attacks against the hierarchical structure of
family and society, designed to achieve a full breakdown of the family.
Nevertheless, Communist China has a new upper class, that is, a group
of people with special privileges. But this upper class is self-per-
petuating not through birth but through cooptation. For the first time in
history an upper class in China has a non-Chinese ideology, and its
members are not representatives of families, but parts of a brotherhood.
The political, social, and ideological developments in the two Chinese
societies today are too complex to permit predictions. But one thing can
be said safely: the role of the upper class family as it was played in
Chinese history will never be repeated, and the characteristics of the
family as an institution, regardless of class status, will never be the same
as they were through more than two thousand years.

62. For the actual situation in Taiwan see among other studies A. R. O'Hara, *Research on Changes of Chinese Society* (Taipei, 1971), and D. C. Schak, *Dating and Mate-
selection in Modern Taiwan* (Taipei, 1974).

∾ DAVID LANDES

BLEICHRÖDERS
AND ROTHSCHILDS:
The Problem of Continuity
in the Family Firm

The French say, "It's easier to make money than to keep it."
Americans talk of "shirtsleeves to shirtsleeves in three generations."
The image of the wheel of fortune, ever turning and raising some while
humbling others, taking all of us through a cycle of prosperity and
poverty, is almost ubiquitous, at least in Western societies, and is partly
an expression of envy, partly an egalitarian ideology (cf. "pride goeth
before a fall"), partly a statement of fact.

A case study illustrative of one subcategory of this rise-and-fall
phenomenon is the problem of continuity in business. That is, what is it
that makes or permits a family to persist over generations in the
management of an enterprise? In particular, what are the determinants
of continuity when the business is successful and the family line
unbroken? Obviously a certain number of enterprises fail or do badly
and have to be liquidated; hence rupture of continuity. And certain
families fail to produce heirs, or at least capable heirs; hence again,
rupture of continuity. But these constitute a relatively straightforward
subset of the larger set and need not concern us here. The really
interesting questions arise when the ingredients of continuity are there:
the firm is doing well; there are members of the family available to
manage it; and even so, there is a rupture.

One of the best places to look for and study this problem is in those branches of the economy where family enterprise continues to be an effective, competitive form. (In the others, where increasing scale has made the joint-stock, public corporation indispensable, the impersonal economic factors drown out the other determinants of continuity.) One such branch is merchant banking, where personal connections and family reputation are still valuable business assets, so that many of the great names of yesterday are still to be reckoned with: Rothschild, Lazard, Hambro, Mallet, Worms. Sometimes, to be sure, the name is a pious cover for new men, a symbol of tradition and experience. Yet the very fact that in this business names are worth keeping is evidence of the real commercial value of the ancestral legacy.

One such merchant bank is Arnhold and S. Bleichröder, a composite firm produced by the merger of two German houses, S. Bleichröder of Berlin and Gebrüder Arnhold of Dresden. The bank is flourishing today in New York. There are no longer any Bleichröders in it: their interest was bought out two generations ago; and even then they had long since ceased to play a significant role in management. Since then, their descendants—those, that is, who survived the Holocaust of the 1940s—have vanished into anonymity. Their name has remained, however, as part of the *raison sociale* of the firm, because the house, as Bleichröders, had once been the greatest private bank in Germany and a power in international finance, and one does not abandon that kind of heritage lightly. The history of the family is a fascinating case study in continuity, not only for itself, but for the light it sheds on the larger phenomenon.[1]

Who were Bleichröders? We do not know, though our very ignorance on this score is evidence that they were of modest origins. For even in Jewry, where family names are a comparatively recent import, adopted from or imposed by the non-Jewish world, families characterized by a history of learning or accomplishments can trace their ancestry back many generations. But the first Bleichröder we know was the father of

1. The best history of the Bleichröder bank is still an article I wrote some years ago as an interim report on my research in the archives of the house: "The Bleichröder Bank: An Interim Report," Leo Baeck Institute, *Year Book V* (London, 1960), pp. 201-20. This will be superseded, especially for the period after 1860, by Fritz Stern's forthcoming book: *Gold and Iron: Bismarck's Banker Bleichröder*. The article that follows owes a great deal to my long collaboration with Professor Stern on this subject, as well as to numerous discussions with the late Frederick Brunner, partner in Arnhold and S. Bleichröder and owner-curator of the personal and business papers of Gerson Bleichröder.

Samuel, himself the founder of the bank. This was Gerschon Jacob, whom we first hear of in Berlin in the 1760s. Where he came from is not certain: the family tradition speaks of the village Bleicherode, in the Harz mountains, whence the name derived.

Nor is it certain how and why he came to Berlin, a city where Jews were not permitted to settle except by explicit authorization, either as *Schutzjuden*, that is, as protected Jews, or as employees of a *Schutzjude* or of the Jewish Community *(Gemeinde)*.[2] Gerschon Jacob was in the latter situation: he was at that time a, or more probably, *the* gravedigger of the *Gemeinde*.

He did not stay a gravedigger. He married a Miss Aron, daughter of one of the more fortunate *Schutzjuden*, and through this marriage got access to funds and connections that enabled him to try his hand at business. He opened a buckle factory at Wriezen, a small city near Berlin, and when this did poorly, he turned his hand to the import and manufacture of perfume and cosmetics, securing for the purpose a patent as court perfumer. Yet in spite of this privilege, Gerschon Jacob did not do well, and in 1802 he petitioned the King to be released from this role. "I do not," he admitted, "have the commercial skill generally imputed to my people."[3] Gerschon retired and we do not hear from him again. He died in 1812.

His son Samuel then had to start almost from scratch. Scraping together some money from some of his relatives, he opened, in 1803, a small *Wechselstube* (exchange office) and *Lotteriegeschäft* (lottery agency) that eventually became the *Bankhaus* S. Bleichröder. We know something about the early years of the enterprise because Samuel's first official account book, covering the years 1806-24, has been saved. It tells the story of a little shop handling small transactions for friends, relatives, and passersby: gulden or marks banco into Thaler or the reverse; gold into silver, silver into gold. These were years of war and occupation, and Berlin saw the troops of many nations come and go.

2. There were in 1750 about one hundred *Schutzjuden* in Berlin, who counted with their families about 20 per cent of the 2,188 Jewish residents of the city (about 2 per cent of total population). For a list of the Jews authorized to reside in Berlin in 1750, see Ismar Freund, *Die Emanzipation der Juden in Preussen*, 2 vols. (Berlin, 1912), 2: 56-60. On the Jewish population of Berlin and Brandenburg in the second half of the eighteenth century, see F. W. A. Bratring, *Statistisch-topographische Beschreibung der gesammten Mark Brandenburg*, 3 vols. (Berlin, 1804-09), 1: 33.

3. General-Directorium, Manufact.-und Commerz-Colleg., *Acta des Manufacturs Collegii*, Galanterie Waaren-Fabriken, Berlin, vol. 320, no. 89, Protokoll of 29 April 1802.

Inevitably, they were good years for money changers, and the transactions handled by Samuel Bleichröder increased in number and size. Even more important, by the end of the first decade the first current accounts appear: the *Wechselstube* had become a bank. The holders of these earliest current accounts were mostly from Breslau, the trading center for Silesia and much of southern Poland, a city whose annual wool market was the source of substantial money flows in and out of the area—hence a demand for correspondents in Berlin and elsewhere to dispose of commercial bills or furnish specie as needed. More interesting, however, about these accounts is the early appearance in them of assets in the form of securities: money was coming into Berlin to be invested in state and local funds, domestic and foreign, and S. Bleichröder was beginning to learn the role that was to make his fortune, that of buyer and seller on the young but hyperactive Berlin Exchange.

It is probably in this connection that he came to the attention of the Rothschilds. In 1830 Amselm Salomon, son of Salomon Mayer of Vienna, came to Berlin to negotiate a conversion loan with the Prussian government on behalf of the Rothschilds. He gave Samuel Bleichröder some buy orders in Russian-English bonds, orders that were almost surely not easy to fill. (The Rothschilds, as the richest of all merchant banks, expected to pay less than others for the same commodity.) Yet Samuel seems to have done as well as or better than could be expected, for these first orders were followed by others, which Samuel energetically, but humbly, solicited; and in a matter of years, Bleichröders became the principal agents of Rothschilds in Berlin.

This was a major turning point in the history of the house. Bleichröders received only 1/4 percent commission from the purchase and sale of securities, and 1 per mill (1/10 of 1 percent) on exchange transactions.[4] Even so, the turnover generated substantial profits, while the relation to the world's premier banking house gave rise to all manner of lucrative business connections. One can follow this process

4. Archives N. M. Rothschild & Sons, London, Special Bleichröder File, letter from S. Bleichröder to N. M. Rothschild, Berlin, 31-8-1831. This and some two dozen other letters were shown to me by Edmund de Rothschild, and I was permitted to make handwritten copies. They undoubtedly constitute a small portion of the correspondence between the two houses. Application to see the remainder of the correspondence was denied, at first on the ground that there was nothing else of interest, then on the ground of the inaccessibility of the archives during building alterations at New Court.

clearly, if only incompletely, over the next few decades: the ties to other major banking firms like Sal. Oppenheim Jr. & Co. of Cologne; the increasing volume of the buy and sell transactions on the Berlin Exchange (by the 1850s Bleichröders were the quasi-official brokerage and issue house for two of Germany's largest railways, the Rheinische Eisenbahn and the Köln-Mindener Eisenbahn); the increasingly frequent appearance of the Bleichröder name in advertisements of payment of dividends and interest, and collection of installments on subscriptions. The story of the rise of Bleichröders in these decades is the story of the rise of the Berlin Exchange to first place in Germany, with a quasi-monopoly of trading in the rail and industrial issues that took the place of funds as the staples of the modern capital market.

The next major step in the rise of Bleichröders was the decision around 1860 of Otto von Bismarck, then Prussian ambassador to St. Petersburg, to bank with the house. Why he did so is not certain: the story has it that he was looking for a Jewish banker (though politically an anti-Semite in his earlier career, Bismarck was very hardheaded in money matters); that he consulted Meyer Carl von Rothschild, whom he had come to know during his stay in Frankfurt as Prussian representative to the German Bundestag; and that Carl recommended Gerson Bleichröder, son of Samuel, who had become a partner of the bank in 1847 and senior partner on the death of Samuel in 1855.[5]

Bismarck was hardly an important client to begin with. He was not wealthy, and Bleichröders were occupied primarily with small collections and remittances on his behalf. But within two years he returned to Berlin as Minister-President and began a twenty-eight-year period of direction of the Prussian and then the German state. During those years his ties to his banker were extraordinarily close, based on complete confidence, reciprocal respect, and a sophisticated appreciation on both sides of the contribution of the other. If anything, the relationship became more intimate with time as both men grew older and tended to grow away from those around them; they shared a past that others could not possibly enter into or understand.

Even as prince-president, Bismarck was not an important client for

5. Samuel had two sons, Gerson and Julius. Both were brought into the firm, but the two parted amicably, with Julius setting up his own small bank while Gerson continued the paternal house. For a time each held a large share in the other's firm. The story that follows concerns only Gerson and his branch of the family. The story of Julius and his descendants is utterly different.

himself, though he did become more wealthy in time, thanks to gifts of land from the nation and Crown.[6] But a man who was banker to Bismarck was a man to know, so that this connection brought in its wake many others, just as the Rothschild connection had earlier. At the same time, a personal tie to the prime minister gave rise to the opportunity to be useful to the state. Thus Gerson Bleichröder played a critical role in enabling Bismarck to finance his wars against Denmark and Austria when the Prussian Landtag refused to vote military credits, and Bismarck never forgot this service. Years later, after his own retirement, he answered a journalist (Anton Memminger) who asked why he had persisted in maintaining a financial relationship that gave rise to nasty suspicions and fed the slanders of anti-Semites by recalling that Bleichröder had helped him when he stood "almost as close to the gallows as to the throne."[7] It was a hyperbolic image, but there is no question that Bismarck's career, if not his skin, was saved by Prussia's victories.

Bleichröder later took a hand in a large number of official and quasi-official transactions: the fixing and collection of the French war indemnity of 1871 (an operation, incidentally, that gave him a striking experience of Prussian hypocrisy in money matters); the rescue of German (and particularly Junker) investments in the ill-fated Rumanian railway venture of Strousberg; the salvage of German colonial and trading interests in the South Seas; the creation of the Reichsbank; the nationalization of the railways. There is no need here to review this list in detail. Suffice it to say that the firm became richer and more important every year. We do not have any of the official balance sheets, but a limited series of notes and a unique statement in one of the letters show a tenfold growth in profits in the 1860s (after Bismarck), while everything we know about the economy of the Empire and the transactions of the bank would indicate substantially higher returns in the years that followed. By the end of his life Gerson von Bleichröder (he was ennobled in 1872 for his services in the Rumanian affair) was the richest man in Berlin, perhaps the richest in Germany. The only person who could compete with him was Alfred Krupp.

6. On the history of Bismarck's personal fortune, the best source is Fritz Stern, "Gold and Iron: The Collaboration and Friendship of Gerson Bleichröder and Otto von Bismarck," in Stern, *The Failure of Illiberalism: Essays on the Political Culture of Modern Germany* (New York, 1972), pp. 58-73; again, this will be superseded by the forthcoming volume. See also Alfred Vagts, "Bismarck's Fortune," *Central European History* 1 (1968): 203-32.

7. Otto von Bismarck, *Gesammelte Werke*, 2nd ed. (Berlin, 1926), 9: 86.

Gerson did not find it easy to handle wealth and power. There is a saying that goes by the name of Heine's Law, that Jews are like the people among whom they live, only more so. Gerson had the German love of rank and power, which means the universal human love of these attributes and then some; and to that must be added the inevitable inebriation of the Jew-outsider rising to unprecedented influence in a society that was still profoundly antisemitic. In principle and in law, the Jews of Germany were "emancipated" in the course of the nineteenth century and raised to a position of civil equality; but it is not easy to legislate against the hearts and wills of the citizenry, so that no sooner had the long process of normalization been completed (not until the 1860s), than the rise of a virulent racist antisemitism called all the gains into question and laid the basis for the genocide of the 1930s and 1940s.

Bleichröder's ascension flew directly in the face of this swelling current of resentment and hatred and only served to inflame it. For Gerson Bleichröder was not only a Jew but a particularly dangerous example of the species. He was a banker—in Germany designated moneylender or usurer—making money from money, serving the state in order to manipulate and loot it, battening on the noble pecuniary innocence of decent Christians. (We are all familiar with this old, tiresome, but dangerous stereotype.) To the high society of Bismarckian Prussia, the Bleichröders were pushy, disagreeable upstarts. Many of the most distinguished figures in this society, scions of the oldest noble families, were quick enough to make use of Gerson's services, to sell him information and good will, to importune him for tips and favors and shares in deals, to smoke his cigars and eat his caviar. But they mocked him behind his back, and the more they sacrificed dignity and pride to mammon, the more they projected the blame on him and sought to humble his dignity and pride.[8]

Under the circumstances, it is not surprising that Gerson should have been somewhat contaminated by the prevalent prejudices and have given at times evidence of self-hatred. Fritz Stern cites a Berlin police report of 1874, which must be taken with the usual grain of salt:

8. A good example of this sponger's contempt was the behavior of Bismarck and his entourage during Bleichröder's visit to the Prussian camp at Versailles in 1871. See the memoirs of Bismarck's aide: Moritz Busch, *Tagebuchblätter,* 3 vols. (Leipzig, 1899), 2: 110, 125, 161. Compare also Rudolf Vierhaus, ed., *Das Tachbuch der Baronin Spitzemberg* (Göttingen, 1960), pp. 88, 128, 130, 138. On the general implications of corruption *cum* scapegoating in imperial Germany, see Fritz Stern, "Money, Morals, and the Pillars of Society," in *The Failure of Illiberalism,* pp. 26-57.

Mr. von Bleichröder, who since his elevation to nobility almost bursts with pride and who publicly no longer entertains his former friends and associates, keeps himself apart from them even in his walks: on his promenades in the Sieges-Allee, he walks on the western side, instead of on the eastern with the great majority of the promenaders, who are almost all Jews. Asked why he walked on the other side, he is said to have answered that the eastern side smelled too much of garlic. Several of Bleichröder's former acquaintances heard of this remark and a few days ago took him to task for it on the promenade, and things didn't go very smoothly then.

It is all there: the cutting-off of old friends (disidentification) in order to reassure new; the imputation of stereotypical negative characteristics to those forsaken; the use of a culinary-olfactory discriminant that distills and reduces differences of money and mores into sensory fundamentals.

In all fairness, Gerson never did forget he was a Jew; nor, in spite of occasional rumors to the contrary, did he ever abandon his faith. He was, of necessity, something of a *shtadlan* or intercessor between the Jewish community and the authorities, especially in Jewish efforts to curb antisemitism. He was only moderately successful, in part because even those authorities who deplored and feared popular agitation sympathized *in petto* with the message of anti-Jewish propaganda. Aside from that, however, Bleichröder was never a leader of the Jewish community, which he clearly felt he had outgrown. His aspirations were to another world, and his sense of superiority to his coreligionists could not but communicate itself to them and, even more, to his own family.

What of his family? Gerson and his wife Emma, née Guttentag, had three sons and one daughter. We know little of their childhood and schooling, little of the character of their family life. Gerson was a very busy man and may have seen little of his children, but he did save in his personal files a number of documents attesting to their passage of certain milestones, indicating some kind of interest in their achievements. He brought all his sons into the firm, as his father had taken him in, to learn the business and to take his place some day at the head of the house.

Unfortunately for him, his children were exposed to wider perspectives. As the children of the most important and powerful banker in the kingdom, they moved in exalted circles and could reasonably aspire to positions of the highest status. In nineteenth-century Prussia, this did not mean banking. It meant a military connection—if not a regular army career, then a commission as a reserve officer, preferably in one of the elegant cavalry or guards' regiments. It meant ownership and exploitation of a noble estate, a *Rittergut,* with all the privileges of rank and authority thereunto appertaining. It meant membership in the landed gentry, not only by virtue of one's property but also of one's personal status. For the Bleichröders, whose family title was brand new, this implied an effort to marry into older families—the immemorial trade-off of money for prestige.

The hardest nut to crack was the military: Prussians were used to commoners as *Rittergutsbesitzern* [owners of noble estates];[9] they had even learned to accept "misalliances" of money and blue blood, but they took the army seriously.[10] Gerson's oldest son Hans wanted to serve as an officer in one of the royal guards' regiments, the kind of unit that never took Jews and almost never commoners. (In some elegant cavalry units, the only commoner in the officers' mess was the veterinarian.) Gerson arranged the matter, obviously in the face of bitter resistance. The appointment was a small sensation, unheard of, so much so that about a year later a British diplomat found occasion to comment on it to Herbert von Bismarck, the son of the Chancellor. Herbert made quick to correct any false impressions: the Jew, he noted, had not lasted long. "We precious soon hunted him out."[11] (Herbert hated Gerson von Bleichröder with a vengeance, in large part because Gerson, at the behest of the Chancellor, had intervened in a romance that the Old Man disapproved of.) Apparently it was not a successful experiment.

There is one apocryphal story that may or may not concern the young Bleichröder (it has come down to us without names). *Se non e vero, e*

9. See the classic analysis by Hans Rosenberg, "Die Demokratisierung der Rittergutsbesitzerklasse," in *Zur Geschichte und Problematik der Demokratie* (Berlin, 1958), pp. 459-86.

10. The diplomatic corps was more penetrable. In 1908 Reichskanzler Bülow, writing with satisfaction concerning the appointment of a Goldschmidt-Rothschild, son of the new Baron Maximillian von Goldschmidt-Rothschild (son-in-law of Friedrich Wilhelm von Rothschild), noted the difference between the two services: "We now have this fine, hard-working man in the diplomatic service. I have sent him to London, and he always brings us the best intelligence, but there is no way of making him a reserve officer in Germany . . . .", Kurt Pritzkoleit, *Wem gehört Deutschland: Eine Chronik von Besitz und Macht* (Vienna, Munich, and Basel, 1957), p. 52. Maximillian was ennobled in 1903, raised to a baronage in 1906—the first Jew to be elevated to this status and remain a Jew.

11. Stephen Gwynn and Gertrude M. Tuckwell, eds., *The Life of the Right Honorable Sir Charles W. Dilke,* 2 vols. (New York, 1917), 1: 433. According to Bismarck, the young Hans was expelled from his regiment because he was promenading a whore before the Palace on the day of an attempted assassination of the Emperor and was required by circumstances to take off the wounded monarch's coat while in bad company—bad luck, that; but the penalty of a characteristic flaw. *Gesammelte Werke,* 9: 86.

ben trovato: it describes the kind of contretemps that was almost bound
to happen in such a situation. This young officer, Jewish, was the son of
a very wealthy businessman (banker?), only recently ennobled. He
wanted to win the approval of his fellow officers, so he arranged to have
his father invite the entire officers' corps of the regiment to a *grand
dinner*—all, that is, except one officer who could not call himself *von.*
Came time to sit down to table, and the colonel remarked that this
particular officer was missing. "Where," he asked the host, "is
Lieutenant So-and-so?" "Oh," came the answer, "I didn't invite him. I
thought we would prefer to be among ourselves [*unter uns*]." At which
the colonel gave a signal, and all the officers rose from table and left the
house.[12]

A monumental *gaffe.* If it didn't happen, it nevertheless expressed, by
its very existence as a story that must have been the delectation of vin-
dictive little minds, the self-destructive artificiality of Jewish social aspirations in the Prussian environment.

These early efforts of the Bleichröders to penetrate the circles they
did business with were apparently clumsy and only moderately successful. This, of course, only stimulated them to further efforts. The
children bought themselves estates and, beginning with one of the
daughters, began to marry into the houses of central European nobility.
Each of these marriages entailed a Christian ceremony, and if not the
formal apostasy of the Bleichröder partner, at least a Christian
education for the children. There was no place for Jews in this milieu.

Thus the generations were sealed off, the younger from the older.
Gerson, who suffered from failing vision from the 1860s on, eventually
to the point of blindness, spent his lunch hours eating in the office by
himself; his sons were off at their clubs, with their friends, or with their
mistresses.[13] In a rare moment of introspection, Gerson reflected on his

12. Something had happened. The Baroness Spitzemberg notes in her diary (18 February 1873) that owing to an incident of the previous year, the officers of several regiments were boycotting the Bleichröder receptions; and without uniforms, no ball was
possible. Vierhaus, ed., *Das Tagebuch der Baronin Spitzemberg,* p. 138. Was this
another incident? And did it serve as the basis for the story that was being spread around
by provincial newspapers in the late 1870's for the delectation of those middle-class
Untertänen who were the strongest support of Prussian hierarchy? Thus in *Neue allge-
meine Zeitung für Franken and Thüringen,* 25 April 1879 (Bleichröder Archive, Box 6).

13. Gerson's first two grandchildren were born out of wedlock to his eldest son Hans
and Marie Brebeck, the daughter of a non-Jewish launderer. In 1904, a decade after his
father's death, Hans married Marie, and Hans Jr. threw a champaign party for his
classmates to celebrate his newly-gained legitimacy. These and other details of personal
history were given to Fritz Stern by an old friend of the Bleichröder children.

failure with his children: "The boss noted," his secretary writes, "that in the education of his own children he had come to recognize, with the best intention and reflection, that a different method would be more appropriate for the present age, and hence he did not tie them to the house, gave them even in their younger years great freedom, and did not anxiously shield them from contact with the modern world. 'I meant well, but now I have to recognize that I was wrong.' " And the secretary added: "Must he not from time to time have a feeling of loneliness? Are there not days when he barely sees or talks to one of his four children, when none takes the time to keep him company?"[14]

Commensality was an important feature of a working partnership in the nineteenth century, just like common partners' offices with the desks side by side or opposite within the same room, and every important decision taken together on the spot. Gerson came to rely more and more on a young cousin, Leopold Schwabach, a specialist in market operations, to run the firm alongside him and in his absence (as he grew older, he traveled more and more for his health). Schwabach was tough, nervy, no respecter of rank and dignity, and far enough behind Gerson in the *cursus honorum* to be immune to the temptations of the larger society. He inherited the senior post after Gerson's death, and his son Paul after him. (It was Paul who eventually drove and bought out the Bleichröder heirs, who had little to contribute to the firm but the money they had inherited from their father.) Paul himself was later ennobled, allegedly for personal services to the Emperor: he made Wilhelm, a passionate sailor, a gift of a beautiful yacht. By the interwar period the Schwabachs were arriving at the point that the Bleichröders had reached some fifty years earlier; and if the Nazis had not cut short the career of the bank in the thirties, the third-generation Schwabach, Paul Jr., could not have kept it going. He too was caught in the assimilationist web—this time in circumstances that made a satisfactory resolution impossible. He wanted to marry Carmen von Wedel, a descendant of an old Junker family. Paul Jr. was a Christian and half gentile by his mother; but the Nuremberg laws forbade the union, and a petition to the Minister of the Interior for an exception as *Halbarier* (half Aryan) was turned down after more than a year of special pleading and string-pulling. Reluctantly, Paul Jr. tried, with the help of

14. Kühlow notes from reminiscences of Gerson von Bleichröder, 17 May 1882 (in Bleichröder Archive, Box 6), translated and cited by Fritz Stern in *Gold and Iron* [forthcoming].

Alfred Duff Cooper and Duncan Sandys, to obtain permission to reside permanently in Britain. Before the new arrangements could be consummated, he died suddenly, at the age of thirty-five—some said, of a broken heart. Certainly he had lost his ability to cope with this Moloch of a fatherland. His father, crushed by an avalanche of personal, business, and political disasters, died soon after, on the morrow of the great pogroms of November 1938 (the *Cristallnacht*).

As for the Bleichröders, they pursued their task of spending what their fathers had made. All went well until 1933, when the racism of the regime brought them back to a past they thought they had left behind. They took shelter at first behind their mixed ancestry, for most of them were by now only part Jewish. As the years passed, however, the Nazis, encouraged by the indifference or inaction of the outside world, broadened and intensified the persecution. By 1939 the government was hunting down "Mischlinge" as well as full Jews and was moving them to camps in the east, a preliminary to what was to become the Final Solution. The Bleichröders, who had almost come to think of themselves as German, now found themselves defined as Jews. In desperation, they wrote to the Nazi authorities asking to be exempted from the new decree in recognition of their services to their country. We have two of these letters, signed in good Prussian fashion at each echelon of the Nazi hierarchy (one of the signatories is Adolf Eichmann, no less, then Head of Department IV B 4, for Jewish Affairs, in the Reichssicherheits-Hauptamt).[15] The most interesting thing about these petitions is the grounds advanced by the Bleichröders to justify their exemption. They made no mention of the bank and its substantial services to Prussia and Germany—even those services, like the mobilization of funds to finance Bismarck's wars, that might have appealed to militarists. Rather, they spoke of their own service in the German army in the Great War, then of their participation in the right-wing Freikorps attack on the worker occupants of the Vulcan shipyard and their support for National Socialism. The letters were signed "Heil Hitler." None of this sufficed to aryanize them in the eyes of their persecutors. The final answer was No.

They were not liquidated. Because of their service and wounds in

---

15. Germany, Ministry of the Interior, Reichssicherheits-Hauptamt, Department IV B 4, letters of Curt von Bleichröder to Frick, 7 January 1942; Edgar von Bleichröder to Frick, 23 January 1942; Radthe [?] to Eichmann, 29 January 1942; Müller to Radthe [?], 7 May 1942.

World War I, they were exempted from deportation, but notified that, in the course of the final settlement [Bereinigung] of the Jewish question, they would be confined in an old folks' ghetto within the boundaries of the Reich. In the event, they and other members of the family were able to flee to Switzerland, whence they returned to Germany after the war to fight with one another over what was left of their patrimony. Apparently there were still Bleichröders residing in the Federal Republic; but they will not answer mail relating to the family or acknowledge any tie to the past. This is the ultimate rootlessness.

Why did the Bleichröders behave as they did? The question can be answered in part by contrasting them with their sponsors, the Rothschilds. Here was a family that did not start from a position of anonymous poverty: the Rothschilds can trace their ancestry back for two hundred years before Meyer Amschel; and Meyer Amschel himself (though he began, like his brothers, as a modest trader in second-hand goods), studied originally to be a rabbi. There were a number of rabbis in the Rothschild lineage, and it is this that in Jewish tradition spells *yichos* (hereditary distinction).

This distinction was converted to fame, notoriety, and power by Meyer Amschel's success as merchant banker. The Rothschilds rose to the first position in the world of high finance in the space of two decades—an incredibly short time in a slower world. The Rothschilds themselves do not see it that way. I once had occasion to write that in Frankfurt the Rothschilds rose in a decade "from upstarts to undisputed rulers of the market" (that was just Frankfurt). I was called to task by the head of the British bank, who pointed to a drawing, not contemporary, of Meyer Amschel receiving in his house the Landgrave of Hesse-Cassel: "Look at the house," he said. "That was no house of an upstart." Meyer Amschel, he insisted, was a substantial merchant.[16]

I tell this story because it conveys that lively sense of family and

16. See the comparable sensitivity to the allegation that the family built its fortune by successful speculation with the treasury of the Kurfürst of Hesse, confided to Meyer Amschel Rothschild to protect it from Napoleon. The energetic refutation is in Christian Wilhelm Berghoeffer (an employee of the Bank), *Meyer Amschel Rothschild, der Gründer des Rothschildschen Bankhauses*, 2d ed. (Frankfurt am Main, 1923), pp. 129-34. The Berghoeffer biography is one of only two books on the family and firm written with their approval and co-operation. The other is Bertrand Gille, *Histoire de la Maison Rothschild*, 2 vols. (Paris, 1965-1).

dynastic distinction that continues to this day to be perhaps the salient Rothschild characteristic.[17] Meyer Amschel had it to an extreme degree, and it inspired his entire conception of the firm and its relationship to the outside world. When he died, his greatest concern was that the brothers stay together and that the firm continue in the family. No daughter or son-in-law was to have any part of the business; nor was any daughter or son-in-law to have any right to inquire into the records or conduct of the firm. Any daughter so forgetful of her obligations to her father as to disobey this injunction was simply to be cut off from any inheritance (over and above moneys already received in the father's lifetime). The will made specific reference to Napoleonic Code, which called for equal division, and affirmed quite arbitrarily that all concerned recognized that these arrangements satisfied the legal requirements.[18]

The brothers took this legacy seriously. The family crest shows it: one fist holding five arrows. There is the well-known story of young Montefiore, brother-in-law of Antony (son of Nathan), who wanted to enter the firm; the consent came grudgingly and on impossible conditions—he would have to change his name to Rothschild. For a member of one of the great Sephardic dynasties, older and more distinguished than the Ashkenazic Rothschilds, the demand was totally unacceptable. The young man knew when he was not wanted.

This sense of special status was reinforced by the success of subsequent decades. The Rothschilds became, as it were, the new kings of the Jews and in this capacity received all kinds of honor, and were the targets of all kinds of opprobrium. (This explains in part their extraordinary sensitivity: they see themselves as the leading representatives of the larger group and correctly interpret much of the criticism directed toward them as manifestations of, or fuel for, antisemitism. Hence their unwillingness to open their archives, and their destruction of those early records that might put the House in an unfavorable light.) The family has, until very recently, always maintained its Jewish faith, and this almost as a point of honor. Older members of French aristocratic society

17. Joseph Wechsberg, *The Merchant Bankers* (1966; Pocket Book ed., 1968), p. 275, cites Jacob de Rothschild's reply to the question, "What is it like to be 'a Rothschild'?" "I don't think it's very different from being someone else. One is, of course, acutely aware of bearing the name. My upbringing taught me to respect it. And one is left with a strong wish to sustain and enhance its traditions." Jacob was then (and now) partner in N. M. Rothschild & Sons, London.

18. Berghoeffer, *Meyer Amschel Rothschild,* pp. 201-5.

(le gratin) can tell of visits from Rothschilds who moved like kings with a whole retinue of retainers, including cooks to prepare kosher meals in the proper vessels and serve them on their own plates. This observance has substantially weakened since the days of Meyer Amschel or Amschel Meyer, but the loyalty to the faith and coreligionists is still strong, partly because it is hard for a Rothschild to pass into the anonymity of the gentile world, and partly because the Jewish community will not release them that easily.

The uniqueness of the family as a Jewish family, in conjunction with its close social ties to the highest non-Jewish circles, posed from the start an interesting problem: whom could a Rothschild marry? The answer, more often than not, was another Rothschild. Few other Jews were acceptable; and, especially at first, no non-Jew, however wealthy or highborn, would do. Hence frequent alliances between Rothschild cousins or between uncles and nieces. This policy of strict endogamy had to be relaxed eventually, for love laughs at dynastic constraints, and the Rothschild daughters began losing their hearts to the elegant young men who visited their homes.[19] But while women could be permitted to marry out in this manner (could be dowered off and sent on their way), the men, who were charged with the continuity of the House, were expected to find their partners within the faith. This, they have in fact continued to do, until this last generation when there has been a general liberation from old constraints, not only in regard to marriage but to the admission of outsiders into partnership. It is still Rothschilds who manage the remaining branches in London and Paris, but they share control, and the ability of the family to maintain its place under these new circumstances remains to be tested over time. Before, the family and the House were unique in their isolated pride; now the bank is a partnership somewhat like other partnerships.[20]

19. One of the few insights into this dilemma is offered in Lady Battersea [Constance Rothschild, daughter of Anthony, granddaughter of Nathan], *Reminiscences* (London, 1923). The book is remarkably candid and has for epigraph some lines of John Bunyan: "Some said, 'John, print it'; other said, 'Not so.' Some said, 'It might do good'; others said, 'No,' " Even so, there are aspects of the story that have not been published and can be learned only by reading the manuscript papers in the British Museum (add. Ma. 47954-55); and even there some of the more personal passages have been blacked out with india ink. See also Lucy Cohen, *Lady de Rothschild and Her Daughters* (London, 1935).

20. The first outsider admitted to partnership in the London house was David Colville in 1960. He was followed by Michael Bucks, who had worked his way up from copy boy, and Philip Shelbourne, a barrister specializing in taxation and a complete outsider. In the meantime, a large share of the Paris bank is held by Le Nord, a holding company

Along with pride of name and place went a certain arrogance in business. The Rothschilds have always been demanding of business associates (including other Rothschilds), peremptory with subordinates (even those more or less independent correspondents who were important bankers in their own right: Belmont in New York, Lambert in Brussels, Bauer in Madrid, and Bleichröders in Berlin), and brusque with outsiders to the point of rudeness.[21] They have not been easy people to do business with; but they have been good people to do business with—correct, exact, often imaginative, with a purse to match their vision. A good many firms, including some of the greatest merchant banks of the nineteenth century, built their fortunes on their ties to Rothschilds.

The point is that their manners (or lack thereof) were just the other side of their sense of family and self. They made more than their share of enemies. Given their preeminence, some of this was inevitable; but they put together an international team of extraordinary energy and initiative and held it together for a century and more. More important, they held themselves together, while other family firms were converted, absorbed, or dissolved, and did so in spite of a steady attrition due to the lure of other pursuits and the inevitable variations in personal ability and performance. As Jacob de Rothschild put it: "We are especially proud that the bank has remained in the family for six generations. The Rothschilds must have had ability—and the good fortune to produce in each generation a few first-rate bankers. The degree of success achieved by any merchant bank cannot for long exceed that of the people responsible for running it."[22] In this they have been unique: one can think of a few family firms that have lasted almost as long, but none of comparable scope, none that demanded so much of its members and exposed them to such tempting alternatives.

Admittedly, the Rothschilds are a special, polar case, and one may well ask what inferences can be drawn therefrom. The answer is that it is precisely because they represent an extreme example of cohesion and

---

descended from the now nationalized Chemin de Fer du Nord, the most properous railway in France and a Rothschild fief from its creation. Shares in Le Nord are publicly traded. For a fascinating view from within of the partial, very partial, opening of the firm to outside (nonfamily) participation, see Ronald Palin (he rose from copy boy to secretary of N. M. Rothschild & Sons), *Rothschild Relish* (London, 1970).

21. The above is based on extensive reading in the correspondence of the Paris house, as well as personal experience in London.

22. Wechsberg, *Merchant Bankers,* p. 276.

continuity that one may distill generalities from their experience; just as the history of the Bleichröders offers a polar, hence specially illuminating, example of the reverse. The two dynasties represent a kind of dualism: rootlessness vs. roots; anxiety vs. assurance; haughtiness vs. pride; outer vs. inner-directedness. At the heart of continuity, I submit, is the question of identity and self. The Rothschilds knew who they were and where they came from, and therefore, where they were going; by the third generation, the Bleichröders had changed their minds about who they were, or at least who they wanted to be, and had lost their way.

What is the significance of all this for economic performance and development? The problem is not an easy one to deal with because of a complex balance of advantages and disadvantages, both to the persons and families concerned, and to the impersonal performance of the economy or a particular branch thereof. An attempt at starting on an answer can be made by stringing together what seems to be relevant considerations.

First, the presumed advantages of continuity are (1) the continued employment of capital in the enterprise, and (2) the continued availability of talent to the enterprise. This may take the form of talent in the pure sense; or special knowledge; or good will and its implied connections.

Where these conditions are present, it is clear that a breach of continuity can imperil if not destroy an enterprise; and that family firms are thus peculiarly subject to fluctuations in dynastic talent, biological accident, and the like. (Hence, the common practice today of insuring the lives of partners.)

But what of the larger picture: the branch of industry or trade; the region (in the territorial sense); the economy as a whole? Here the consequences are less clear-cut. Let us try, for the sake of simplification, two principal cases. In the first, enterprise is the work of a small atypical group—a religious minority; or resident aliens; or a privileged group with special ties to the State—whereas the society as a whole does not generate entrepreneurs (for the very reason that makes the atypical group necessary). This is an old story, and it is not an uncommon situation even now: witness the role of alien entrepreneurs such as the Chinese in southeast Asia, Indians in Africa, and Westerners in much of the Third World. In such instances, breaches of continuity can be serious on the macro level; thus the efforts of the French monarchy to encourage noblemen to engage in business enterprise, or the specification in patents of nobility that the grant was conditional on continuity. This same concern was exhibited by the Prussian government in its efforts during the eighteenth century to sustain some kind of status boundaries in the distribution of social, political, and economic functions.

In the second case, enterprise is widely distributed. These breaches of continuity can then be seen as a vehicle for the renewal of the business elite. The incapable, indifferent, or hostile are weeded out and their places are taken by hungrier men. Even then, however, things are not so simple. One can distinguish two possibilities:

(1) The indifferent or incapable remain in the firm, where they adulterate the quality of the management. This was the case of Bleichröders once Gerson's sons matured, and especially after his death. For all the talent of Schwabach, his opportunities were constrained by the presence of the Bleichröder heirs. Note, moreover, that this kind of difficulty can arise even when the heirs are not active partners.

One might argue that insofar as there were entrepreneural failings in the British economy of the late nineteenth century, they often took this form.

(2) The heirs pull out altogether (or are pushed out), clearing the way for the new men. On the level of the enterprise, this kind of hemorrhage can be crippling. This is what happened to Bleichröders after a series of lawsuits in the 1920s finally led to the separation of the family from the bank. The firm never recovered its prewar strength and influence and found it desirable eventually to merge with Gebr. Arnhold of Dresden.

On the macro level, however, this kind of turnover can be an effective cathartic, so long as there are entrepreneurs ready to take the places of those who retire and vehicles for these new men. This, along with its great capacity to mobilize capital, is the chief contribution of the immortal, impersonal joint-stock company: it is not dependent on the health, intelligence, or inclination of a genetic pool. And as Jeffreys notes in his dissertation on the history of the joint-stock corporation in Britain, many partnerships converted in the mid-nineteenth century for just this reason; the family was tired or played out, so a company took over.[23] The history of merchant banking is full of these stories of joint-stock banks gobbling up the older private houses: this is the way Rothschilds of Frankfurt went out in 1903, when Willy died and no one in the family could be persuaded to move to Frankfurt and keep the *Stammhaus* going.

In general, then, the significance of continuity for macroeconomic performance is mixed and has varied with historical circumstances. It was undoubtedly far more crucial in the earlier, precorporate phase of industrial and commercial development. (Recall in this connection the Weber thesis and Tawney's passing reference to puritan faith as an armor against the derision and temptation of an older, competitive value system.)[24] It has been more important in those fields where a sense of tradition and name are valuable business assets, as guarantees of quality if not quantity of performance. Merchant banking is one such field, and it is no coincidence that in spite of the efficiency and resources of the great corporate banks, there remains an important niche for private houses. Publishing is probably another; hotel and restaurant management another; and there are no doubt many more. Note that the value of family continuity in such fields cannot always be measured in terms of money: a hamburger chain can serve many more people than a first-class restaurant; and joint-stock bankers could afford from the start to be far less fussy about their promotions than the older merchant banking houses, and hence could be and were far more active.

This introduction of quality considerations, not always measurable in money terms, raises the question of the larger significance of continuity—to the society as well as the economy. Given a flow of talent and resources away from business into other spheres of activity or leisure, what is the balance in terms of macrosocial performance? Here presumably everything would depend on the nature of the trade-off.

23. James B. Jefferys, "Trends in Business Organization in Great Britain since 1856, . . ." (Ph.D. thesis, London School of Economics, 1938).

24. The *locus classicus* is Max Weber, *The Protestant Ethic and the Spirit of Capitalism*, which appeared in German in 1904-05 and was first translated into English in 1930. It triggered a debate that still goes on—one of the few truly seminal works in social science. Weber argues, in brief, that Protestants of the Calvinist variety were moved by anxiety concerning salvation to develop an ethic of everyday behavior that fostered assiduous devotion to business and rational accumulation of capital for productive use; and that this mode of behavior, once become an end in itself, was a prodigious stimulus to capitalist development. The thesis, inevitably, gave rise to ardent controversy. Among the books engendered thereby was R. H. Tawney, *Religion and the Rise of Capitalism* (New York, 1926). The discussion of the contest with the older value system will be found in chapter 4.

The Bleichröders, in a society dominated by an arrogant, crude, militaristic, antisemitic elite, chose to repudiate themselves (in effect, castrated themselves) in the hope of making themselves acceptable to the enemy; by the 1930s, they look very ugly.[25]

On the other hand, one can cite any number of instances of remarkable achievement by the members of business clans in public service, the professions, arts and letters, science and teaching; and often, particularly in the past, these roles have been opened to them only by the business success of their ancestors. In this sense, breach of entrepreneurial continuity has been an instrument of political, social, and intellectual innovation.

What all this seems to add up to is that the behavior of businessmen and their heirs is, like all other social behavior, partly determined by the tacit or expressed ideology these actors bring to their roles—their self-image, their self-esteem, their force of personality—and partly to the place accorded to them, the image held of them, the opportunities opened to them by the world around them. Societies get, on the whole, the businessmen and business families they deserve. It probably says something for British society of the nineteenth century that it turned out Goschens and Barings; or that American society in this century has produced Rockefellers and Kennedys; and it is no accident that Imperial and then postwar Germany produced the Bleichröders.

25. More venial is the lapse of one man, whose grandparents had made a fortune in clothing manufacture in San Francisco—his obituary gave as his highest achievement his expertise as a judge at dog shows. This isn't ugly; it's just a descent into the oblivion of triviality.

DOMESTIC IDEALS

AND SOCIAL BEHAVIOR:

Evidence from Medieval Genoa*

That human personality and behavior, and ultimately history itself, are shaped by the character of a society's domestic life is a premise that underlies the importance historians now assign to the household. Its demographic configurations, it is held, influence the socializing of children, generational attitudes, sex roles, and affective kin ties; and the fact that these configurations can be assessed as early as the fifteenth century in some areas of Europe adds to their allure.[1] Yet the formative nature of the household on personality and behavior in past time remains more a theory than an axiom. It might well be argued that in assigning to the household such important functions, we are often assigning to the past the conditions of the present. To take just one example, can we be confident that young children were socialized in the households, extended or otherwise, of Renaissance Florence when so many were sent out at birth to wet-nurses, and when we are so ignorant of their later upbringing?[2] Indeed Ariès's distinction between medieval

*Parts of this approach were first worked out and presented in a lecture in 1972 at the Institute for Research in the Humanities at the University of Wisconsin, which had awarded me a fellowship for the year; and I am grateful to its Director and Fellows for both their award and their hospitality. I must also thank the Canada Council for a grant that allowed me to microfilm certain of the notarial registers on which this study is based.

1. The already classic statement of the case is Laslett's Introduction to *Household and Family in Past Time,* ed. Peter Laslett with Richard Wall (Cambridge, 1972), pp. 1-81, which is supported by the volume's essays and bibliography.

2. See, for example, James Bruce Ross, "The Middle-Class Child in Urban Italy, Fourteenth to Early Sixteenth Century," in *The History of Childhood,* ed. Lloyd de-Mause (New York, 1974), pp. 183-96.

and early modern childhood rests on a denial of the medieval household's socializing role.[3]

It might further be pointed out that household statistics cannot sufficiently convey either the important influence on human behavior of domestic and social ideals or the real tensions encountered in households and among families whose demographic shape does not conform to such exemplary patterns. Volumes can be devoted to the influence and strains imposed by the dominance of such social and domestic standards in our own day when, for example, statistically significant single individuals and extended families alike have been constrained by the conventions of the child-oriented nuclear family. And it is not simply a modern problem. Alberti's *Della Famiglia* and similar treatises from post-plague Florence which extol the joys of family life in a large household with strong and extended kin ties point to the importance of a similar tension between demographic realities and ideals of family organization in earlier societies.[4] Even before the plague had introduced a period of such dramatic demographic change, ordinary rates of medieval mortality placed strains on the household as death brutally separated actual family organization from its ideal.

The role of the household within such a society can be discerned in at least one form of documentation, notarial acts. These records, which are abundant for the cities of southern Europe from the thirteenth century, uniquely reflect human behavior among all social groups in a variety of situations, public and domestic. Through marriage contracts and dowry pledges, divorce proceedings and legitimations, commercial contracts and apprenticeships, wills and estate inventories, guardianship and emancipation acts, real estate transactions and arbitration agreements, we can recapture the life cycle both of individuals and of domestic groups. Genoa has one of Europe's oldest and fullest notarial archives with registers which begin in 1156 and which become both numerous and continuous from the beginning of the thirteenth century.[5] The relation in Genoa proposed here between social behavior and the ideals

3. Philippe Ariès, *Centuries of Childhood,* trans. Robert Baldick (New York, 1962), pp. 365-69.

4. See David Herlihy, "Mapping Households in Medieval Italy," *Catholic Historical Review* 58 (1972): 15-20.

5. For a fuller statement of the extent and value of the Genoese and other European notarial archives, see Diane Owen Hughes, "Toward Historical Ethnography: Notarial Records and Family History in the Middle Ages," *Historical Methods Newsletter* 7 (1974): 61-71.

and realities of family and household organization is drawn from an analysis of all the extant notarial documents of the twelfth century and of selected thirteenth- and fourteenth-century registers.

The two social groups of merchant aristocracy and artisans have been chosen for study primarily for reasons of identification. Aristocratic surnames, in common use from the twelfth century, let us trace descent with some certainty; and the trade names of artisans supply one means of classifying a part of the vast majority of the Genoese population slower to adopt fixed surnames.[6] The division is tied, of course, to differences in wealth. The merchant aristocrats, often descendants of the families that had come to dominate the Ligurian countryside in the tenth and eleventh centuries, ruled the city with an eye to profit and almost without interruption from Genoa's first large scale commercial ventures of the twelfth century until its economic and political reversals of the fourteenth.[7] The dowries of their women, their testamentary bequests, their houses in the city—all show how much richer they were than Genoa's artisans, a group which never attained the wealth or prominence of their Tuscan counterparts, even when they rose to control the government in the fourteenth century. The average aristocratic dowry in twelfth-century Genoa was nine times that of the artisan; bequests for aristocratic soul outran by seven times those for that of an artisan; and the great house of the aristocrat cost over ten times what artisans paid for their humbler quarters.[8]

But it is not a division based exclusively on wealth. The growing prosperity of local industry in the thirteenth century, although it did not much alter the general picture, did nevertheless allow some members of

6. Artisan surnames become fairly reliable by the fourteenth century. In the thirteenth century artisans generally had a second name, but it often changed drastically from one generation to the next. Thus Baldus Ayguinus' son was Willelmus de Curtemilia de Peçolo *(Documenti intorno alle relazioni fra Alba e Genova, 1141-1270,* ed. Arturo Ferretto, 2 vols. [Biblioteca della società storica subalpina, 23 and 50, 1906, 1910], 1:251); and Rubeus Gardinus' son was Gardinus de Garexio (Archivio di Stato, Genoa [hereafter, A. S. G.], Notary Ugolino di Scarpa, II, f. 92r).

7. A brief interruption was the artisan-backed government of Guglielmo Boccanegra from 1257 until 1262. Here, as even in the more permanent governmental changes of the fourteenth century, the relations between aristocrats and the new rulers were closer than rhetoric might suggest. See, for example, *Annali genovesi di Caffaro e de' suoi continuatori,* ed. Luigi Tommaso Belgrano and Cesare Imperiale di Sant' Angelo (Fonti per la storia d'Italia, 11-14bis, 1890-1929), 4: 25, n. 3.

8. Averages based on the extant acts, both published and unpublished, of the twelfth-century notaries. For a precise list, see *Cartolari notarili genovesi (1-149):* Inventario (Pubblicazioni degli Archivi di Stato, 22 and 41, 1956 and 1961).

certain trades (most notably the drapers, butchers, and notaries) to attain an aristocratic style of life, one which was often capped by an
aristocratic marriage.[9] And if most aristocrats were rich, some, like Isa-
bella Mallone, who tended her family's ovens and along with her
grandson was remembered in the will of a merchant who lay dying in
1258 in the nearby house of a tailor, were poor enough to be given
charity not only by their own relatives but even by their merchant and
artisan neighbors.[10] A climate of social mobility and a lack of economic
specialization combine, moreover, to confuse easy categories and to
make social groups more fluid and chimerical than any arbitrary division can ever suggest. Aristocratic De Fornari, who, if their fortunes
had ever rested on bread, had long ago abandoned their ovens, draper-
wine merchants, apothecary-loansharks, or merchant-bankers are
recurrent testimony to the difficulty of social classification.[11]
Nevertheless, while recognizing their variety—and indeed the large
part of the Genoese population they exclude—a comparison of these
two important and fairly distinct groups lets us chart some of the
relations between domestic ideals and social behavior in an early
population about which it has often seemed difficult to be precise.

Within Genoa, the unquestionable aristocratic ideal was the joint
patriarchal family, which formed the basic unit of a larger patrilineage; and this ideal shaped the city itself. Genoa's landscape, like
those of other Italian cities, was dominated by towers, which had impressed early visitors such as Benjamin of Tudela in the twelfth
century and which continued to strike foreigners such as Pero Tafur
as late as the fifteenth.[12] These were the fortifications of a series of
aristocratic family compounds, which expressed architecturally the
aristocratic ideal of family organization. Gathered in adjacent houses,
which often faced a small square, several branches of a family shared
common fortifications, market, shops, *loggie, curia,* baths, and church.
Remains of some houses and estate inventories give us a glimpse of their
interiors: generally one main, central room, the *caminata,* served for the

9. As, for example, when Salvagia Doria was married in 1342 to the son of a butcher
(A. S. G. Notary Bartolomeo de Bracelli e Francesco de Silva, f. 124v).

10. A. S. G. Notary Corrado Capriata, I, f. 21v.

11. As was pointed out long ago by Robert Reynolds, "In Search of a Business Class in
Thirteenth-Century Genoa," *Journal of Economic History* 5, supplement (December,
1945).

12. *The Itinerary of Benjamin of Tudela,* ed. and trans. Marcus Nathan Adler
(London, 1907), p. 5; Pero Tafur, *Travels and Adventures, 1435-1439,* ed. and trans.
Malcolm Letts (New York, 1926), p. 27.

family's eating and entertaining, off or above which there was a kitchen. On the next floor was a mezzanine *(medianus)*, off or above which were the family's bedrooms *(camerae);* and off or above them were the rooms for servants and slaves. Goldthwaite's eloquent comments on the lack of attention given to the aristocratic urban house in medieval Florence can also be applied to Genoa. If by the fifteenth century, the family had begun to lavish considerable wealth and imagination on its internal decoration, filling the variously painted rooms with tapestries, bits of furniture, and secular and devotional works of art, the inventories nevertheless show that their domestic possessions were far less inventive, less expensive, and less numerous than, for example, their clothes.[13] Private ease was subordinated to public display; and the single house was subordinated to the family enclave.

The notarial records suggest that under ideal conditions sons lived together in such houses at least until their father's death and often after it, introducing their wives and children into the common house. Their widows were given the right to remain as long as they did not reclaim their dowries, and widowed sisters who had reclaimed their dowries were given the right to return.[14] But demographic, physical, and psychological impediments constantly undercut the ideal. Some Genoese aristocrats were unable to produce a male heir while others left six or even more.[15] By the fifteenth century, many of the great houses of the Genoese aristocracy, some of which had facades over two hundred feet wide, could easily accommodate such families. But it would have been more difficult in the much smaller houses of earlier centuries. In 1267 Giacomo Spinola's house just outside Genoa in Cornigliano was a modest thirteen feet wide and forty-eight feet long, a size common for many aristocratic houses within the city, as the medieval remains still show.[16] The limitations of space imposed by such dwellings must often have encouraged sons to find new quarters when marriage made their father's house seem too crowded. The five-way division among his sons in 1278 of the estate of Nicolà Doria actually embraced twenty-eight

13. Luigi Tommaso Belgrano, *Della vita privata dei Genovesi*, 2nd ed. (Genoa, 1875), pp. 40-5; Emilio Landiani, *Vita privata genovese nel Rinascimento* (Atti della società ligure di storia patria [hereafter A. S. Li.], 47, 1915), pp. 65-116, 230-41, 247-58; Richard A. Goldthwaite, "The Florentine Palace as Domestic Architecture," *American Historical Review* 77 (1971): 977-1012.

14. See Diane Owen Hughes, "Urban Growth and Family Structure in Medieval Genoa," *Past and Present* 66 (1975): 13-17.

15. See, for example, Natale Battilana, *Genealogia delle famiglie nobili di Genova*, 3 vols. (Genoa, 1825-33).

16. Belgrano, *Della vita privata dei Genovesi*, pp. 13-14, n. 1.

males who fought six years later at Meloria.[17] If sisters, wives, and widowed mothers were added to this number, we should probably arrive at a family size for the immediate descendants of Nicolà (including the affinal relatives that lived with them) of close to fifty, a sizable number even for the ample Doria houses in the Piazza San Matteo. The pressure of numbers was undoubtedly intensified by the often underestimated psychological stresses of joint family life. If Ugone Embriaco was unusual in being summoned before the consuls of Genoa in 1144 to swear that he would not kill or maim his father's brother, the hostilities that could fester in these enclosed, familial quarters nevertheless provided added incentive to movement.[18]

There is no indication in Genoa, however, that estate division or the abandonment of communal living drastically altered the tenor of aristocratic family life. How significant, for example, was the Doria division of 1278 when the eldest son Branca, granted his father's great house at San Matteo, lived, probably with a brother or two, within a stone's throw of his closest paternal relatives; when the sons of Branca's late brother were awarded in Domoculta (an agricultural area controlled by the Doria just north of San Matteo) a great house whose improvement had been largely paid for by Branca and whose fields bordered on those of their uncle Rizzardo?[19] And just as communal living arrangements allowed for diverse individual enterprise, so too separate houses by no means signalled the end of joint economic activity. Ingone Gentile, like other Genoese aristocrats in a similar position, continued to act in a senior capacity in the business enterprises of both of his married nephews, the sons of his late brother Daniele, even after they had left the paternal house, one in February 1345, the other in November.[20]

17. A. S. G. Notary Bongiovanni de Langasco, I, f. 9r; Jacopo Doria, *La Chiesa di S. Matteo in Genova* (Genoa, 1860), pp. 250-58; and see Arturo Ferretto, *Codice diplomatico delle relazioni fra la Liguria, la Toscana e la Lunigiana ai tempi di Dante (1265-1321)*, 2 vols. (A. S. Li., 31, 1903), 2: 38-9.

18. *Codice diplomatico della Repubblica di Genova*, ed. Cesare Imperiale di Sant' Angelo, 3 vols. (Fonti per la storia d'Italia, 77, 79, 89, 1936-42), I, nos. 133 and 170.

19. A. S. G. Notary Bongiovanni De Langasco, I, f. 9r. One of Branca's brothers, Babilano, had acquired a neighboring house by 1286, and in the same year one of the heirs to the property at Domoculta bought from his uncle Branca land adjoining it at San Matteo—probably to build a house in the family's central enclave (A. S. G. Ugolino Scarpa, II, ff. 5v-6r).

20. A. S. G. Notary Tommaso Casanova, IX, ff. 11v, 13v, 119v-121r; and see generally Hughes, "Urban Growth and Family Structure in Medieval Genoa," pp. 19-20.

It was not within the walls of the house but within the shelter of the family enclave that the Genoese aristocratic family seems to have lived most fully. Unlike the palazzi of the sixteenth century, whose commodious internal space encouraged the domestication of many activities, the austere, often cramped houses of the medieval period pushed their inhabitants outdoors, into the family enclave. The facilities of such enclaves indicate the extent to which they, rather than the household, provided the focus for aristocratic family life. Its towers protected families within from the constant factional warfare that marked Genoa's political and social life. The shops *apotecae* and *bottecae)* and storage facilities *(voltae)* on the ground floor of the houses within it, the market on which it often impinged, its ovens, and often its gardens provided economic outlets and communal domestic facilities. Its bath became a center for family gossip while its *loggia* were a more public place for family meetings and festivities. Its church was a building dedicated to private family worship and, like the *loggia,* which was often decorated with family emblems, provided a means of family identification through plaques inscribed to the ancestral dead, through ever more splendid tombs and monuments, and through a constant hum of masses sung to mark the anniversaries of the deaths of its members.[21]

Their original wooden buildings were converted in the thirteenth and fourteenth centuries into elegant stone structures which formed an architecturally unified whole. A stunning example is the partially restored Doria square at San Matteo where the Doria were living and accumulating land by the twelfth century and where by the fourteenth century the great houses of the family's leader faced the small square and backed on tiny streets which contained scores of smaller houses for less important members of the lineage group. Its focal point was then, as it is today, the church of San Matteo, which Marino Doria had secured as a

21. Most noble squares seem to have contained a bath from early times. See *Il cartolare di Giovanni Scriba,* ed. Mario Chiaudano and Mattia Moresco (Documenti per la storia del commercio e del diritto commerciale italiano, 1-2, 1935 [hereafter Giovanni Scriba], nos 505, and Francesco Podestà, *Il colle di San Andrea in Genova* (A. S. Li., 33, 1901), p. 263, n. 1. On the *loggia* and emblems, see Belgrano, *Della vita privata dei Genovesi,* p. 46, n. 2; and for churches, see Mattia Moresco, "Le parrocchie gentilizie genovesi," in *Scritti di Mattia Moresco* (Milan, 1959), pp. 1-27. Finally, on the noble enclave generally, see Ennio Poleggi, "Le contrade delle consorterie nobiliari a Genova tra il XII secolo e il XIII secolo," *Urbanistica* 42-43 (1965): 15-20. For examples of masses and monuments, frequently mentioned in noble wills from the end of the thirteenth century, see the wills of Colombo Bestagno (A. S. G., Notary Bartolomeo de Bracelli, ff. 101v-201r) and Ansaldo Lomellino (A. S. G., Notary Tommaso Casanova, IX, ff. 7v-11r).

private family church in 1125 and which contained tributes to the
family's heroes and housed its dead.[22] By the fourteenth century, of
course, the Doria had become great aristocrats: Branca's son Bernabò,
a captain of the people in Genoa, had married Eleanora Fieschi, whose
uncle was Pope Hadrian V; and his granddaughter married a Sforza.[23]
But even at its lower reaches, the enclave was the aristocratic ideal of
family organization expressed in stone. The city's notarial acts let us re-
construct similar if less splendid quarters for almost every aristocratic
family in the city and let us follow their devolution within the family for
five or more generations.[24]

If the individual buildings in these enclaves lack the integrity and
care for internal detail that become evident later in Renaissance
domestic architecture, it is precisely because the emphasis was on the
joint enterprise, on the unity of the whole—a unity that was maintained
even when, as in the case of the Doria square, the buildings were
constructed in different centuries. And as this architectural unity
sacrificed individual buildings to the concept of a compound, so too
Genoese aristocratic households were dominated by the lineage group.
The lineage provided a structure for family continuity and solidarity in
a society where high mortality constantly threatened the stability of
smaller units.

Although the lineage is not an easily definable economic unit, customary inheritance practices among the aristocracy made it a net for
property, and it extended naturally out beyond household walls. In the
fifteenth century the governors of the commune had, for example, to
carefully state that for their administrative purposes (to collect a tax on
legacies imposed on all but members of the immediate *familia*), " . . .
by his family is understood everyone . . . who stays or lives in that
testator's house, receiving either nourishment or clothing or salary, and
not anyone else, even if he is from the testator's lineage or albergo, who
does not so live in the testator's house."[25] In the absence of sons, estates

22. Doria, *La chiesa di S. Matteo in Genova, passim.*
23. Ferretto, *Codice diplomatico delle relazione fra la Liguria, la Toscana e la Lunigiana*, 2: 33, 89-90.
24. A brief sketch of some is provided in Poleggi, "Le contrade delle consorterie nobiliari a Genova."
25. . . . intelligatur de sua familia omnis persona que . . . staret et habitaret in
domo ipsius testatoris ad vitum sive vestitum sive ad salarium et non aliqua alia persona
etiam si esset de stirpe progenie vel albergo ipsius testatoris que dicto modo non staret in
domo testatoris predicti," *Statuto dei padri del commune della repubblica genovese*, ed.
Cornelio Desimoni (Genoa, 1885), p. 103.

were given to brothers, grandsons, and nephews. Male aristocratic testators in the twelfth century never left their estates outside this circle; and almost without exception, they named no residual heirs, expecting their property to descend (or ascend) through the lineage, a practice which continued throughout the Middle Ages.[26] Aristocratic property rarely left the lineage group. While members of the same aristocratic family—often as distant as fourth or fifth cousins—might hold property jointly, they seldom can be found holding with those outside it.[27]

Politically, the lineage provided its members with the military strength and social organization necessary to guarantee their individual and collective privileged status in a society whose factional strife, economic opportunity, and social mobility seemed constantly threatening. The structured lineage with its hierarchy of leaders, who lived in the enclave's great house or houses and who organized both its defense and its political and social alliances in the twelfth century, seems to have flourished best, both then and in later centuries, among those aristocratic families most politically active in the city.[28] Nicoloso Doria could enter into negotiations in 1200, as leader of the Doria, for all of his house *(de domo mea)* as Rabella Grimaldi could contract politically in the fourteenth century for all of the Grimaldi, by then Grimaldi both by blood and by formal association.[29]

In aristocratic families whose political role in Genoa was less intense, formal leadership is often harder to discern. Yet the aristocratic lineage's physical identity in the city through its enclave, its group identity in a political faction, and its remarkably constant economic and social dealings over several generations (sometimes over centuries) with a particular group of families all suggest that lineage structure exerted controls even where the structure itself is hidden. The Della Volta, for example, one of twelfth-century Genoa's most powerful families whose

26. In the one exception in the dozen extant wills made by male aristocrats in the twelfth century, the testator named his daughers as residual heirs. This may have compensated for the low dowries, which had deprived at least one of them of an aristocratic husband, *Giovanni Scriba,* nos. 984, 1041. In a telling departure from aristocratic testamentary inexplicitness, the rich—but not aristocratic—Nicolà de Viali, to preserve the family property in the city and his newly acquired villa in the country (symbols of his aristocratic pretensions), allowed rights only of usufruct to any heirs more distant than his yet unborn children; usufruct rights that were to descend in the male line "usque infinitum" (A. S. G. Notary Tommaso Casanova, X, ff. 23r-v, 176r-177r).

27. With the significant exception of property that passed through women, usually in the form of dowry, less often as legacies.

28. Hughes, "Urban Growth and Family Development in Medieval Genoa," pp. 7-9.

29. A. S. G. Ms. 102 (Diversorum), f. 131v; Notary Tommaso Casanova, IX, f. 138v.

lineage structure is clear and striking in that period, had close economic and social relations with the neighboring Mallone, a partnership reinforced in the late thirteenth and early fourteenth centuries, when the Della Volta's political fortunes were in decline and its lineage structure and leaders are less discernible, through the formation by the two families, along with the Cattaneo and Soldano, of the contractual clan, or *albergo*, Cattaneo.[30]

The *albergo* is perhaps the final proof in Genoa of the strength of the lineage as the aristocratic social ideal. For when in the late thirteenth and fourteenth centuries factional strife, declining economic opportunity, and the demographic consequences of rapid aristocratic emigration and, finally, of the catastrophe of 1348, made inroads into the stability of the lineage and its power to support its constituent families, these families generally moved together into a new, artificial lineage or clan, called in Genoa an *albergo*. Although individual joint families usually contracted and entered by themselves, it was the larger sense of lineage that encouraged most families of the same name, if often of enormously distant relationship, to join the same *albergo* and to create with their new, artificial kinsmen (who were usually their most immediate aristocratic neighbors in the city) an enlarged enclave in which, as a fifteenth-century tax register clearly shows, almost all its members lived.[31]

Artisan families, like artisan houses, were different from those of the aristocracy; and artisans seem to have had a genuinely different view of family life from their aristocratic co-citizens. Social ideals are, in some ways, harder to define for this social group; for often artisans may have lacked the economic means to effect them. Is the apparently smaller size of the artisan family, for example, a product of social intention, or did the later marriage age encouraged by craft training combine with poorer living conditions to deny artisans the large families they may have favored?[32] But if considerations such as these should make us careful about drawing social ideals from majority behavior, certain features of artisan family organization are nevertheless striking.

30. A. S. G., Cart. 48, ff. 85v, 105r; Cart. 50, ff. 13r, 19r-v, 21v, 23v, 29r; Cart. 77, f. 174r.; Ferretto, *Codice diplomatico delle relazione fra la Liguria, la Toscana ela Lunigiana*, 2: 241, 258, 318.

31. Jacques Heers, *Le clan familial au moyen âge* (Paris, 1974), pp. 160-61.

32. See Hughes, "Urban Growth and Family Structure in Medieval Genoa," p. 23 and n. 80.

From their first appearance in the twelfth-century city, artisans settled individually rather than in extended family districts. The real estate
contracts of the twelfth and thirteenth centuries almost never show artisan kinsmen living in adjoining houses or buying and selling neighboring real estate. This was undoubtedly a feature of immigration,
which seems in Genoa to have been, at least in its early stages, a rather
solitary undertaking.[33] If by the fourteenth century the inevitable expansion of certain families and the transfer of property within them
modified this for some, physical alienation from kinsmen outside the
household was, however, intensified for a growing number of artisans
who were forced to rent accommodation with leases that expired at the
end of three or four years.[34] It was also intensified by the dispersal of
trades throughout the city. Since Genoese artisans frequently placed
their sons (and their daughters) in trades different from their own, their
children were likely to seek accommodation elsewhere in the city, in a
district where, in the absence of kinsmen, fellow tradesmen became
their chief support.[35]

When the artisan reached beyond the walls that contained his
household, he, unlike the aristocrat, reached away from kin ties into the
very public city. Only the parish church offered some protective shelter;
and if its square, its altar, and its priests were there for all, artisans
seem to have been particularly aware of the benefits it offered, turning
to its priests in the absence of kinsmen as witnesses and counsellors and
using its square in the absence of a private *loggia* for their meetings.[36]
Not only were kinsmen physically distant, the memory of their ancestors must also have been harder to recall. By the fourteenth century
most aristocrats chose to be buried not just in the family's church but,
like Danino dei Ultramarini in 1345, in the tombs of their ancestors.[37]

33. Ibid., pp. 21-25.

34. For example, A. S. G., Notary Giovanni de Fossato, I, f. 118r; Notary Angelino de
Sigestro, II, f. 252r; Notary Giovanni de Vegio, I, pt. 2, f. 148r. Few are for shorter
periods and almost none for longer ones.

35. This can be traced both from actual apprenticeship documents (although this dis-
torts conclusions since fathers who trained their sons at home, as Frederick Lane once
pointed out to me, would not make such a contract) and from the remarkable frequency
with which artisan sons cite their father's trade in addition to giving his name, a subject
which I treat in some detail in "Kinsmen and Neighbors in a Medieval City," forthcoming in a collection tentatively entitled *The Medieval City*.

36. *Liber magistri Salmonis, 1222-26,* ed. Arturo Ferretto (A. S. Li, 36, 1906), pp.
550-51; Heers, *Le clan familial au moyen âge,* pp. 149-51.

37.   . . . *in monumento antecessorum,* A. S. G. Notary Tommaso Casanova, IX, f.
27r.

Artisans, even those as rich as the draper Percivale di Campomorono, who gave his two daughters dowries that approached a noble level, almost never so stipulated in their wills.[38] Buried without monument at their parish churches or at the even more public cathedral of San Lorenzo, there were fewer commemorative masses to keep alive their memory and fewer kinsmen there to hear them if they were sung.

Whatever the actual construction of a particular artisan household—whether stem, joint, conjugal, or another type—it was this household, rather than any ties of kinship that might extend beyond it, that was central to the artisan's concept of family life. The shoemaker who, although he had two brothers living in 1190, left the major part of his estate, including the house in which he lived, to the shoemaker who shared in his business (and who probably lived in his house), naming the parish church as his residual heir, did something that no aristocrat would ever have done.[39] And he was not alone: a surprisingly high 14 percent of artisan testators, in the absence of direct heirs, chose in the twelfth century to leave their estates to non-relatives.[40] In some cases this may represent a means for survival in old age in a world where the fragility of the household left many exposed. The household's changes seldom left the aristocrat without support. If there were no members of his immediate household to shelter him, the larger lineage arranged for his care. The sale in 1345 to Benedetta Ceba of a house in the Ceba enclave was, for example, conditional on her granting Oddoardo Ceba, her kinsman who had been awarded usufruct rights in half of the house, GL8 1/2 annually.[41] Artisans, more susceptible to the vagaries of the household and obviously terrified of a poor and lonely old age, were sometimes forced to make, among other things, reciprocal arrangements with friends, fellow tradesmen, and neighbors, as the widow Agnese did in 1233 when she entrusted her small estate to a neighboring artisan, who, in turn, made her his heir.[42]

The conjugal bond defined the artisan household. Its importance can be seen in the fact that in the twelfth century wives were made heirs by their artisan husbands in 23 percent of the extant wills, sometimes even in the presence of children, an award the aristocracy never contem-

---

38. For Percivale, see A. S. G., Notary Giovanni Galli, III, f. 107r.

39. *Oberto Scriba de Mercato, 1190,* ed. Mario Chiaudano and Raimondo Marozzo della Rocca (Notai liguri del secolo XII, 1, 1938) [hereafter, *O. S., 1190*], no. 50.

40. Based on twenty-four extant wills.

41. A. S. G., Notary Tommaso Casanova, XI, ff. 224r-v.

42. A. S. G., Cart. 19, ff. 54r-v.

plated.[43] And it can probably also be seen in the fact that artisans seem
to have indulged in wife-beating, whereas aristocrats, who lived in
households bound by patriarchal authority, more often directed their
hostilities toward their fathers and uncles.[44] The bond between husbands and wives may have been fostered by the demands of artisan life
in which women often worked beside their husbands or supplemented
his income by practising a trade of their own. And it was certainly supported by the conjugal fund established at marriage by the woman's
dowry and the husband's return gift, or *antefactum,* which for all but
the richest artisans were roughly equal contributions both to support
the marriage itself and to keep the wife in widowhood.[45]

The centrality of the conjugal family can also be seen in artisan attempts to overcome its limitations. Although some artisan families in
the fourteenth and fifteenth centuries, particularly after 1339 when the
aristocracy's exclusion from government broadened their own political
participation, attempted to combat demographic and economic incur-
sions into the household by forming, like the aristocrats they aped, artificial lineages, or *alberghi,* most found other solutions. Even the few
popular *alberghi,* more a home of rich merchants than rich artisans,
seem to have had a different social texture from their aristocratic counterparts, one which indicates certain basic structural differences
between aristocratic and artisan families: when Cristoforo Tonso, in
the fifteenth century, entered the popular *albergo* of the dei Franchi
(first established in 1393), he enrolled himself and his sons; his action
did not immediately change the status of other kinsmen. When the Ceba
entered the noble *albergo* of the Grimaldi in 1448, however, Nicolà
Ceba entered for himself, his sons, grandsons, and great grandsons, and
for six other heads of branches of the Ceba lineage.[46] These were,
furthermore, more associations of neighbors than of neighboring lineages. The popular *alberghi* of the dei Franchi and the Giustiniani
were, in the later Middle Ages, the two that housed the largest

43. The discovery of a few more wills increased the figure given in "Urban Growth
and Family Structure in Medieval Genoa," p. 25.

44. A. S, G., Notary Corrado de Castello, VIII, f. 116r; Notary Maestro Salomone, II,
f. 369v; Richard D. Face, "Lanfranco Cigala of Genoa: the Career of a Delinquent,"
Medievalia et Humanistica (1963), pp. 77-85; and above, p. 6.

45. See, for its early history, Hughes, "Urban Growth and Family Structure in
Medieval Genoa," pp. 13-15, 24-25.

46. A. Ascheri, *Notizie intorno alla reunione delle famiglie in alberghi* in Genova
(Genoa, 1846), pp. 69-70; Heers, *Le clan familial au moyen âge,* p. 92.

number of separate families in the city, drawing as they did on smaller neighboring families rather than larger lineage groups.[47]

But entrance into an *albergo* was an event that touched no more than a few of the grandest families. Most found other solutions to ease the recurrent strains on the household of mortality, retirement, and economic need; ones that, when they had any familial overtones, were founded in a conjugal base. In the twelfth century, for example, artisans, though decidedly not aristocrats, frequently extended their families either by requiring that adult sons support their retired parents or by insisting that sons-in-law, in return for dowry, move into their wives' houses, working for their parents and submitting to their authority.[48] Were artisans reluctant to submit to any but those who, like their sons but not like their sons-in-law, were part of the conjugal family?[49] Nor does the joining of brothers or brothers-in-law to form a contractual family (the *atterèment* or *frérèche*), found in the Genoese countryside and common elsewhere in rural Europe in the later Middle Ages, seem to have been favored by the city's artisans.[50] It has been observed that "the sibling tie and the conjugal tie are opposed forces."[51] Was the strength of the conjugal tie among artisans in medieval Genoa sufficient to direct contractual familial arrangements toward it, thus binding parents and children (especially sons), but not brothers, sisters, or more distant kinsmen? Did indeed the primacy of the marital bond, ideally distinguished by the marital affection recommended by the canonists, make artisans more reluctant than either their rural or

47. See Ascheri, *Notizie intorno alla reunione delle famiglie in alberghi, passim.*

48. *O. S., 1190,* nos 5, 141-44, 563; *Giovanni Scriba,* nos 314-15, 633-36, 644-45, 710, 818-20, 952.

49. In rural Neuchâtel in the fifteenth century, uxorilocal marriage usually saw the husband entering his wife's family *loco filii;* but sometimes other arrangements were made: Dominique Favarger, *Le régime matrimonial dans le comté de Neuchâtel du XVe au XIX siècle* (Neuchâtel, 1970), pt. 2, ch. 1.

50. *Documenti genovesi di Novi e Valle Scrivia,* ed. Arturo Ferretto (Bibliogeca della società storica subalpina, 50-51, 1909-10), n. 823; Robert Boutrouche, *La crise d'une société. Seigneurs et paysans du Bordelais pendant la Guerre de Cent Ans* (Paris, 1963), pp. 119-22; Emmanuel Le Roy Ladurie, *Les paysans de Languedoc,* 2 vols. (Paris, 1966), 1: 160-8; Christiane Klapisch and Michel Demonet, " 'A uno pane e uno vino': la famille rurale toscane au début de XVe siècle," *Annales, E. S. C.* 27 (1972): 899-901.

51. By J. D. Freeman, "The Family System of the Iban of Borneo," in *The Developmental Cycle in Domestic Groups,* ed. Jack Goody (Cambridge, 1971), p. 42; and for perceptive comments, see Robert Wheaton, "Family and Kinship in Western Europe: The Problem of the Joint Family Household," *Journal of Interdisciplinary History* 5 (1975): 619-21.

aristocratic neighbors to contemplate adoptive arrangements that lay beyond it?[52]

One might, of course, see this emphasis on the conjugal bond and the existence of smaller household groups and less elaborate kin structures as nothing more than the product of reduced circumstances, which could support neither the great aristocratic household nor the patrilineage that guaranteed its status. There is certainly evidence for such a view. Analyses of the Florentine *catasto* of 1427 show, for example, that both in the city and its *contado* the incidence of extended households increased with wealth.[53] Within Genoa the house of a rich notary or draper, like Percivale di Campomorono, which when he lay dying in 1330 housed his wife, his six children, and at least one slave, was more likely to have retained a married son or two—who would undoubtedly have yielded more readily to his authority under his roof than if they lived elsewhere—than was the smaller house or rented quarters of a poorer artisan.[54] Indeed, it is the less prestigious trades that exhibit the most consciously conjugal characteristics. The woolworkers, who carried on modest businesses near the rapid streams at either side of the city, for example, correspond remarkably well, in their husband-wife business transactions, their individual dwellings, and their apparent freedom from extensive kin ties, to the conjugal ideal.[55] Yet even Percivale di Campomorono, as he made his will and freed his slave, was surrounded not by his kinsmen but by neighbors and fellow craftsmen.

So long as artisans did not accumulate sufficient wealth to pass, if they chose, for aristocrats, they seem genuinely to have cherished the strong bond between husband and wife. The records of their marriage settlements give us one means of measuring this. Unlike aristocrats who in the twelfth century withdrew marital support from their wives, as they had begun to do elsewhere in Italy, artisan husbands continued to grant their wives, on the receipt of their dowry, a substantial return gift *(antefactum)*. In the twelfth century almost 50 per cent of these artisan

52. As the valid test of the marriage: see J. T. Noonan, "Marital Affection in the Canonists," *Studia Gratiana* 12 (1967): 479-509.

53. Christiane Klapisch and Michel Demonet, " 'A uno pane e uno vino': La famille rurale toscane au début du XVe siècle," *Annales. E. S. C.* 27 (1972): p. 884.

54. A. S. G., Notary Giovanni Galli, III, ff. 107r-108r.

55. Roberto Lopez, "Le origini dell'arte della lana," in *Studi sull'economia genovese nel Medio Evo* (Documenti e studi per la storia del commercio e del diritto commerciale italiano, 8, 1936), pp. 114-15.

antefacta equalled or exceeded the amount the woman brought to the marriage as dowry; and well over 70 per cent were more than half its value, as compared with 44 per cent in aristocratic marriages.[56] In the following centuries, moveover, the difference between artisans and aristocrats became even more striking. As aristocratic dowries outstripped the return gift by eight, ten, or twelve times, artisan *antefacta* maintained a rough equality with the dowry, even as artisan dowries rose in value. In the second half of the thirteenth century, the average artisan dowry was about GL71 and the average artisan *antefactum*, about GL50, compared with GL24 and GL19 respectively in the previous century; but what these figures may obscure is the fact that in almost 80 percent of these cases artisan men were awarding their brides an *antefactum* that equalled or exceeded the value of their dowry, a rise of about 30 percent over the late twelfth century.[57] And even this figure may be distorted by a number of rich drapers, notaries and butchers who were awarding their daughters dowries on a noble scale but who were prevented, by the law of 1143 which set a limit of GL100 on all Genoese *antefacta,* from giving equal return gifts to their wives.[58] The many artisans who gave their wives an equal settlement at marriage broke another requirement of that law which allowed no *antefactum* to rise above one-half the stated value of the dowry, a requirement that other citizens who received dowries at an artisan level were significantly less inclined to ignore. Only 43 per cent of other citizens who in these acts acknowledged receipt from their wives of dowries that fell within the artisan range awarded them an equal return gift. Thus artisan devotion to a balanced conjugal fund, as perhaps artisan devotion to the conjugal bond, should be seen as more than simply a reflection of their economic status. With the possible exception of artisans from the greatest trades, it may have distinguished this social group not only from the city's aristocrats but also from the majority of its humbler citizens.

To see what effect these proposed social ideals, aristocratic adherence to the patrilineage and artisan devotion to the conjugal bond, had on actual social behavior within medieval Genoa, consider the history of

56. See Hughes, "Urban Growth and Family Structure in Medieval Genoa," p. 24.

57. These figures are based on the extant contracts found in A. S. G., Cart. 49, 78, 82, Notary Angelino de Sigestro, Notary Filippo di Saolo, Notary Palodino de Secto, I, Notary Bartolomeo de Fornario, Notary Oberto de Langasco, Notary Antonino de Quarto, Notary Giberto de Nervio, I.

58. *Codice diplomatico . . . Genova,* I, no. 153.

revealing, if often ignored, members of the aristocratic and artisan family group, namely its children and its wives. They shared the vital role of bearing and transmitting the family line. Yet they shared as well, through both customary and legal restrictions, a certain incapacity. Neither women or children could act without counsel, for example; and both, according to the moral wisdom of the age, were to be submissive to the authority of other household members. Although central members of the family, they were also peculiarly vulnerable to the claims of the larger family group as it tried to enforce and refine familial ideals and to foster suitable social behavior among those upon whom it could exert some claim.

The childrearing practices of aristocrats and artisans emphasize the difference in their attitudes toward family life. Among artisans, whose children normally spent their first year or two at their mother's breast, the nursing bond complemented the maternal; but it competed with it in aristocratic households, where babies were commonly received by wet nurses. Numerous aristocratic wills from the thirteenth century on make special bequests to the testator's "mamma," the source, as the colloquial name may suggest,[59] not only for milk but for the early motherly affection that artisans would expect, as the nurse's almost total absence from their lists of charitable bequests reveals, from their natural mothers.[60] Although it is not easy to judge from the existing sources whether aristocratic children were nursed at home or sent away, as they were in Renaissance Florence, a fourteenth-century will that re-members a particular "mamma" for those at Zemignano suggests that some at least had a rural base, perhaps near the villas that, by the fourteenth century, most aristocrats possessed in the Genoese countryside.[61]

59. Like the Greek μάμμα meaning breast or mother (and grandmother), *mamma* resembled and recreated the first childish calls for food and attention, whose sound is similar in countless societies: see Roman Jakobson, "Why 'Mama' and 'Papa' " in *Selected Writings*, (The Hague, 1962), 1: 538-45, and Edmund Leach, "More about 'Mama' and 'Papa' " in *Rethinking Kinship and Marriage*, ed. Rodney Needham (A. S. A. Monograph, 11, 1971), pp. 75-98. It was a term applied at least occasionally to nurses in ancient Rome, as it was both commonly and formally in medieval Genoa: *Statuta Genuensis*, lib. 4, cap. 67, p. 117v. The *mamme* of Genoa were also called *baiule*, as they were in Florence.

60. For two thirteenth-century bequests, see *Le carte di Santa Maria delle Vigne di Genova, 1103-1393,* ed. Gabriella Airaldi (Genoa, 1969), no. 89, and Roberto Lopez, *Benedetto Zaccaria, ammiraglio e mercante* (Messina, 1932), pp. 243-4. For an exception, see *Liber magistri Salmonis, 1222-26,* pp. 7879-, where Oberto de Grocola, who was probably an artisan, had a *baiula* who invested small sums with him.

61. A. S. G. Notary Tommaso Casanova, IX, ff. 132r-v.

Nor do artisan wills make mention of the nurses or governesses whom so many aristocrats remembered on their deathbeds.[62] The wills suggest that within aristocratic families, whatever their demographic shape, the nurse made a much more lasting impression on girls than on boys. Aristocratic women, who had moved from home and produced families of their own, remembered both their own and their children's nurses; but they are never mentioned in the wills of men. Nicolosa di Guisolfo, who lay ill in 1345, remembered both her nurses and those of her two children; but her husband Filippo di Savignone, who had lain dying just a month earlier, did not.[63] The creation of a household of her own in which she employed nurses for her own children probably called up memories of the nurse she had left at home; and bits of her clothing and jewelry made natural bequests. But perhaps, too, boys were earlier removed from their nurse's care, into school, into merchant training, even into battle, beside their fathers, brothers, and uncles.

Whatever the possible demographic consequences of different nursing practices within aristocratic and artisan households, by which aristocratic mothers may have been freed to devote themselves more quickly to new pregnancies and larger families and by which artisan fertility may have been reduced, their psychological impact was undoubtedly significant.[64] The absence of nurses in the artisan household, even where less specialized servants were employed, surely created a more intense early bond between mothers and children than in the households of aristocrats. Yet in a society where childbirth so often left households motherless, the aristocrat had a surrogate that artisans must often have lacked to ease the loneliness of loss and the almost inevitable adjustment to a stepmother.

It is hard to measure the mark made by early childhood experiences, for entry into the documents was seldom made before young adulthood. And by that time the reversed adolescences of aristocrats and artisans had probably intensified those experiences. At adolescence, or even before, aristocratic boys were recalled from their nursery exile to be immersed in family concerns and trained in the family business; whereas artisan boys (and frequently girls as well) were often pushed out of the nest into apprenticeship to spend their adolescence and young

---

62. The so-called *nutrices*.

63. A. S. G. Notary Tommasa Casanova, IX, ff. 21r-v, 58r.

64. According to the hypothesis advanced by J. C. Russell, "Aspects démographiques des débuts de la féodalité," *Annales. E. S. C.* 20 (1965): 1118-27.

adulthood with fellow tradesmen rather than their kinsmen. If the patriarchal discipline of aristocratic training could be harsh and stulti-
fying, it may have been preferable to that of an alien master, whose
feared disciplines reverberate through the formulaic conditions of apprenticeship contracts, masters assuring the parents of prospective ap-
prentices that they will "give discipline only as a master should discipline his pupil," although at least one contract amends "pupils" to
"servants."[65] And both the clauses that guarantee the apprentice's
service both day and night and every day (or at least on the usual
working days of a particular trade) and the precise conditions governing
runaways suggest that the master's household was more like a workshop than a home.[66] Did these years (six or seven on the average in the
twelfth and thirteenth centuries) away from home in harsh surroundings at an emotionally sensitive age, years in which many artisans were
expressly forbidden the privilege of marrying, reinforce the memory of
their boyhood homes and give birth to the desire to recreate them? And
might latent hostility toward parents who had placed them in apprenticeship have strengthened the new bonds they forged with the
wives they married on release from their term, while it weakened those
older bonds that bound them to their parents?

For artisans, marriage and economic independence seem usually to
have arrived together, after the years of apprenticeship were over. For
aristocrats, however, coming of age was an almost imperceptible
process in which the arrival of social and economic independence could
often lag behind recognition of their sexual maturity through marriage.
The period's wills stipulate that aristocratic daughters were to be married by fifteen or sixteen, and many were married younger.[67] If families
anticipated a slightly later marriage age for sons, their marriages were
nevertheless seldom delayed in medieval Genoa, as they seem to have

---

65. A. S. G., Notary Bartolomeo de Fornario, f. 12r.

66. Runaways were to be returned by their fathers or guardians, usually within eight
days of their notification of the apprentice's flight: A. S. G. Notary Bartolomeo Fornario,
IV, f. 39r; *Documenti genovesi di Novi e Valle Scrivia*, no. 807. Some parents tried to
lighten the service aspects of apprenticeship as Margarita di Sant' Agnese did in 1326, for
example, when she secured from her son's master the guarantee that he would not be required to carry water to the house (A. S. G., Cart. 51, ff. 132r-v).

67. Occasional wills stipulate a marriage age as early as twelve: A. S. G. ms. 102
(Diversorum), f. 233v; and some aristocratic marriages completed at or soon after that
age: Belgrano, *Della vita privata dei Genovesi*, p. 412; Roberto Sabatino Lopez, "Familiari, procuatori e dipendenti di Benedetto Zaccaria," in *Miscellanea di storia ligure in
onore di Giorgio Falco* (Milan, 1962), pp. 227-30; A. S. G. Notary Tommaso Casanova,
IX, ff. 120r-121r; XI, f. 108r.

been in Renaissance Florence, until a decade or more separated husbands from their childbrides.[68] Although marriage could significantly
expand the social and business circle to include new affinal relatives (as
in the case of the seventeen-year-old Eliano Marocelli and Orieta de
Negri, whose marriage in 1326 immediately drew de Negri investment
to Marocelli business enterprises), and although marriage more than
occasionally coincided with the groom's emancipation from his father's
potestas, the basic patriarchal orientation of the family and its economic
life allowed the new couple little real independence.[69]

The apparent freedom that emancipation bestowed is often,
moreover, an illusion. The communal government viewed as legal
minors all boys under the age of twenty; but it recognized a second category before full adulthood of young men over twenty who were still in
their father's *potestas,* removal from which was usually expected at the
age of twenty-five (the age of full legal majority) by a formal act of
emancipation.[70] Many Genoese seem never to have been emancipated,
however, while some, like the seventeen-year-old groom of Orieta de
Negri, who was styled the emancipated son of Domenico Marocelli,
were emancipated with noticeable haste. In this case, as in numerous
others, emancipation may have been demanded by the bride's relatives
to protect her dowry in the event of her husband's death from the claims
of his kinsmen, an important consideration for the orphaned Orieta.[71]
But the documents also suggest that many aristocratic emancipations in
Genoa were little more than means of securing for the family a form of
limited liability; for emancipation freed fathers from responsibility for
the debts (and criminal activities) of their children. This may have been
Leo Cataneo's intention in emancipating, in 1331, his undoubtedly
young son Raimondino, who was specifically enjoined by the authorities to refrain from commercial partnership for at least three
years.[72] And it almost certainly lay behind the unusual emancipation in
1308 of Grimalda, the daughter of Pietro Lercari, to allow her to borrow on the same day GL300 from Gotifredo de Negri.[73] Aristocrats, un-

68. Herlihy, "Mapping Households in Medieval Italy," pp. 15-17.

69. A. S. G. Notary Tommaso Casanova, XI, ff. 153r-154r.

70. "Breve dei consoli di Genova," nos. 17, 28, 72, ed. Franco Niccolai, *Contributo
allo studio dei più antichi brevi della compagna genovese* (Milan, 1939), pp. 106-7, 112;
Manlio Bellomo, "Communita e comune in Italia negli statuti medievali *super emancipa-
tionibus,*" *Annali di storia del diritto* 8 (1964): 81-106.

71. And see *Giovanni Scriba,* nos. 989-90, 996, 1166.

72. A. S. G., Notary Bartolomeo Bracelli e Francesco de Silva, f. 228v.

73. A. S. G., Cart. 77, f. 86r.

like *popolani,* seldom awarded their sons substantial settlements at emancipation, and the act itself seems to have provoked remarkably little change in the orientation of their business lives.[74]

It was neither marriage nor the beginning of a business career, the joint signal of artisan adulthood, but rather a father's death that could push aristocratic sons toward independence. When sons were married and mature, this often prompted the division of an estate among brothers and their establishment of separate, if usually neighboring households.[75] And both the sizeable inheritance and the freedom from patriarchal control that their father's death could bring them sometimes encouraged that independent commercial daring for which Genoese merchant aristocrats—on the strength of only a few cases—have become so well known. The familial situation of two notable cases suggests that it might be useful to study the relationship between the absence, for reasons of either death or incapacity, of paternal control and the creative application of commercial talents in Genoa. Was it their father's death in 1300, as they were about to come of age, that allowed the Pessagno brothers to turn the direction of the family's commercial interests away from the East toward the galley trade with northern Europe that their father had consistently ignored? It was a new direction that allowed at least two of them to make their mark in the West: Antonio rivalled the Frescobaldi as royal bankers in England and rose in 1317 to the office of seneschal in Aquitaine, while Manuele became in the same year Portugal's first admiral of the largely Genoese fleet he had recruited.[76] And although the earlier success in the East of Benedetto and Manuele Zaccaria, (through their administration and control of the alum mines of Phocea) is, like that of the two Pessagno brothers, a tribute to their native commerical abilities, the notorious misfortunes of their father Folcone—his double abductions, first in 1252 during their adolescence, when he had to be rescued by the communal army; then thirteen years later, after his sons had begun their careers, when the promise of a GL5000 ransom secured his release—

74. *Giovanni Scriba,* nos. 314-15, 633-36, 644-45, 710, 818-20, 952; *O. S., 1190,* nos 5, 141-4.

75. Estate division was not, however, dependent on a father's death. Sometimes sons even divided part or whole of the paternal goods while the father was still alive, see A. S. G., Notary David de S. Ambrosio, I, f. 63r, for the division by the three sons of Zaccaria de Castello; but this seems to have been rare.

76. Diane Owen Hughes, "Antonio Pessagno, Merchant of Genoa" (Ph. D. diss., Yale University, 1967), pp. 1-31, 74-75, 85-110, 141-44.

suggest a slightly foolish figure whom his sons came to despise. Perhaps the tension between the partriarchal ideal and Folcone's behavior is reflected in Manuele's derisive testamentary bequest to his father of GL10, the amount that some aristocrats left to loyal servants.[77]

The different meanings that artisans and aristocrats might draw from their domestic cycle and the configurations of their household can be further refined by studying certain features of their wives' behavior, both within the house and outside it. Greater maturity at marriage frequently combined with valuable skills to award artisan wives, as we have seen, central places within their households, a place that may have been warmed by affection. While it would be foolish to deny the prominence of arranged marriages among artisans as well as aristocrats, the more frequent absence of artisan fathers from the marriage negotiations of their children in the twelfth century may indicate greater freedom in the selection of a mate.[78] It is an artisan who first appears in the extant notarial records to exercise the marital choice that the church was coming to advocate by running to her priest to refuse her assigned partner.[79]

In her importance as a mother, and in her value as an unpaid partner, lay the artisan wife's claim to authority within a conjugal household. But even when the couple did not set up an independent household, the not infrequent uxorilocal marriages among artisans, sometimes prompted by the advantage to both sides of a marriage between an apprentice and his master's daughter, undoubtedly gave some artisan wives a kind of superiority over their husbands in the new complex household.[80] If the exercise of this authority within the home has gone largely unrecorded, it is reflected in the occasional identification in the fourteenth century of artisans (but never aristocrats) by both their father's and mother's names in the joint business contracts so frequently entered into by artisan husbands and wives, and in the remarkably independent investment in the city's commerce by artisan women that fill the notarial records.[81]

77. Lopez, *Benedetto Zaccaria, ammiraglio e mercante; Annali genovesi,* 4: 9, 73; Lopez, "Familiari, procuratori e dipendenti di Benedetto Zaccaria," pp. 222-23 (for his will of 1271).

78. See Hughes, "Urban Growth and Family Structure in Medieval Genoa," p. 22.

79. *Lanfranco (1202-1226),* ed. H. C. Krueger and R. L. Reynolds (Notai liguri del secolo XIII, 6, 1953), no. 1503.

80. See, for example, *O. S., 1190,* nos. 502-3; *Lanfranco (1203-1226),* no. 1233.

81. One artisan wife even stood witness to a notarial act of her husband—one of the few women who ever so appear in the extant witness lists: A. S. G. Cart. 15, f. 3v.

The importance of lineage and status considerations, which encouraged families to seek balanced alliances, left aristocratic women with less choice in a husband. This is most apparent at the height of aristocratic society, as in the marriages arranged on the same day in 1282 between Branca Doria's niece Pietrina and Percivalle Fieschi, and between Percivale's young sister and Pietrina's brother Saladino, a widower with three children.[82] But if the political consequences of balanced matches were less significant in other families, their economic and social advantages (not least the equal exchange of dowries that they entailed) made them attractive throughout Genoa's merchant aristocracy. They served, for one thing, as a minimal guarantee of a woman's rights in a lineage group which, since aristocratic marriage was almost exclusively endogamous and virilocal, she entered as an alien.[83]

The wife's position between lineages must often have been tragic in a city so often consumed by factional, lineage-based strife, especially when marriage was used as a means of easing hostilities between lineages. Giovanna Embrone was undoubtedly not alone in becoming a widow at her brothers' hands. Her particular trials began just before her husband's assassination in 1226 when she was taken back into her brothers' house to make a will in which she excluded her young daughter by Nicolà Embrone and made her three brothers her heirs; and they may not have ended when, after her husband's death, she entered the convent of the Hospitalers. Her brothers soon appeared to persuade her to demand release from her vows on the grounds that she had been "out of her mind" with grief when she made them.[84] But even when feuds and political strife did not divide families, the wife's position was delicate. Her youth, and often that of her husband, told against them both when they lived their first married years as children in the authority of the husband's father, a figure who seldom seems to have inspired the devotion of his daughters-in-law. If not every woman was as antagonistic as Alda di Sori, who in her will of 1217 inserted special

82. Ferretto, *Codice diplomatico delle relazioni fra la Liguria, la Toscana e la Lunigiana*, p. xxxviii.

83. There are very few exceptions that I have found. Buongiovanni Malfigliastro's son Giovanni, when he married up into the city's aristocracy, did swear to live with his mother-in-law, *Giovanni Scriba*, nos. 989-90, 996; but if his upward mobility encouraged uxorilocal marriage, most other mixed-status marriage were virilocal. And the marriage between two Spinola in the mid-thirteenth century, as that between two Zaccaria in 1342, is unusual, A. S. G., Notary Filippo di Saulo, I, f. 46r; Notary Tommaso Casanova, XI, f. 105r.

84. *Annali genovesi*, 3: 19; *Liber magistri Salmonis, 1222-26*, pp. 458, 553.

clauses to keep her father-in-law from her goods, it is nevertheless striking how seldom any aristocratic woman mentions in her will the father-in-law or mother-in-law whose house she so often shared.[85]

The dowry appeared in Genoa in the eleventh and twelfth centuries as a means of avoiding paying out money to the increasingly alien wives, that a tightened lineage was producing, by instead granting endowment to daughters.[86] But it became a way of guaranteeing that daughter's rights in her husband's home. If the dowry in Genoa did not grant her kinsmen an assured place in the family counsels that concerned her and her children, as it did in Siena, it does seem to have given them the right to continue to interest themselves in her economic welfare, especially if the dowry was being seriously mismanaged.[87] Moreover, growing emphasis on the clothes and jewels which formed that part of her dowry known in Genoa as the *guarnimenta,* the part which seems to have shown its greatest increase among aristocrats in the later Middle Ages, may reflect, among other things, aristocratic attempts to secure the property and dignity of married daughters within their new homes; for unlike the dowry proper, which was controlled by her husband or his father, the *guarnimenta* was hers to display.[88]

Aristocratic, unlike artisan, wives did not participate actively in the commercial Genoa whose citizens' devotion to profit has been seen as touching both sexes.[89] Their extradotal money was invested in the enterprises of their husbands, fathers, brothers, and other relatives; but the investments were generally small and infrequent. Of the 180 investors in Genoa's overseas trade (an aristocratic monopoly) recorded in the more than thirteen hundred acts of Genoa's first extant notarial register in the decade from 1155 to 1164, only fifteen were women, all occasional investors who usually entrusted their small sums to a relative or his factor; a sign of their commercial incapacity which the thirteenth- and fourteenth-century registers confirm.[90] If some aristocratic wives in

85. *Le carte di Santa Maria delle Vigne di Genova, 1103-1392,* no. 89.
86. See Hughes, "Urban Growth and Family Structure in Medieval Genoa," pp. 13-15.
87. D. Bizzarri, "Il diritto privato nelle fonti senesi del secolo XIII," *Bollettino senese di storia patria* 33-34 (1926-7), p. 248.
88. *Statuto dei padri del comune della repubblica genovese,* pp. 71-75, 151-52, for decrees against rising *guarnimenta.*
89. See, for example, Roberto Lopez, "Aux origines du capitalisme gènois," *Annales d'histoire économique et sociale* 9 (1937): p. 443; William N. Bonds, "Genoese Noblewomen and Gold Thread Manufacturing," *Medievalia et Humanistica* 17 (1966): 79-81.
90. Hilmar C. Krueger, "Genoese Merchants, their Partnerships and Investments, 1155 to 1164," in *Studi in onore di Armando Sapori* (Milan, 1957), 1: 259, n. 6.

the twelfth and early thirteenth centuries acted as their husbands' commercial agents in the city, like the women of the Bulgaro family or or like Alda Nepitella, Sofia Stregghiaporco, and Sibilia Embriaco, all of whom handled extensive economic transactions for their husbands, they were exceptional. Some were from families whose entrance into the aristocracy had been recent, while the active role of others can be explained by particular and unusual domestic circumstances.[91] And by the fourteenth century their participation may have contracted. A register from the mid-fourteenth century of the notary Tommaso Casanova, who had a particularly aristocratic clientele, contains not one aristocratic wife who acted as her husband's business agent.[92]

Only in widowhood did aristocratic wives come of age. The contrast between their widowhoods and those of the city's artisan women shows the extent to which domestic ideals shaped their conception of their new domestic role and status. The conjugal bond broken, a young artisan wife frequently met the economic stringencies and undoubted loneliness of widowhood by early remarriage. The income from her dowry, usufruct rights in her husband's estate, and even her more than occasional position as his chief beneficiary were not enough in many artisan homes, especially where there were no sons to assume his place, to overcome the absence of the household's chief support. Any Genoese widow had the legal right to reclaim her dowry and *antefactum* and return to her own family; but her artisan brothers may have been as reluctant to receive this extra burden in Genoa as they seem to have been in

91. All but Sibilia were from families whose aristocratic status was recent, and she appeared briefly only while her husband and his nephew were both involved in delicate negotiations in Sicily. For the Bulgaro women, see *Giovanni di Guiberto (1200-1211)*, ed. M. W. Hall-Cole, H. C. Krueger, and R. L. Reynolds (Notai liguri del secolo XII, 4, 1940), nos. 636, 1083-85, 1090, 1299, 1606-7, 1942; A. S. G. ms. 102 (Diversorum), ff. 162r-v. For Alda Nepitella and Sofia Stregghiaporco, *Giovanni di Guiberto (1200-1211)*, nos. 1955, 1390, 2010; A. S. G. ms. 102 (diversorum), f. 169v. For Sibilia Embriaco, A. S. G. ms. 102 (Diversorum), f. 206r.

92. Register IX, which contains almost entirely the acts of this notary in the 1340's. Other registers of the same notary contain a few examples of aristocratic wife-agents, but the assignment is usually brief, and the amounts small. Husbands, especially those absent on business, sometimes found wives who were heiresses in their own right difficult to control: Dominguina, the wife of Paolo Usodimare had inherited at least GL 2250 from her Vivaldi relatives when her husband, as he was about to journey to Sicily, forced her to make a will in which she awarded him GL 1050 and made their daughter her heir (with rights of reversion to Paolo). If she changed the will before his return to Genoa, moreover, the legacies were to be distributed immediately as *donationes inter vivos* (A. S. G. Notary Tommaso Casanova, XI, ff. 124r-125v). Although the heiress Dominguina appears as one of the most active aristocratic wives in the acts of Tommaso Casanova in 1343, she dealt almost exclusively in communal stock and almost always acted through her husband: X, ff. 12v, 19r-v, 36r, 43r-v.

fourteenth-century Pisa, where fathers often insisted in their wills on their married daughters' right to return to their natal home.[93] The reluctance of her own kinsmen to receive the artisan widow may have combined to encourage her remarriage by her attractiveness, and that of not only her dowry but an *antefactum* of equal worth, to a bachelor or widower with children who might find in a less experienced woman fewer substantial assets.

Children from a first marriage went with their mothers, who had usually been appointed their legal guardians, into the new household. Sometimes second husbands contracted with their widow-brides to provide for her children from the earlier marriage, as Giovanni di Bargagli did when he agreed, in accepting his wife's GL160 dowry in 1324, to feed and clothe her daughter Benedetta.[94] More often, however, they were absorbed without official notice into the new household, although their mother alone continued legally to act for them.

Lineage considerations within the aristocracy made widowhood for a woman with children a permanent state and a way of life, which set her apart from other women of her social group. Childless widows might, and often did, retrieve their dowries and their GL100 *antefacta* to return to their fathers' homes and the marriage market, where their scarcely improved fortunes (since aristocratic *antefacta* were set so low and since aristocratic husbands rarely awarded their wives additional legacies), their more advanced age, possible suggestions of barrenness, and their sexual experience must have dimmed their prospects. Widows with children were, however, bound by them to their husband's home and to a celibate life; for when they remarried, they gave up their rights of guardianship and usually left their children behind to be cared for by their guardians within the lineage. Lineage identity effectively weakened a mother's position as a full, natural parent; for in Genoa she could increasingly fulfill her parental role, even when her husband was dead, only within his house, surrounded by his kinsmen.

93. Archivio di Stato, Pisa, Archivio degli Ospedali Riuniti di Santa Clara, ms. 2545, ff. 35r, 72r-73r, 106v-107r, 238r-239r.

94. A. S. G. Cart. 12, pt. 2, ff. 220v-221r. New husbands may have been more disposed to receive stepdaughters than stepsons—or their own kin, more willing to give them up: The *catasto* of Pisa in the early fifteenth century lists far more stepdaughters than stepsons, *Il catasto di Pisa del 1428-29*, ed. Bruno Casini (Pubblicazioni della società storica pisana, 2, 1964), nos. 120, 644, 868, 893, 923, 926, 946, 954, 1092, 1232, 1344, only the last of which is a stepson.

Oberto Malocello stands alone in the extant notarial acts from the twelfth century in giving his wife—a young second wife whose difficulties in the already adult family from his first wife he may have anticipated—guardianship of their children whether or not she remarried; just as Lanfranco Lercari stands alone in agreeing to support a stepson.[95] In the following centuries the moral sanctions against the remarriage of aristocratic widows increased until, by the fourteenth century, a son like the sixteen-year-old Cataneo Calvo, whose widowed mother had deserted him to marry Domenico Lercari, would specifically cut her out of his will, leaving her only the GL100 that were probably her *antefactum*.[96] And by the following century, Pero Tafur noticed that as a general, and surprising, rule in Genoa, "Widows do not take a second husband, and if they do they suffer in their reputation."[97]

That great majority who chose to bow to custom and preserve the widowed state enjoyed a freedom which, unlike artisan women, they had never known before. Most received what Giuletta Strallera insisted on in a formal contract: that she be mistress of her home, where she promised to remain unless her sons or their wives mistreated her, a constant possibility in aristocratic households where resentment against a widowed mother who controlled an undivided estate until the sons came of age was undoubtedly strong and where no patriarch stood to protect her.[98] Not only did widows share in the upbringing and training of their children, many became some of the most active "businessmen"

95. *Giovanni Scriba*, no. 761; A. S. G., ms. 102 (Diversorum), f. 181r. In 1222 Ansaldo, count of Lavagna, had a stepdaughter; but in spite of his title and possible authority in Lavagna, he had not entered the ranks of Genoa's merchant aristocracy (*Liber magistri Salmonis*, pp. 189, 230-31).

96. A. S. G. Notary Tommaso Casanova, X, f. 218r. Another aristocratic widow who remarried suspected that the kinsmen of her first husband, Gaspare Grimaldi, would deprive their daughter of the dowry that her father had assigned her in his will: A. S. G. Notary Bartolomeo Bracelli e Francesco de Silva, ff. 140v-141v.

97. *Travels and Adventures, 1435-1439*, p. 29.

98. A. S. G. ms 102 (Diversorum), ff. 129v, 133r. Some aristocrats in the fourteenth century wrote long and specific instructions into their wills: Angello Lomelino, the father of three daughters and eleven sons, threatened to cut out any heir who tried to touch his wife's assigned usufruct in his house in Genoa and at his villa at Carignano (A. S. G. Notary Tommaso Casanova, XI, ff. 62v-64r); Giovanni Pinelli made certain that his wife had the key and control of the garden between his two houses in Genoa, and he admonished his son, who lived in the adjoining house, neither to enclose nor wall it in an attempt to impede her passage and dominion (*ibid.*, ff. 10v-11v); and Nicolà de Viali, in his climb toward an aristocratic life, assured his wife of her choice of a room in his recently acquired villa and the use of its kitchen (*ibid.*, ff. 176r-177r).

in the city. The great women investors in the extant acts of the early
thirteenth century were all widows: Drua Stregghiaporco, who invested
well over GL1000 between 1201 and 1206 in the overseas trade to
Spain, Africa, and the East; Giardinia Boleto, who invested GL615 in
similar ventures; and Mabilia Lecavella, who sold wine from her land
in Quarto to the king of France, disposed of land in the countryside,
leased commercial property in the city, sent over GL325 in four
contracts during 1205-6 to Africa and the East, and trained her children
in their father's business.[99] All have their counterparts in the com-
mercially active widows of the thirteenth and fourteenth centuries. It
was not aristocratic women generally, but only the widows among
them, who shared in the commercial world of medieval Genoa.

Demography, personality, and circumstance shaped these patterns to
individual families and households. A young and timid bride knew a
different husband from a woman whose long and devoted career as a
wife had won her special solicitude from the aristocratic husband whom
she had lived with from childhood; whereas a young second, or even
third, wife often seems to have inspired in aristocrats particular
conjugal affection, sometimes strong enough to destroy the natural lineage considerations that drew no distinction between the sons of different wives. Ansaldo Cigala's long will of 1264, in which he outlined
the delinquent career of his son Lanfranco, seems to have been his way
of justifying his disinheritance of both Lanfranco and his sisters in favor
of the children of his second marriage, who were to share his estate
equally with their mother.[100] And a second wife's widowed mother,
perhaps more the age of her daughter's husband, sometimes won an
unusual place in the affairs of her daughter's household. For example,
when Ansaldo Lomellino made his will in 1345, he appointed (in addition to three nephews) as guardians of his five children by a second
marriage, not only his young wife, but also his widowed mother-in-
law.[101] Likewise, artisan sons trained in their father's craft and drawn
into a family shop probably had, as their wills sometimes indicate, more

99. Drua: *Giovanni di Guiberto (1200-1211)*, nos. 482, 484, 486, 617, 787, 851, 1408,
1852-54; Giardinia: *ibid.*, nos. 608, 803-4, 806, 923, 950-51, 1140-41, 1215, 1266-68,
1342, 1409, 1721, 1941; Mabilia: *O. S., 1190*, no 271; *Guglielmo Cassinese (1190-92)*,
ed. M. W. Hall, H. C. Krueger, and R. K. Reynolds (Notai liguri del secolo XII, 2,
1939), nos. 94-95, 183; *Giovanni di Guiberto (1200-1211)*, nos. 3, 197, 1087, 1610-11.
    100. Face, "Lanfranco of Cigala: the Career of a Delinquent," *passim.*
    101. A. S. G. Notary Tommaso Casanova, IX, ff. 7v-11v.

complex family obligations than those sent out individually to separate trades.[102]

But variety should not obscure the patterned differences in social behavior that awareness of domestic ideals produced in medieval Genoa. A single momentous event in the domestic cycle, such as the death of a father, can serve to illustrate the ways in which domestic ideals can influence social behavior and form human emotions. In artisan households, the loss of a father frequently drove sons into new homes, homes that would be, if they were not already, soon filled with children whose father was not their own. Their mother's remarriage would probably provoke neither social shame in her children nor a substantial change in her own position, as she sought restoration of the conjugal bond. It may indeed have been widowhood itself that could produce the most significant strains in the artisan household.

For aristocrats, however, such a loss in childhood might encourage, especially in households where the dead father had already assumed some authority, the development of their mother's powers both in and outside the home, as it might eventually free them to develop a business style of their own. Secure within their enclave, aristocratic sons seldom knew a stepfather, and no children from outside their lineage would be expected to share their house or their mother's affections. Her remarriage in defiance of custom might shame them, but it would upset neither the direction of their training nor the composition of the kin group that formed their most intimate society.

102. See, for example, the exclusion by a fourteenth-century carpenter of a wife in favor of a brother who shared the same trade: A. S. G., Notary Giovanni Galli, III, f. 37r.

∽ JOAN W. SCOTT and LOUISE A. TILLY

WOMEN'S WORK

AND THE FAMILY IN

NINETEENTH CENTURY EUROPE *

There is a great deal of confusion about the history of women's work outside the home and about the origin and meaning of woman's traditional place within the home. Most interpretations of either question depend on assumptions about the other. Usually, women at home in any time period are assumed to be non-productive, the anti-thesis of women at work. In addition, most general works on women and the family assume that the history of women's employment, like the history of women's legal and political rights, can be understood as a gradual evolution from a traditional place at home to a modern position in the world of work. Some historians cite changes in employment op-portunities created by industrialization as the precursors of legal emancipation. Others stress political rights as the source of improved economic status. In both cases, legal-political and economic "emanci-pation" usually are linked to changes in cultural values. Thus William Goode, whose *World Revolution and Family Patterns* makes temporal and geographic comparisons of family patterns, remarks on what he calls "the statistically unusual status of western women today, that is, their high participation in work outside of the home." He maintains that previous civilizations did not use female labor because of restrictive cultural definitions. "I believe," Goode writes, "that the crucial crystallizing variable—i.e. the necessary but not sufficient cause of the

* A somewhat different version of this paper appreared in *Comparative Studies in So-ciety and History* and is reprinted with permission of the Cambridge University Press.

145

betterment of the western woman's position—was ideological: the gradual logical philosophical extension to women of originally Protestant notions about the rights and responsibilities of the individual undermined the traditional idea of 'woman's proper place'."[1]

Yet Goode makes no systematic effort to validate his statements with historical data. If, however, notions about individual rights did transform cultural values and lead to the extension of rights to women, and if work opportunities for women stemmed from the same source, we should be able to trace an increase in the number of women working as they gained political rights. The only long period for which there are any reliable labor force statistics for any populations (whether of cities or countries) is the nineteenth and twentieth centuries. These should serve our purpose, however, since women gained political rights in most European countries only in the twentieth century. If we examine the figures for three European countries during the nineteenth and twentieth centuries, we find no confirmation of Goode's belief. In Great Britain, a Protestant country, the civil status of women was reformed through the married women's property acts of the late nineteenth century and political emancipation in the form of suffrage came in 1918. In 1851 and 1861, about 25 percent of British women worked; in 1921, the figure was still about 25 percent. In both Catholic France and Italy, women's legal rights within the family were severely limited until after World War II. Immediately after the war, constitutional changes granted women the right to vote. In France, in 1866, 25 percent of women worked; in 1896, 33 percent worked and in 1954, 30 percent worked, down from a high of 42 percent in 1921. In Italy, the highest percentage for women's employment outside the home (before 1964) was in 1901.[2]

There are several conclusions to be drawn from these figures. First, there was little relationship between women's political rights and women's work. The right to vote did not increase the size of the female labor force, neither did the numbers of women in the labor force dra-

1. William Goode, *World Revolution and Family Patterns* (New York, 1963), p. 56. Ivy Pinchbeck makes the opposite point (that occupational changes played a large part in women's emancipation) in the preface to the reprinted edition of her book, *Women Workers and the Industrial Revolution, 1750-1850* (New York, 1969), p. v.

2. T. Deldycke, H. Gelders, J. M. Limbor, *La Population active et sa structure,* under the supervision of P. Bairoch (Brussells, 1969), p. 29-31. The figures given for Italy indicate that 1881 had an even higher proportion of women working. The 1901 census, however, has been shown to be more reliable, especially in designating occupation. In 1881, census categories tended to overestimate the numbers of women working. In 1901, about 32.5 percent of Italian women worked.

matically increase just prior to their gaining the vote. Moreover, great numbers of women worked outside the home during most of the nineteenth century, long before they enjoyed civil and political rights. Finally, rather than a steady increase in the size of the female labor force, the pattern was one of increase followed by decline.

What then is the source of Goode's inaccurate conception? It stems above all from a model that projects middle class experience and middle class values as representative of all experience and all values. It generalizes a particular class experience into one which represents "western civilization." And it projects backward in linear fashion, twentieth century values and experiences. As a result, Goode fails to make important distinctions about women, work and values and he therefore misrepresents their history. Middle class women formed an insignificant part of the female labor force in nineteenth and early twentieth century Europe, although their numbers began to increase in that period.[3] If we ask: 'which women worked?' and 'what kind of work

3. The percentage of women in "middle class" (white collar) occupations—teachers, nurses, shop assistants, secretaries, and civil servants—increased in England between 1881 and 1911, while the percentage of women employed in working class occupations fell.

	1881	1911
Middle Class Occupations (percent)	12.6	23.7
Working Class Occupations (percent)	87.4	76.3

Lee Holcombe, *Victorian Ladies at Work* (Hamden, Conn., 1973), p. 216, shows that although mid-Victorian ideologies about women's place and women's dependent position in the patriarchal family were still being publicized, middle class women were increasingly entering the labor force. The reasons lie in demographic and economic realities, not ideology. The first of these was the surplus of unmarried or "redundant women," in Harriet Martineau's phrase. These women, to whom the sex ratio denied husbands and for whom male mortality denied fathers and brothers, had to work. Furthermore, the expansion of the tertiary sector in England provided jobs for these women, and for working class women who could take advantage of increased educational opportunities. In Holcombe's analysis, the development of feminist ideology about women's work accompanied change and justified it. It did not precede it or cause it in any sense.

In France, there was a similar move into "middle class" occupations in the twentieth century. Francis Clark, *The Position of Women in Contemporary France* (London, 1937), pp. 74-75, gives the following figures for the female percentage in selected occupations:

	1906	1926
Typists, copyists, accountants	22.8	54.8
Workers in hospitals, convalescent homes, etc.	73.2	76.1
Postal service	22.4	30.5
teachers (state)	48.5	59.2
teachers (private)	68.7	71.4

did they do?,' we discover that not only are Goode's facts wrong, but his model of social change is inappropriate as well.

The women who worked in great numbers in the nineteenth century were overwhelmingly members of the working and peasant classes. Most held jobs in domestic service, garmentmaking or the textile industry. In 1841 and still in 1911, most English working women were engaged in domestic or other personal service occupations. In 1911, 35 percent were servants (including laundresses), 19.5 percent were textile workers and 15.6 percent were engaged in the dressmaking trades.[4] In Milan, according to the censuses of 1881, 1901, and 1911, a similar concentration of women in domestic service existed, with garment-making ranking second and textiles much less important than in England.[5] Similarly in France, (excluding agriculture) textiles, garmentmaking, and domestic service were the chief areas of female employment. In France, 69 percent of working women outside agriculture were employed in these three fields in 1866: domestic service, 28 percent; garmentmaking, 21 percent; textiles, 20 percent. In 1896, the proportions were altered, but the total was 59 percent; domestic service, 19 percent; garmentmaking, 26 percent; textiles, 14 percent.[6]

Despite very different rates of industrialization in England, France, and Italy, the evidence strongly suggests that women in all three cases did not participate in factory work (except in textiles) in large numbers. Rather, economic and social changes associated with urban and industrial development seem to have generated employment opportunities in a few traditional sectors in which women worked at jobs similar to household tasks. The economic changes leading to high employment of women included the early industrialization of textiles and the nineteenth century pattern of urbanization, with cities acting as producers of and markets for consumer goods and as places of employment for domestic servants.[7] The expansion of consumer goods

4. Pinchbeck, *Women Workers,* p. 315; E. L. Hutchins, *Women in Modern Industry* (London, 1915), p. 84.

5. Louise A. Tilly, "Women at Work in Milan, Italy—1880-World War I" (Paper presented to the American Historical Association Annual Meeting, New Orleans, December 28, 1972). The national distribution of women workers, in Italy as a whole, showed textiles more important than domestic service as an employer of women. Domestic servants were disproportionately concentrated in cities, textile production outside cities.

6. Calculated from data in Deldycke *et al., La Population active,* p. 174. Agricultural activity was unimportant in England and in the city of Milan, so French figures are made comparable by excluding agriculture.

7. By industrialization we mean the process by which secondary and tertiary economic activity, over time, gain in importance in an economy. This is accompanied by an increased scale of these activities and consequent increasing productivity per capita.

production involved the growth of a large piecework garment industry. Production moved from the workshops of craftsmen to the homes of people who sewed together precut garments. This change in the process of production generated employment opportunities for large numbers of women. The subsequent decline of this method of producing ready-made goods and its replacement by factory production, as well as the decline of textiles and the growth of heavy industry, led to lower female participation in the work forces of all three countries we have examined.

The kinds of jobs available to women were not only limited in number and kind, they also were segregated, that is, they were held almost exclusively by women.[8] The women who held these jobs were usually young and single. In Milan, about 75 percent of women aged fifteen to twenty worked in 1881 and 1901. In female age groups over twenty, employment in textile manufacture and garmentmaking declined sharply, presumably as women stopped work after marriage. The only female occupation with appreciable proportions (50 percent or more) of workers over thirty years of age was domestic service, in which celibacy prevailed.[9] In Great Britain, similar age patterns are evident in the scattered available data. Most women operatives in the Lancashire cotton mills in 1833 were between sixteen and twenty-one years old. Only 25 percent of female cotton workers were married in the Lancashire districts in 1841. Hewitt argues for an increase in proportions, either married or widowed, among cotton operatives peaking sometime in the 1890s and declining thereafter. The highest fraction of married women in this occupation was about one third.[10] The much less specialized labor force of London in the 1880s was aged primarily between fifteen and twenty-five years.[11]

When census figures finally provide marital status, some big national differences can be noted. In 1911, while 69 percent of all single women in Britain worked, only 9.6 percent of married women did.[12] In 1896, 52 percent of all French single women were in the labor force, and 38

8. See Edward Gross, "Plus ca change . . .? The Sexual Structure of Occupations over Time," *Social Problems* 16 (Fall, 1968): 198-206.

9. Census data from 1871 to 1901 analyzed in Louise A. Tilly, "The Working Class of Milan, 1881-1911" (Ph.D. diss., University of Toronto, 1974).

10. Miriam Cohen, "The Liberation of Working Class Women in England?" (Paper, History Department, University of Michigan), p. 15; Hutchins, *Women in Modern Industry,* pp. 81-82; Edward Cadbury, M. Cecile Matheson and George Shann, *Woman's Work and Wages. A Phase of Life in An Industrial City* (Chicago, 1907), p. 219; Margaret Hewitt, *Wives and Mothers in Victorian Industry* (London, 1958), p. 17.

11. Pinchbeck, *Women Workers,* pp. 197-198.

12. Deldycke, *et al., La Population active,* p. 169.

percent of married women.[13] Although our evidence is impressionistic and scattered, it looks as though fewer married women worked as industrialization advanced (at least in the pre-1914 period). Thus Britain, the more advanced industrial country in 1911, had the lower proportion of married women workers; on the other hand, in France, where both agriculture and manufacturing were organized on a smaller scale than in Britain, more married women were in the labor force.

Why did women work in the nineteenth century and why was the female labor force predominantly young and single? To answer these questions we must first examine the relationship of these women to their families of origin (the families into which they were born), not to their families of procreation (the family launched at marriage). We must ask not only how husbands regarded their wives' roles, but what prompted families to send their *daughters* out into the job market as garment workers or domestic servants.

The parents of these young women workers during industrialization were mostly peasants and, to a lesser extent, urban workers. When we examine the geographic and social origins of domestic servants, one of the largest groups of women workers, their rural origins are clear. Two-thirds of all the domestic servants in England in 1851 were daughters of rural laborers. For France, we have no aggregate numbers, but local studies suggest similar patterns. In his study of Melun, for example, Chatelain found that in 1872, 54 percent of female domestic servants were either migrants from rural areas or foreigners.[14] Theresa McBride calculated that in Versailles from 1825 to 1853, 57.7 percent of female domestic servants were daughters of peasants. In Bordeaux, a similar proportion was obtained: 52.8 percent. In Milan, at the end of the nineteenth century, servants were less likely to be city born than any other category of workers.[15]

If cultural values were involved in the decisions of rural and lower class families to send their daughters to work, we must ask what values they were. Goode's loose references to "values" obscure an important

13. Ibid., p. 185

14. Abel Chatelain, "Migrations et domesticité feminine urbaine en France, XVIII siècle-XX siècle," *Revue d'Histoire économique et sociale* 47 (1969): 521; E. Royston Pyke, *Golden Times* (New York, 1970), p. 156.

15. Teresa McBride, "Rural Tradition and the Process of Modernization: Domestic Servants in Nineteenth Century France" (Ph.D. diss., Rutgers University, 1973), p. 85, Tilly, "Working Class of Milan," p. 129-130. McBride found that in Versailles in the same period only 19.5 percent of female domestic servants were from working class families.

distinction between modern middle class values and preindustrial lower class values. Goode assumes that the idea of "woman's proper place," with its connotations of complete economic dependency and idealized femininity is a traditional value. In fact, it is a rather recently accepted middle class value not at all inconsistent with notions of "the rights and responsibilities of the individual." The hierarchical division of labor within the family which assigned the husband the role of breadwinner and the wife the role of domestic manager and moral guardian emerged clearly only in the nineteenth century and was associated with the growth of the middle class and the diffusion of its values.[16] On the other hand, as we will demonstrate at length below, traditional ideas about women, held by peasant and laboring families, did not find feminine and economic functions incompatible. In the preindustrial Europe described by Peter Laslett and in contemporary premodern societies studied by anthropologists, the household or the family is the crucial economic unit.[17] Whether or not all work is done at home, all family members are expected to work. It is simply assumed that women will work, for their contribution is valued as necessary for the survival of the family unit. The poor, the illiterate, the economically and politically powerless of the past operated according to values which fully justified the employment of women outside the home.

We are arguing then, contrary to Goode, that preindustrial values, rather than a new individualistic ideology, justified the work of working class women in the nineteenth century. In so doing, we are not merely

16. Philippe Ariès, *Centuries of Childhood: A Social History of Family Life,* trans. Robert Baldick (London, 1962); J. A. Banks, *Prosperity and Parenthood. A Study of Family Planning Among the Victorian Middle Classes* (London, 1954); J. A. and Olive Banks, *Feminism and Family Planning in Victorian England* (New York, 1964), all associate the idea of these separate feminine characteristics with the middle class. John Stuart Mill made a compelling argument for granting political equality to women while recognizing feminine preferences and qualities which distinguish women from men. See J. S. and H. T. Mill, *Essays on Sex Equality,* ed. Alice Rossi (Chicago, 1971). For analysis of hierarchical patterns, see Susan Rogers, "Woman's Place: Sexual Differentiation as Related to the Distribution of Power," (Paper, Anthopology Dept. Northwestern University, April, 1974).

17. Peter Laslett, *The World We Have Lost* (New York, 1965). Among the many anthropological and historical studies of pre-industrial societies are George Foster, "Peasant Society and the Image of the Limited Good," *American Anthropologist* 67 (April, 1965): 293-315; Conrad Arensberg and Solon Kimball, *Family and Community in Ireland* (Cambridge, Mass., 1968); Ronald Blythe, *Akenfield, Portrait of an English Village* (New York, 1968); Edgar Morin, *The Red and the White: Report from a French Village* (New York, 1970); Mack Walker, *German Home Towns: Community, State and General Estates, 1648-1871* (Ithaca, New York, 1971).

disputing his analysis, we are rejecting the model of social change on which he bases that analysis. Goode's model (a standard one for theorists of development) assumes a one-to-one connection between cultural values and social change. He argues, in effect, that ideological changes led directly and immediately to structural and behavioral changes. We also reject the antithesis of Goode's argument which says that material changes in economic, political or social structures led directly and immediately to changes in values and behavior. It, too, is based on a model which assumes that change in one realm necessarily and directly leads to change in another. Thus Engels tells us that the coming of capitalism excluded women from "participation in social production" and reduced their role and status to that of servants in the home. Proletarian women are exceptions to this description because in industrial society they are engaged in social production. Nonetheless, in both instances Engels makes a direct connection between economic change and changes in values and status.[18]

Our examination of the evidence on women's work in the nineteenth century has led us to a different understanding of the process which led to the relatively high employment of women outside the home in nineteenth century Europe. The model we use posits a continuity of traditional values and behavior in changing circumstances. Old values coexist with and are used by people to adapt to extensive structural changes. This assumes that people perceive and act on the changes they experience in terms of ideas and attitudes they already hold. These ideas eventually change, but not as directly or immediately as Goode and Engels would have us believe. Behavior is less the product of new ideas than of the effects of old ideas operating in new or changing contexts.[19]

Traditional families then, operating on long-held values, sent their daughters to take advantage of increased opportunities generated by industrialization and urbanization. Industrial development did not affect all areas of a given country at the same time. Rather, the process can best be illustrated by an image of "islands of development" within an underdeveloped sea, islands which drew population to them from the

18. Frederick Engels, *The Origins of the Family, Private Property and the State,* ed. Eleanor B. Leacock (New York, 1971), p. 81.

19. Our notion is a variation of the one presented by Bert Hoselitz: "On the whole, the persistance of traditions in social behavior . . . may be an important factor mitigating the many dislocations and disorganizations which tend to accompany rapid industrialization and technical change." Bert Hoselitz and Wilbert Moore, *Industrialization and Society* (Paris, 1966), p. 15.

less developed areas.[20] The values of the less developed sector were imported into the developing sector and there were extended, adapted, and only gradually transformed.

As peasant values were imported, so was the behavior they directed. And work for the wives and daughters of the poor was a familiar experience in preindustrial societies. No change in values, then, was necessary to permit lower class women to work outside the home during the nineteenth century. Neither did industrialization "emancipate" these women by permitting more of them to work outside the home. And, given the fluctuations in the size of the female labor force especially, it is difficult to see any direct connection between the work of peasant and working class women and the political enfranchisement of all women.

Since most women workers were of rural origin, an attempt at reconstructing the historical experience of women workers during the early stages of industrialization should begin by examining the peasant or family economy whose values and economic needs sent them into the job market.

Commentators on many different areas of Europe offer strikingly similar descriptions of peasant social organization. Anthropologist and social historians seem to agree that regardless of country, "the peasantry is a preindustrial social entity which carries over into contemporary society specific elements of a different, older, social structure, economy and culture." The crucial unit of organization is the family, whose "solidarity provides the basic framework for mutual aid, control and socialization." The family's work is usually directed to the family farm, property considered to belong to the group rather than to a single individual. "The individual, the family and the farm appear as an indivisible whole . . . . Peasant property is, at least *de facto,* family property. The head of the family appears as the manager rather than the proprietor of family land."[21]

20. W. Arthur Lewis, "Economic Development with Unlimited Supplies of Labour," in *The Economics of Underdevelopment,* eds. A. N. Agarwala and S. P. Singh (New York, 1963), p. 408.

21. Teodor Shanin, "The Peasantry as a Political Factor," in *Peasants and Peasant Societies; Selected Readings,* ed. T. Shanin (Penguin Books, 1971), pp. 241-44. A similar analysis of the peasant family in mid-twentieth century can be found in Henri Mendras, *The Vanishing Peasant. Innovation and Change in French Agriculture,* trans. Jean Lerner (Cambridge, Mass., 1970), p. 76: "The family and the enterprise coincide: the head of the family is at the same time the head of the enterprise. Indeed, he is the one because he is the other . . . he lives his professional and his family life as an indivisible entity. The members of his family are also his fellow workers."

These descriptions of Eastern European peasants are echoed by Michael Anderson in his comparison of rural Lancashire and rural Ireland early in the nineteenth century. He suggests that in both cases the basis of "functional family solidarity . . . was the absolute *interdependence* of family members such that neither fathers nor sons had any scope for alternatives to the family as a source of provision for a number of crucially important needs."[22] Italian evidence confirms the pattern. Although in late nineteenth century Lombardy a kind of *frereche* (brothers and their families living together and working the land together) was a frequent alternative to the nuclear family, the household was the basic unit of production. All members of the family contributed what they could either by work on the farm, or, in the case of women and the young, by work in nearby urban areas or in rural textile mills. Their earnings were turned over to the head of the household; in the case of brothers joined in one household, the elder usually acted as head. He took care of financial matters and contractual relationships in the interests of all.[23] For Normandy in the eighteenth century, Gouesse's recent study has described the gradual evolution of reasons given for marriage when an ecclesiastical dispensation had to be applied for. At the end of that century, grounds such as "seeking well-being," or "desire to live happily" became more common. Goesse considers these differences of expression rather superficial; what all these declarations meant, although few stated this explicitly, was that one had to be married in order to live. "The married couple was the simple community of work, the elementary unit." In nineteenth century Brittany, "all the inhabitants of the farm formed a working community . . . linked one to the other like the crew of a ship."[24]

Despite differences in systems of inheritance and differences in the amount of land available, the theory of the peasant economy developed by Chayanov for nineteenth century Russia applies elsewhere. The basis of this system is the family, or more precisely the household—in Russia, all those "having eaten from one pot." It has a dual role as a unit of production and consumption. The motivations of its members,

22. Michael Anderson, *Family Structure in Nineteenth Century Lancashire* (Cambridge, 1971), p. 96.
23. Giunta per la Inchiesta Agraria e sulle condizioni della Classe agricola, *Atti* (Rome, 1882), vol. vi, fasc. ii: 552, 559; fasc. iii: 87, 175-76, 373, 504, 575.
24. Y. Brekilien, *La vie quotidienne des paysans en Bretagne au XIXe siècle* (Paris, 1966), p. 37. Jean-Marie Gouesse, "Parenté, famille et marriage en Normandie aux XVIIe et XVIIIe siècles," *Annales. Economies, Sociétiés, Civilisations* 27e Année (July-October, 1972): 1146-74;)

unlike capitalist aims, involve "securing the needs of the family rather than . . . making a profit." The family's basic problem is organizing the work of its members to meet its annual budget and "a single wish to save or invest capital if economic conditions allow."[25]

Members of the family or household have clearly defined duties, based in part on their age and position in the family and in part on their sex. Sex role differentiation clearly existed in such peasant societies. Men and women not only performed different tasks, but they occupied different space.[26] Most often, although by no means always, men worked the fields while women managed the house, raised and cared for animals, tended a garden, and marketed surplus dairy products, poultry, and vegetables. There was also seasonal work in the fields at planting and harvest times.[27] Martin Nadaud, a mason from the Creuse, expressed a husband's expectation for his wife this way:

We know there are countries where women marry with the oft-realized hope of having to work only in the house; in France, there is nothing of the sort, precisely the contrary happens; my wife, like all other women of the country was raised to work in the fields from morning until night and she worked no less . . . after our marriage . . .[28]

Of course the wives of masons from the Creuse were in a peculiar position. Their husbands were gone for long periods of time building houses in Lyons or Paris. They had to do all agricultural chores since the division of labor in the Creuse was between women who handled

25. Basile Kerblay, "Chayanov and the Theory of Peasantry as a Specific Type of Economy," Shanin *Peasants and Peasant Societies,* p. 151, and *A. V. Chayanov on the Theory of Peasant Economy,* eds. Daniel Thorner, Basile Kerblay and R. E. F. Smith (Homewood, Ill., 1966), pp. 21, 60. See also Henriette Dussourd, *Au même pot et Au même feu: etude sur les communautés familiales agricoles du centre de la France* (Moulins, 1962).

26. For the most part, men worked outside the home. They performed public functions for the family and the farm. Women, on the other hand, presided over the interior of the household and over the private affairs of family life. Separate spheres and separate roles did not, however, imply discrimination or hierarchy. It appears, on the contrary, that neither sphere was subordinated to the other. This interpretation is, however, still a matter of dispute among anthropologists. See Lucienne A. Roubin, "Espace masculin, espace feminin en communauté provencale," *Annales, E. S. C.* 26 (March-April, 1970): 540; Rogers, "Woman's Place", and Rayna Reiter, "Men and Women in the South of France: Public and Private Domains" (Paper, New School for Social Research, 1973).

27. Pinchbeck, *Women Workers,* part 1 *passim.;* Alain Girard and Henri Bastide, "Le budget-temps de la femme mariée à la campagne," *Population* 14 (1959): 253-84.

28. Martin Nadaud, *Mémoires de Leonard, ancien garcon macon* (Paris, 1895, reissued 1948), p. 130. Agricole Perdiguier recalled that his father made his daughters work in the fields: "Madeleine and Babet worked with us, like men." *Mémoires d'un compagnon* (Paris, 1964), p. 33.

most of the agricultural tasks and men whose primary work was as artisans in the cities. Women's work on the farm was so important there that at one point Nadaud's family tried to arrange a marriage for him with a girl whose mother was widowed. That way, the Nadaud family farm would acquire two female hands instead of one.

Despite the peculiarity of the Creuse, however, Nadaud's expectation that women would work seems typical of peasant economies. Eilert Sundt's reports on the Norwegian peasantry in the mid-nineteenth century show that women were needed as workers, so experienced and often older women were the choice of young men as wives. Sundt wrote, "the material progress of a family depended as much upon the wife as upon the husband."[29] And Frederic Le Play, describing marriage customs of Slavic peasants noted that "the peasant takes a wife to augment the number of hands in his family."[30]

Women labored not only on the farm, but at all sorts of other work, depending in part on what was available to them. In most areas their activity was an extension of their household functions of food provision, animal husbandry, and clothesmaking. Documentation of this can be found in almost every family monograph in the six volumes of Le Play's *Les Ouvriers Europeens.* There was the wife of a French vineyard worker, for example, whose principal activity involved the care of a cow. "She gathers hay for it, cares for it and carries its milk to town to sell." Another wife worked with her husband during harvest seasons and "washed laundry and did other work . . . for farmers and landowners in the neighborhood." She also wove linen "for her family and for sale." Other women sewed gloves or clothing; some took in infants to nurse as well.[31] In the regions surrounding the silk-weaving city of Lyon, the wives and daughters of farmers tended worms and reeled silk.[32] Similarly, in Lombardy, seasonal preoccupation with the care of the hungry worms filled the time of women and children in the household.[33]

Work of this type was a traditional way of supplementing the family income. Indeed, Le Play insisted on including all activities of family members in his budgets because, he argued, "the small activities un-

---

29. Quoted in Michael Drake, *Population and Society in Norway, 1735-1865* (Cambridge, 1969), pp. 145, 139-40.
30. Frederic Le Play, *Les ouvriers européens,* 6 vols. (Paris, 1855-1878), 5: 45.
31. Ibid., 6: 145, 127, and 5: 261, respectively.
32. Arthur Dunham, *The Industrial Revolution in France* (New York, 1935), p. 170.
33. Marie Hall Ets, *Rosa, The Life of an Italian Immigrant* (Minneapolis, 1970).

dertaken by the family are a significant supplement to the earning of the principal worker." In fact, he often noted that not only did women work harder than men, but they contributed more to "the well-being of the family."[34] Often women's work meant the difference between subsistence and near starvation. Pinchbeck cites a parish report on rural women who, in a time of economic crisis, could find no work: "In a kind of general despondency she sits down, unable to contribute anything to the general fund of the family and conscious of rendering no other service to her husband except that of the mere care of his family."[35]

In non-farming and some urban families a similar situation seems to have prevailed. In fact, Chayanov's description of the peasant economy seems a fitting characterization of pre-industrial working class social arrangements. In *The World We Have Lost,* Peter Laslett describes the household as the center of production. The workshop was not separated from the home and everyone's place was at home. In the weaver's household, for example, children did carding and combing, older daughters and wives spun, while the father wove. In the urban worker's home, a similar division of labor often existed. Among Parisian laundry workers, for example, the entire family was expected to work, although women were uniquely responsible for soaping and ironing. This kind of business, in fact, was as well run by women as by men. And parents willed their shops and their clientele to their daughters as frequently as to their sons.[36] Wives of craftsmen sometimes assisted their husbands at their work of tailoring, shoemaking, and baking. Sometimes they kept shop selling the goods and keeping accounts. The wives of skilled cutlery workers served as intermediaries between their husbands and their masters. They not only picked up materials for their husbands to work on at home and transported finished products back to the employer, but they also negotiated work loads and wages.[37]

When the husband worked away from home, women engaged in enterprises of their own. Like their rural counterparts, urban working class women contributed to the family economy by tending vegetable

34. Le Play, *Les ouvriers européens,* 3: 8 and 6: 109, respectively.
35. Pinchbeck, *Women Workers,* p. 59. See also R. H. Hubscher, "Une contribution a la connaissance des milieux populaire ruraux au XIXe siècle: Le livre de compte de la famille Flahaut, 1811-1877," *Revue d'histoire économique et sociale* 47 (1969): 361-403.
36. Le Play, *Les ouvriers européens,* 5: 386.
37. Ibid., 3: 281. Le Play adds that "For each day of work . . . the women transport twice, a weight of about 210 kilograms a distance of one kilometer" (3: 161).

gardens, raising animals (usually some pigs and hens), and marketing the surplus. Some women set up cafés in their homes, others sold the food and beverages they had prepared outside. A Sheffield knife maker's wife prepared a "fermented drink called 'pop', which she bottled and sold in summer to the inhabitants of the city."[38] These are early nineteenth century examples, but Alice Clark refers to gardening and the garment trades in seventeenth century England; she cites another expedient of poor women, "selling perishable articles of food from door to door."[39] This practice continued in the nineteenth century. Le Play details the work of a German miner's wife who "transported foodstuffs on her back. Two times a week she goes to [the city] where she buys wheat, potatoes, etc. which she carries (10 kilometers) . . . Some of this food is for her household, some is delivered to wealthy persons in town, the rest is sold [for a small profit] at the market."[40] Among the popular classes in eighteenth century Paris and Bordeaux, "it was generally accepted that womenfolk had an important part to play in the domestic economy. Most took a job to bring in an additional income."[41] They worked as domestics, laundresses, seamstresses, innkeepers, and beasts of burden, hauling heavy loads many times a day. They also begged and smuggled if they had to. "The importance of the mother within the family economy was immense; her death or incapacity could cause a family to cross the narrow but extremely meaningful barrier between poverty and destitution."[42] The popular culture which valued the work of women existed in France during much of the nineteenth century.[43]

The indispensable role of women was demonstrated, too, by the fact that in many communities, widows could manage a farm alone (with the assistance of a few hired hands) whereas widowers found the task al-

38. Ibid., 3: 325.

39. Alice Clark, *The Working Life of Women in the Seventeenth Century* (London, 1919), pp. 150, 209.

40. Le Play, *Les ouvriers européens*, 3: 106-7.

41. Alan Forrest, "The Condition of the Poor in Revolutionary Bordeaux," *Past and Present* 59 (1973): 151-52.

42. Olwen Hufton, "Women in Revolution, 1789-1796," *Past and Present* 53 (1971): 92.

43. Edith Thomas, *Les Petroleuses* (Paris, 1963), pp. 73-79. The fleeting history of social concern and legislation during the Paris Commune of 1871 shows these values reflected in popular radicalism. Although women were not granted political equality by the Communards, illegitimate children were granted legal claims parallel to those of legitimate children. Among the institutions set up by the women of the Commune themselves were day nurseries for working mothers.

most impossible.[44] It is also demonstrated vividly in times of financial hardship. Hufton insists that women were the first to feel the physical effects of deprivation, in part, because they denied themselves food in order to feed the rest of the family. Other observers describe a similar situation. The report Anderson cites from Lancashire is representative of conditions in Italy, England, and France: "an observation made by medical men, that the parents have lost their health much more generally than the children and particularly, that the mothers who most of all starve themselves, have got pale and emaciated."[45]

The role women played in the family economy usually gave them a great deal of power within the family. Scattered historical sources complement the more systematic work of contemporary anthropologists on this point. All indicate that while men assume primacy in public roles, it is women who prevail in the domestic sphere. Hufton even suggests they enjoyed "social supremacy" within the family.[46] Her suggestion echoes Le Play's first-hand observation. In the course of his extensive study of European working-class urban and rural families (carried out from the 1840s-70s), he was struck by the woman's role. "Women are treated with deference, they often . . . exercise a preponderant influence on the affairs of the family. (La communauté)" He found that

44. Susan Rogers, "The Acceptance of Female Roles in Rural France" (Paper, Anthropology Dept., Northwestern University, 1972), pp. 95-96; Anderson, *Family Structure,* p. 95; Leonard Covello, *The Social Background of the Italo-American School Child* (Leiden, 1967), quotes a Sicilian proverb: "If the father is dead, the family suffers; if the mother dies, the family cannot exist," (pp. 208-9). A French version of this is, "Tant vaut la femme, tant vaut la ferme," quoted in Plan de Travail, 1946-7, *La Role de la femme dans la vie rurale* (Paris, 1946).

45. Hufton, "Women in Revoltion," p. 91-93, Tilly, "Working Class of Milan," p. 259, Anderson, *Family Structure,* p. 77, Laura Ohren, "The Welfare of Women in Laboring Families: England, 1860-1950," *Feminist Studies* 1 (Winter-Spring, 1973): 107-25.

46. Hufton, "Women in Revolution," p. 93, Susan Rogers, "Female Forms of Power and the Myth of Male Dominance: A Model of Female/Male Interaction" (Paper, Anthropology Dept., Northwestern University, 1973); Rémi Clignet, *Many Wives, Many Powers; Authority and Power in Polygynous Families* (Evanston, 1970); Ernestine Friedl, "The Position of Women: Appearance and Reality," *Anthropological Quarterly* 40 (1967): 97-108; Evelyn Michaelson and Walter Goldschmidt, "Female Roles and Male Dominance Among Peasants," *Southwestern Journal of Anthropology* 27 (1971): 330-52; Rayna Reiter, "Modernization in the South of France: The Village and Beyond," *Anthropological Quarterly* 45 (1972): 35-53, Joyce Riegelhaupt, "Salaoio Women: An Analysis of Informal and Formal Political and Economic Roles of Portuguese Peasant Women," *Anthropological Quarterly* 40 (1967): 127-38. See also Olwen Hufton, "Women and the Family Economy in Nineteenth Century France" (Paper, University of Reading, 1973).

they worked harder and in a more sustained fashion than their husbands and concluded that their work, their energy, and their intelligence "makes them more fit . . . to direct the family."[47]

The key to the woman's power, limited almost exclusively, of course, to the family arena, lay in her management of the household. In some areas, wives of craftsmen kept business accounts, as did the wives or daughters of farmers.[48] Their familiarity with figures was a function of their role as keeper of the household's accounts, for the woman was usually the chief buyer for the household in the market place, and often the chief trader as well. Primitive as this accounting was, it was a tool for dealing with the outside world. Working class women also often held the purse strings, making financial decisions, and even determining the weekly allowance their husbands received for wine and tobacco. Le Play's description of the Parisian carpenter's wife was typical not only of France:

She immediately receives his monthly wage; it is she who each morning gives her husband the money necessary to buy the meals he takes outside the house. To her alone . . . in conformity with the custom which prevails among French workers, are confined the administration of the interior of the home and the entire disposition of the family resources.[49]

Indeed, this practice was so linked to the wife's role that when factories replaced the home as the location of work for craftsmen, factory owners sometimes paid directly "to the wives the wages earned by their husbands."[50] Whether in Lorraine, Brittany, or Lancashire, among Northern English miners, peasants, or London workers, women seem to have dominated family finances and some areas of family decision making. "The man struts, presides at the table, gives orders, but important decisions—buying a field, selling a cow, a lawsuit against a

47. Le Play, *Les ouvriers européens*, 5: 404 and 6: 110, respectively.

48. That sometimes management roles implied literacy as well is indicated in a manuscript communicated to us by Judith Silver Frandzel, University of New Hampshire. It is the account book of a farm in Besse-sur-Barge, Sarthe, undated but from the 1840s, kept exclusively by the daughter of the family. She lists everything, from sale of animals and land to purchase of handkerchiefs, kitchen utensils or jewelry, for which money was spent or received.

49. Le Play, *Les ouviers européens*, 5: 427; see also, 4: 198 for the life history of the tinsmith of Savoy and his wife.

50. Ibid., 6: 110-11. See also Marie José Chombart de Lauwe and Paul-Henry Chombart de Lauwe, *La Femme dans la societe* (Paris, 1963), p. 158.

neighbor, choice of a future son-in-law—are made by *la patronne*."[51] Or, as a retired farmer from a French village remarked to a visiting anthropologist: "The husband is always the *chef d'exploitation* . . . Well, that's what the law says. What really happens is another matter, but you won't find that registered in the *Code Civil*."[52]

It is important here to stress that we speak here of married women. Whatever power these women enjoyed was a function of their participation in a mutual endeavor, and of the particular role they played as a function of their sex and marital status. Their influence was confined to the domestic sphere, but that sphere bulked large in the economic and social life of the family. In this situation, women were working partners in the family enterprise.

Daughters in lower class families were early socialized to assume family and work responsibilities. "Daughters . . . begin as soon as their strength permits to help their mother in all her work."[53] Frequently they were sent out of the household to work as agricultural laborers or domestic servants. Others were apprenticed to women who taught them to weave or sew. In areas of rural Switzerland where cottage industry was also practiced, daughters were a most desirable asset. It was they who could be spared to spin and weave while their mothers worked at home; and they gave their earnings, "as a matter of course to the economic unit, the maintenance of whose property had priority over individual happiness."[54] Whatever her specific job, a young girl early learned the meaning of the saying, "woman's work is never done." And she was prepared to work hard for most of her life. Many a parent's advice must have echoed these words to a young girl, written in 1743:

You cannot expect to marry in such a manner as neither of you shall have occasion to work, and only a fool would take a wife whose bread must be earned solely by his own labor, and who will contribute nothing towards it herself.[55]

Women were expected to work, and the family was the unit of social as

51. Brekelien, *La vie quotidienne*, p. 69. See also Anderson, *Family Structure*, p. 77; Peter Stearns, "Working Class Women in Britain, 1890-1914," in *Suffer and Be Still*, ed. Martha Vicinus (Bloomington, Indiana, 1972), pp. 104, 108; Rogers, "Female Forms of Power", p. 28.

52. Rogers, "Female Forms of Power", p. 21.

53. Le Play, *Les ouviers européen*, 3: 111.

54. Rudolf Braun, "The Impact of Cottage Industry on an Agricultural Population," in *The Rise of Capitalism*, ed. David Landes (New York, 1966), p. 63.

55. Pinchbeck, *Women Workers*, pp. 1-2.

well as economic relationships. These were the cultural values held by families who sent their daughters out to work in the early stages of industrialization.

Women's work was in the interest of the family economy. Their roles, like those of their husbands, brothers and fathers, could be modified and adjusted to meet difficult times or changing circumstances. Here Chayanov's discussion of the limits of self-exploitation is instructive:

> *When our peasant as worker entrepreneur is not in a position to develop an adequate sale of his labor on his own farm and to get for himself what he considers sufficient earnings, he temporarily abandons his undertaking and simply converts himself into a worker who resorts to someone else's undertaking, thus saving himself from unemployment on his own.*[56]

This means that traditional families employed a variety of strategies to promote the well-being of the family unit. Sometimes the whole family hired itself out as farm hands, sometimes this was done only by men, at other times by one or more children. Supplemental work in domestic industry was frequently resorted to by mothers of families in time of greater need or economic crises. That is why such work was so often seasonal or undertaken sporadically. The custom of sending children of both sexes out to serve on other farms, or to work in nearby cities, was yet another expedient—a way of temporarily extending the family beyond its own limited resources in order to increase those resources and thereby guarantee economic survival.

As major structural changes affected the countries of Europe (in the late eighteenth century in England, much later in France and Italy) these strategies were adapted and new ones were developed, in the face of new pressures and opportunities, to attain the traditional goals of the family economy. In the nineteenth century, Western European population growth was causing land shortages in some areas. In addition, rationalized large-scale agriculture was putting marginally productive lands under great competitive pressure. New forms and methods of industrial production also transformed the location and nature of the work done by rural and urban craftsmen. In this situation, it became increasingly necessary for family members, but particularly for children, to work away from home. The development of domestic industry and rurally-located textile mills, and the expansion of urban

56. Thorner, *et al.*, *A. V. Chayanov*, p. 40.

populations (with their increased demand for consumer goods and domestic services), provided opportunities for these people to work.

In Lombardy, for example, peasants had long practiced labor intensive farming on small holdings. During the nineteenth century, peasants were increasingly unable to support their growing families on these holdings. They seized options similar to the temporary expedients they had customarily employed. Women and girls, whose work on the farm was less productive than that of men, went to work in nearby rural silk mills. Others went to Milan as domestic servants or garment workers, into what were essentially self-exploitative, low-paying, marginally-productive jobs. The point was to make enough money to send home.[57]

In the hinterland of Zurich, described by Rudolf Braun, another sort of strategy developed. Originally among landed peasants all family members worked to make ends meet—as domestics, as soldiers, or as quasi-servants in the households of their siblings who had inherited land. Everyone turned their money over to the family. "The maintenance of the property had priority over individual happiness . . the question of who got married and at what age, was less an individualistic decision than a family agreement." Demographic and economic pressures made some families landless, others had to supplement their farming with work in rural industry, particularly textiles. In these areas the system of *Rastgeben* arose. It designated the practice of children paying their parents a set amount for room and board. If they did not work at home, but at another house, the children paid the landlady the *rast*. In earlier times such money or work had been given as a matter of course. The practice became formalized, however, and the size of the contribution specified as work relations among family members changed. Braun tells us that modifications of this sort eventually broke down family solidarity.[58] He is undoubtedly right. The important point of the Zurich example for our argument, however, is that in the process of transformation, old values and practices shaped strategic adaptations to new conditions.

Similar examples can be drawn from non-farming families as well. The first industrial revolution in England broke the locational unity of home and workshop by transferring first spinning and then weaving

57. Tilly, "Women at Work"; this pattern of behavior also confirmed for pre-World War I Piedmont, another province of northern Italy, by interviews with several women who went, as young as age ten, to the city of Turin as domestic servants.

58. Braun, "The Impact of Cottage Industry," pp. 61-63.

into factories. Neil Smelser's study of *Social Change in the Industrial Revolution* shows, however, that in the first British textile factories the family as a work unit was imported into the mills. "Masters allowed the operative spinners to hire their own assistants . . . the spinners chose their wives, children, near relatives or relatives of the proprietors. Many children, especially the youngest, entered the mill at the express request of their parents."[59] Of course, this extension of the family economy into factories in early industrialization declined after the 1820s, with increased differentiation and specialization of work. But the initial adjustment to a changed economic structure involved old values operating in new settings.

This is eminently demonstrable in the case of women workers, the single ones who constituted the bulk of the female labor force and the less numerous married women as well. Long before the nineteenth century, lower class families had sent their daughters out to work. The continuation of this practice and of the values and assumptions underlying it is evident not only in the fact of large numbers of single women working but also in the age structure of the female labor force, in the kinds of work these women did, and in their personal behavior.

The fact that European female labor forces consisted primarily of young, single women—girls, in the language of their contemporaries— is itself an indication of the persistence of familial values. Daughters were expendable in rural and urban households, certainly more expendable than their mothers and, depending on the work of the family, their brothers. When work had to be done away from home and when its duration was uncertain, the family interest was best served by sending forth its daughters. Domestic service, the chief resort of most rural girls, was a traditional area of employment. It was often a secure form of migration since a young girl was assured a place to live, food, and a family. There were risks involved also; servant unemployment and servant exploitation were real. Nevertheless, during the nineteenth century, though many more girls were sent into service and moved farther from home than had traditionally been the case, the move itself was not unprecedented. Domestic service was an acceptable employment partly because it afforded the protection of a family and membership in a household.[60]

This was true not only of domestic service, but of other forms of fe-

---

59. Neil Smelser, *Social Change in the Industrial Revolution: An application of Theory to the British Cotton Industry* (Chicago, 1959), pp. 188-89.

60. Chatelain, "Migrations," p. 508.

male employment. In Italy and France, textile factory owners attempted to provide "family" conditions for their girls. Rules of conduct limited their activity and nuns supervised the establishments, acting as substitute parents. *In loco parentis* for some factory owners sometimes even meant arranging suitable marriages for their female operatives.[61] These factory practices served the owner's interests too, by keeping his work force under control and limiting its mobility. At times they also served the interests of the girls' families more than those of the girls themselves, for the girls' wages sometimes went directly to their parents. We do not wish to argue that the factory dormitory was a beneficient institution. The fact that it used the family as model for work and social relationships, and the fact that the practice did serve the *family* interest to some degree, is, however, important.

In the needle trades, which flourished in urban centers, similar practices developed. The rise of ready-made clothing production involved a two-fold transformation of garmentmaking. First, piecework at home replaced workshop organization. Only later (in England by 1850, in France by the 1870s depending on the city and the industry, and in Italy, still later) did new machinery permit the reorganization of the garment industry in factories. In the period when piecework expanded, women found ample opportunity for work. Those who already lived in cities customarily took their work home. Migrants, however, needed homes. So, enterprising women with a little capital turned their homes into lodging houses for pieceworkers in their employ. While these often provided exploitative and miserable living conditions, they nonetheless offered a household for a young girl, a household in which she could do work similar to what she or her mother had done at home.[62]

---

61. Ets, *Rosa*, pp. 87-115; Italy, Ufficio del Lavoro, *Rapporti sulla ispezione del lavoro, l dicembre 1906-30 giugno (1908)* (pubblicazione del Ufficio del Lavoro, Serie C, 1909), pp. 64, 93-94, describes the dormitories and work arrangements in north Italian textile mills; Evelyne Sullerot, *Histoire et sociologie du travail féminin* (Paris, 1968), pp. 91-94; Michelle Perrot, *Les Ouvriers en Grève, France 1871-1890* (Paris, 1974), pp. 213, 328. Recent interpretations of similar American cases are to be found in John Kasson, "The Factory as Republican Community: The Early History of Lowell, Mass." (Paper read at American Studies Convention, October, 1973), and Alice Kessler Harris, "Stratifying by Sex: Notes on the History of Working Women," (Working Paper, Hofstra University, 1974).

62. Eileen Yeo and E. P. Thompson, *The Unknown Mayhew* (New York, 1972), pp. 116-80. See also, Henry Mayhew, *London Labour and the London Poor,* 4 vols. (London, 1861; reprinted London, 1967). Sullerot, *travail féminin,* p. 100, describes the household-like organization of seamstresses in small shops, in which the *patronne* and workers ate *en famille,* with the less skilled workers dismissed, like children, before dessert.

Domestic service, garmentmaking, and even textile manufacturing, the three areas in which female labor was overwhelmingly concentrated, were all traditional areas of women's work. The kind of work parents sent their daughters to do, in other words, did not involve a radical departure from the past. Many a wife had spent her girlhood in service at someone else's house. Piecework and spinning and weaving were also common in traditional households. The *location* of work did change and that change eventually led to a whole series of other differences; but, initially, there must have been some comfort for a family sending a daughter to a far-off city in the fact that they were sending her to do familiar, woman's work.

As parents sent daughters off with traditional expectations, so the daughters attempted to fulfill them. Evidence for the persistence of familial values is found in the continuing contributions made by working daughters to their families. In some cases, as we have seen, factories sent the girls' wages directly home to their parents. In others, girls simply sent most of their money home themselves. In England, it was not until the 1890s that single working girls living at home kept some of their own money.[63] Earlier, on the continent, their counterparts "normally turned over all their pay to the family fund." The daughter of a Belgian locksmith first served her family by tailoring. She habitually gave her family all her earnings "and thus had no savings at the time of her marriage."[64] Irish migrants sent money back from as far away as London and Boston.[65] And, even when they no longer expected to return home to marry and live in their natal villages, French and Italian servant girls continued to send money back home. The servant girls working for the Flahaut family during the period 1811 to 1877 in rural France sent money home to their parents. There were regular arrangements by which Monsieur Flahaut sent foodstuffs instead of money, or paid the rent on the father's farm, or sent clothing and coal directly to the parents of his servant girls. Sometimes, too, younger or unemployed brothers and sisters received these payments which were deducted from the domestic's wages. Hubscher tells us that for certain farmers who rented their lands, their daughters' contributions were "indispensable,

63. Stearns, "Women in Britain," p. 110.
64. Le Play, *Les ouviers européens*, 5: 122.
65. Anderson, *Family Structure*, p. 22; Lynn Lees, personal communication: "The sending back of money seems to have been a standard practice for Irish migrants everywhere. Rural Ireland has been living on the proceeds for several generations."

without them it would have been impossible to cultivate the fields they rented." He adds that the "financial support" of the daughters for their parents "seemed absolutely normal to both" parties. It represented a "strong family solidarity which required a mature and economically independent child to contribute to the support of its relatives."[66] Mill girls in Lombardy also made contributions to their families and, if they lived close enough, the families sent regular baskets of food. According to one autobiographical report, the employer actually sent a man and wagon around to the girls' villages weekly to pick up their families' food baskets.[67]

In Lancashire "considerable contact was maintained" between migrants and their families. Money was sent home, members of the family were brought to the city to live by family members who had "travelled," and sometimes even "reverse migration" occurred.[68] The children of married daughters working in Norwegian cities as domestics were sent home to be raised by grandparents. In this case, the young husband and wife continued to work separately as domestics to save for the future establishment of their own household.[69] Even when whole families migrated to the United States, they carried these traditional practices with them. Willa Cather notes in *My Ántonia* that work by immigrant girls as domestics or farm hands "contributed to the prosperous, mortgage free farms" their parents built in Nebraska.[70]

The cultural values which sent young girls out to work for their families also informed their personal behavior. The increase, noted by historians and demographers, in illegitimate birth rates in many European cities from about 1750 to 1850 can be seen, paradoxically, as yet

66. Hubscher, "Une contribution," pp. 395-96.
67. Ets, *Rosa*, pp. 138-40.
68. Anderson, *Family Structure*, p. 153.
69. Drake, *Population and Society in Norway*, p. 138.
70. Robert Smuts, *Women and Work in America* (New York, 1971), p. 9. See also Virginia Yans McLaughlin, "Patterns of Work and Family Organization: Buffalo's Italians," *Journal of Interdisciplinary History* 2 (Autumn, 1971): 299-314. The predominance of the family interest over that of individuals and the importance of the family as a model for social relationships can be glimpsed in the lives of young working men as well as in those of young girls. The Irish custom of sending money to parents was followed by boys as well as girls. In Italian immigrant families in the U.S., boys and girls turned over their salaries to parents. In French working class families, likewise. The compagnonnage system offered boys sponsored migration and houses in which to live, complete with a substitute family of mère, père and frères. These houses seemed to offer this kind of family setting without the authoritarian aspects of the factory dormitories.

another demonstration of the persistence of old attitudes in new settings.[71] Alliances with young men may have begun in the city as at home, the girls seeking potential husbands in the hope of establishing a family of their own. The difference, of course, was that social customs enforceable at home could not be controlled in the city.

When a girl was far from home, her family had little control over whom she married, or when. The pressure that kept a Swiss daughter spinning at home until she was forty could not affect the choices of a

71. Cf. Edward Shorter, "Illegitimacy, Sexual Revolution and Social Change in Europe, 1750-1900," *Journal of Interdisciplinary History* 2 (1971): 237-72; "Capitalism, Culture and Sexuality: Some Competing Models," *Social Science Quarterly* (1972): 338-56, and, most recently, "Female Emancipation, Birth Control and Fertility in European History," *American Historical Review* 78 (1973): 605-40. Shorter has argued that the increase in illegitimate fertility which began in the mid-eighteenth to late nineteenth centuries in Europe was preceded by a dramatic change in values. This change, he says, was stimulated by rebellion against parental authority and by exposure to "market values" when young women broke with "old traditions" and went out to work. The change was expressed in a new sexual "liberation" of young working girls. They sought self-fulfillment and self-expression in sexual encounters. In the absence of contraception, they became pregnant and bore illegitimate children. We find Shorter's speculations imaginative but incorrect. He makes unfounded assumptions about preindustrial family relationships and about patterns of work in these families. The actual historical experience of young women working in the nineteenth century was not what Shorter assumes it was. When one examines their history and finds that peasant values and family interests sent them to work, and when one examines the kinds of work they did and the pay they received, it is impossible to agree with Shorter that their experience was either radically different from that of women in the past, or was in any sense "emancipating."

Shorter cannot demonstrate that the attitudes changed; he deduces that they did. We show that the behavior from which Shorter deduced changed values was consonant with older values operating in changed circumstances. Illegitimacy rose at least partly as a consequence of a compositional change in population, i.e., the increasing presence of many more young women in sexually vulnerable situations as workers in cities, removed from family protection and assistance. Under these circumstances, illicit liaisons can be seen as alternate families and illegitimate children the consequence of an attempt to constitute the family work unit in a situation in which legal marriage sometimes could not be afforded, or at other times was not felt necessary. Far from their own parents and the community which could have enforced compliance with an agreement to marriage which preceded sexual relations, women were more likely to bear illegitimate children. This is discussed more fully in the text below. See J. DePauw, "Amour illegitime et société à Nantes au XVIIIe siècle," *Annales, Economies, Sociétés, Civilisations* 27e Année (July-October, 1972): 1155-82, esp. 1163. De Pauw shows (1166) that promises of marriage in cases of illegitimacy increased as both illegitimacy and the unions between social equals in the eighteenth century which produced the bastards increased. (In each subsequent version of his argument, Shorter has become less qualified and more insistent about the logic of his argument. Logic, however, ought not be confused with actual historical experience and Shorter has little solid evidence from the past to support his speculation.) See Louise Tilly, Joan Scott and Miriam Cohen, "Women's Work and European Fertility Patterns" (Paper, 1973).

daughter who had migrated to the city. In fact, her migration implied that she was not needed in the same way at home. The loneliness and isolation of the city was clearly one pressure for marriage. So was the desire to escape domestic service and become her own mistress in her own home as her mother had been. The conditions of domestic service, which usually demanded that servants be unmarried, also contributed to illicit liasons and led many a domestic to abandon her child. This had long been true; what was different in nineteenth century Europe was that the great increase in the proportions of women employed in domestic service outstripped increased employment in manufacturing. This meant that, proportionately, more women than ever before were employed in this sector, which was particularly conducive to the production of illegitimate children.

Yet another motive for marriage was economic. Girls in factories were said to be fairly well paid, but most girls did not work in factories. Women in the needle trades and other piecework industries barely made enough to support themselves. (Wages constantly fluctuated in these consumer product trades and declined after the 1830s in both England and France. Women in these trades were also paid half of what men received for comparable work, often because it was assumed that women's wages were part of a family wage, an assumption which did not always correspond with reality.)[72] In the rural households they came from, subsistence depended on multiple contributions. The logical move for a single girl whose circumstances took her far from her family, and whose wages were insufficient either to support herself or to enable her to send money home, would be to find a husband; together they might be able to subsist.

It may well be that young girls became "engaged" to their suitors and then followed what were in many rural areas customary practices: they slept with the men they intended to marry.[73] When they became

72. Charles Booth, *Life and Labour of the People of London* (London, 1902); Yeo and Thompson, *The Unknown Mayhew,* pp. 116-80; France, Direction du Travail, *Les associations professionelles ouvrières* (1903), 4: 797-805; P. Leroy-Beaulieu, *Le travail des femmes au XIXe siècle* (Paris, 1873), pp. 50-145.

73. P. E. H. Hair, "Bridal Pregnancy in Rural England in Earlier Centuries," *Population Studies* 20 (1966-67): 233-43, and "Bridal Pregnancy in Earlier Rural England, Further Examined," *Population Studies* 24 (1970): 59-70; Thomas F. Sheppard, *Lou marin in the Eighteenth Century: A Study of a French Village* (Baltimore, 1971); E. A. Wrigley, *Population and History* (New York, 1969), pp. 61-106; K. R. V. Wikman, *Die Einleitung der Ehe: Eine vergleichende Ethnosoziologische untersuchung uber die Vorstufe der Ehe in den sitten des Schwedischen Volkstums* (Abo, 1937; Acta Academie Aboensis, Humaniora, II).

pregnant, however, the men often either disappeared, or continued living with them, but did not marry them. Sometimes the couple married after the child or children were born. The constraint of the traditional necessity to bring a dowry to her marriage sometimes meant that a woman worked while cohabiting with her lover until the requisite trousseau was put aside. The absence of the moral force of family, local community, and church prevented the fulfillment of marital expectations. Lack of money and severe economic pressures, as well perhaps as different attitudes and expectations on the part of the men, kept them from fulfilling their promise. To Henry Mayhew, the testimony of abandoned women indicates that often (a) there was no money for a proper wedding; (b) the men's jobs demanded that they move on; (c) poverty created a possible emotional stress; and (d) traditional contexts which identified and demanded proper behavior were absent.[74] Young girls, then, pursued mates and behaved with them according to traditional assumptions. The changed context yielded unanticipated (and often unhappy) results.

Even among prostitutes, many of whom were destitute or unemployed servants and pieceworkers, a peculiar blend of old and new attitudes was evident. In preindustrial society, lower class women developed endless resources for obtaining food for their families. Begging was not unheard of and flirtations and sexual favors were an acknowledged way of obtaining bread or flour in time of scarcity. Similarly, in nineteenth century London, prostitutes interviewed by Mayhew explained their "shame" as a way of providing food for their families. One, the mother of an illegitimate boy, explained that to keep herself and her son from starving she was "forced to resort to prostitution." Another described the "glorious dinner" her solicitations had brought. And a daughter explained her prostitution to the author of *My Secret Life* as her way of enabling the rest of the family to eat: "Well, what do you let men fuck you for? Sausage rolls?" "Yes, meat-pies and pastry too."[75]

Not all single working girls were abandoned with illegitimate

74. Yeo and Thompson, *The Unknown Mayhew*, pp. 167-80. For eighteenth century Nantes, De Pauw, "Armour illegitime," pp. 1166-1167, shows how economic promises to find the woman work, or teach her a craft led to liaisons which ended in pregnancy; Thomas, *Les Petroleuses,* pp. 20-22, 76-79, describes common law marriage in the Parisian working class at the time of the Commune.

75. Yeo and Thompson, *The Unknown Mayhew*, pp. 141, 148, 169; E. M. Sigsworth and J. J. Wylie, "A Study of Victorian Prostitution and Venereal Disease," in Vicinus, *Suffer and Be Still,* p. 81.

children, nor, despite the alarm of middle class observers, did most become prostitutes. Many got married and most left the labor force when they did. Both the predominance of young single girls in the female labor force and the absence of older married women reflect the persistence of traditional familial values. When they married, daughters were no longer expected to contribute their wages to their parents' household. Marriage meant a transfer from one family to another and the assumption of some new roles. Single girls, however, carried the values and practices of their mothers into their own marriages. The traditional role of a married woman, her vital economic function within the family economy, sent her into the labor force when her earnings were needed by the household budget. When the income of her husband and children was sufficient for the family's needs, she left the labor force. Mothers of young children would sometimes leave the labor force only after their oldest child went out to work. Over the developmental cycle of the family, this pattern is valid, but in cases of temporary need, such as sickness, or in the case of the death of a money earner, the married woman would go back to work.[76] Even without a money contribution, however, her contribution to the family economy was nevertheless substantial. In London during the 1890s, the wives of the lower classes "had great responsibility. Whether they earned a salary of their own or not, they handled most of the family's money and were responsible not only for food shopping, but for paying the rent, buying clothes, keeping up insurance payments and overseeing school expenses for their children."[77]

Although increasingly the location of work in factories or shops outside the home made such work more feasible for single women, some married women continued to find jobs. Industrialization only gradually transformed occupational opportunities. Old jobs persisted for many years alongside the new. Women who married industrial workers and who lived in cities imported old styles of behavior into new contexts. Much of the work performed by married women was temporary. Anderson describes varieties of domestic employment for married women in Preston in 1851. Many helped their husbands, others ran "a

76. Chayanov and other economic studies of peasantry remark on the concept of "target income." On the demographic reflections of the developmental cycle see Lutz Berkner, "The Stem Family and the Developmental Cycle of the Peasant Household: An Eighteenth-Century Austrian Example," *American Historical Review* 77 (April, 1972): 398-418. Lynn Lees is working on urban applications of the developmental cycle concept with English and Irish workers' families.

77. Stearns, "Women in Britain," p. 104.

little provision shop or beer house." Well over a third of those who worked, he continues, "were employed in non-factory occupations. Many others also worked irregularly or part time" and often were not even listed in official records as having an occupation. Indeed, Anderson's formulation for Lancashire, that "patterns of family structure in towns can only be explained as hangovers from rural patterns," has much wider application.[78] Whether in the cities and towns of Europe or in America, the work patterns of married women resembled older, preindustrial practices. Immigrant women in New England textile mills, for example, were "the only large group of regularly employed married women" other than blacks. Smuts explains that they were attracted by the familiar work of spinning and weaving and, more important, by the opportunity of working with their children. "A mother whose children worked could look after them better if she worked in the same mill."[79] Depending, of course, on their past experience, immigrant women adapted their skills to American conditions. Thus Italian mothers with their children picked fruit and vegetables around Buffalo, New York, an activity reminiscent of southern Italy.[80] Italian women on New York's lower East Side sewed pants or made paper flowers with their daughters at home. Their husbands, lacking these skills, dug ditches and swept the streets. When these same women followed their work into factories and sweatshops, the husbands sometimes kept house and cared for the children. Married Irish women with only agricultural experience became domestics. But many cleaned New York office buildings at night so they could care for their families during the day.[81]

Whether they worked outside the home or not, married women defined their role within the framework of the family economy. Married working class women, in fact, seem almost an internal backwater of

---

78. Anderson, *Family Structure*, pp. 71, 79 respectively.

79. Smuts, *Women and Work in America*, p. 57.

80. Virginia Yans McLaughlin, "A Flexible Tradition: South Italian Immigrants Confront a New York Experience," (Paper, 1973), pp. 8, 11, and McLaughlin, "Patterns," pp. 306-7.

81. Louise Odencrantz, *Italian Women in Industry: A Study of Conditions in New York City* (New York, 1919), p. 19. Odencrantz also describes the concept of the family income (the sum earnings of fathers, mothers, sons and daughters, other relatives, and returns from lodgers) as typical of Italian immigrants in New York. Covello, *Italo-American School Child*, p. 295, describes the resistance of Italian immigrants to school requirements and their haste to send boys out to work. One mother exclaimed, "The law [for school attendance] was made against the family." The father of Louise Tilly, as an Italian immigrant school boy in New York before World War I, and the only member of his family not employed, did the cooking and kept house.

preindustrial values within the working class family. Long after their husbands and children had begun to adopt some of the individualistic values associated with industrialization, these women continued the self-sacrificing, self-exploitative work that so impressed Le Play and was characteristic of the peasant or household economy. Surely this (and not the fact that "husbands gave purpose to married women among the poor") is the meaning of the testimony of a woman from York cited by Peter Stearns: "If there's anything extra to buy such as a pair of boots for one of the children, me and the children goes without dinner—or mebbe only 'as a cop o' tea and a bit o' bread, but Him allers takes 'is dinner to work, and I never tell 'im."[82] As long as her role is economically functional for her family, familial values make sense for the lower class woman. And the role of provider and financial manager, of seamstress and occasional wage earner was economically functional for a long time in working class families.

Perhaps most illustrative is this case history which embodies the collective portrait we have just presented. Francesca F. was born in about 1817 in a rural area of Moravia and remained at home until she was eleven.[83] She had a typical childhood for a girl of her class. She learned from her mother how to keep house and help on the farm, and she learned at school how to read, write, figure and, most important of all, sew. At eleven, she was sent into domestic service in a neighboring town. She worked successively in several different houses, increasing her earnings as she changed jobs. At one house she acquired a speciality as a seamstress. She saved some money, but sent most of it home, and she returned home (to visit and renew her passport) at least once a year.

Until her eighteenth year, Francesca's experience was not unlike young girls' of earlier generations. Her decision to "seek her fortune in Vienna," though, began a new phase of her life. With the good wishes of her parents, she paid her coach passage out of her savings and three days after she arrived she found a job as a maid. She lived for six months with the bourgeois family which employed her. Then she left for a better position, which she held until her master died (six months), and onto yet another job as a domestic for a year.

At twenty, attracted by the opportunities for work available in a big city and tired of domestic service, she apprenticed herself to a wool weaver. He went bankrupt after a year and she found another job. That one she quit because the work was unsteady and she began sewing

82. Stearns, "Women in Britain," in Vicinus, p. 106.
83. Le Play, *Les ouvriers européens*, 5: 9, 16-17, 45, 50-54.

gloves for a small manufacturer. Glovemaking was a prospering piece-work industry and Francesca had to work "at home." Home was a boarding house where she shared her bed with another working girl of "dubious character." Unhappy with these arrangements, Francesca happily met a young cabinetmaker, himself of rural origin with whom she began living. (The practice of sleeping with one's fiancé was not uncommon in rural Moravia according to Le Play.) She soon had a child whom she cared for while she sewed gloves, all the while saving money for her marriage. (Viennese authorities at this time required that workers show they could support a family before they were permitted to marry. The task of accumulating savings usually fell to the future bride.)

Three years after she met the cabinetmaker, they were married. Francesca paid all the expenses of the wedding and provided what was essentially her own dowry—all the linens and household furnishings they needed. The daughter of rural peasants, Francesca was now the mother of an urban working class family. Although the care of her children and the management of her household consumed much of her time, she still managed to earn wages in 1853, by doing the equivalent of 125 full days of work, making gloves. (Although it amounted in Le Play's calculation to 125 days, Francesca sewed gloves part of the day during most of the year.)

As long as piecework was available to her, Francesca F. could supplement her husband's wage with her own work. With the decline of such domestic work, however, and the rise of factories, it would become increasingly difficult for the mother of five young children to leave her household responsibilities in order to earn a wage. Economic conditions in Vienna in the 1850s still made it possible for Francesca to fulfill the role expected of a woman of the popular classes.

Traditional values did not persist indefinitely in modern or modernizing contexts. As families adapted customary strategies to deal with new situations they became involved in new experiences which altered relationships within the family and the perceptions of those relationships. As the process of change involved retention of old values and practices, it also transformed them, but in a more gradual and complex manner than either Goode or Engels implied.

The major transformation involved the replacement of familial values with individualistic ones. These stressed the notion that the individual was owner of him or her self rather than a part of a social or moral whole.[84] They involved what Anderson calls "an instrumental orientation" of family members to their families "requiring recip-rocation for their contribution in the very short run."[85] These attitudes developed differently in different places depending in part on specific circumstances. Nonetheless, the evidence indicates an underlying simi-larity in the process and the final outcome. Sons first, and only later daughters, were permitted to keep some of their earnings. They were granted allowances by their parents in some cases; in others a specified family contribution was set; in still others the child decided what por-tion of the pay would be sent home (and it diminished and became increasingly irregular over time). Anderson points out that in Preston, high factory wages of children reversed normal dependencies and made parents dependent on their children. The tensions created by the dif-ferent priorities of parents and children led to feuds. And in these situa-tions children often left home voluntarily and gladly and "became unrestrained masters of their destiny."[86]

Long distance and permanent migration also ultimately undermined family ties. This, coupled with the pressures of low wages and permanent urban living, and the forced independence of large numbers of young girls, clearly fostered calculating, self-seeking attitudes among them. They began to look upon certain jobs as avenues of social and oc-cupational mobility, rather than as a temporary means to earn some money for the family. Domestic service remained a major occupation for women until the twentieth century in most of Europe. (In fact, in the mid-nineteenth century the number of women employed as domestics increased tremendously.) Nonetheless, as it embodied traditional female employment, a position as a servant also began to mean an opportunity for geographic and occupational mobility. Once the trip to the city and the period of adjustment to urban life had been accomplished under the auspices of service, a young girl could seek better and more renumerative work.[87] Her prospects for marrying someone who made better money in the city also increased immeasurably.

Their new experiences and the difficulties, and disillusionment they experienced, clearly developed in young women a more individualistic and instrumental orientation. They lived and worked with peers

84. C. B. MacPherson, *The Political Theory of Possessive Individualism, Hobbes to Locke* (Oxford paperback, 1964), p. 3.

85. Anderson, *Family Structure*, pp. 131-132.

86. Ibid.

87. McBride,"Rural Tradition"; Chatelain, "Migrations," makes a similar point.

increasingly. They wanted to save their money for clothes and amuse-
ments. They learned to look out for their own advantage, to value every
penny they earned, to place their own desires and interests above those
of their families.

Decreased infant mortality and increased educational opportunity
also modified family work strategies. And instead of sending all their
children out to work for the family welfare, parents began to invest in
their children's futures by keeping them out of the work force and
sending them to school. (Clearly this strategy was adopted earlier for
sons than daughters—the exact history of the process remains to be
described.) The family ethic at once sponsored intergenerational mobility and a new individualistic attitude as well.[88]

A number of factors, then, were involved in the waning of the family
economy. They included the location of job opportunities, increased
standards of living and higher wages, proximity to economic change,
increased exposure and adherence to bourgeois standards as chances for
mobility into the bourgeoisie increased, ethnic variations in work patterns and family organization, and different rates of development for
different regions and countries. The decline of the family as a productive
unit can be dated variously for various places, classes, and ethnic
groups. It reached the European peasant and working classes only
during the nineteenth century, and, in some areas like Southern Italy,
rural Ireland, and rural France, not until the twentieth century. The
usefulness of the family model as a unit of analysis for social relationships and economic decision making, however, has not disappeared.[89]

A great deal more work is needed on the redefinition of family relationships and on the changes in the definition of women's work and
women's place that accompanied it. Clearly many things changed. The
rising standard of living and increased wages for men, which enabled
them to support their families, made it less necessary for married
women to work outside the home. (In early industrialization, such work
also exacted great costs in terms of infant and child mortality.)[90] Even
for single women, economic change reduced traditional work opportu-

88. For an important discussion of changes in family strategies, see Charles Tilly,
"Population and Pedagogy in France," *History of Education Quarterly* 13 (Summer,
1973): 113-28.

89. See, for example, Marc Nerlove, "Economic Growth and Population: Perspectives
of the 'New Home Economics'" (Unpublished Draft, Northwestern University, 1973).

90. Hewitt, *Wives and Mothers*, pp. 99-122 and Appendix I. For France, see the debate surrounding the passage of the Loi Roussel in 1874, regulating wet nursing.

nities, while new jobs opened up for those with more education. After World War I, for example, domestic service was much less important an area of employment for young women. A smaller number of permanent servants who followed that occupation as a profession replaced the steady stream of young women who had constituted the domestic servant population.[91] The rise of factory garment production seems to have limited available work for women in Milan and elsewhere.[92] On the other hand, the growth of new jobs in expanding government services, in support services for business, in commerce, in health services, and in teaching provided work opportunities, primarily for single women, and especially for those with at least a basic education.[93]

There is evidence also that women's role in the household, whether as wives or as daughters, was modified with time. In Britain, women in working class families began to lose control over finances early in the twentieth century, but the process was not complete until World War II. Working girls began to receive spending money of their own only at the end of the nineteenth century. After about 1914, more and more single girls kept more and more of their wages, and wives began to receive a household allowance from their husbands, who kept the rest and determined how it was spent.[94] The rhetoric of some working class organizations also suggests a change in ideas about family roles. Labor unions demanded higher wages for men so that they could support families and keep their wives at home. Some socialist newspapers described the ideal society as one in which "good socialist wives" would stay at home and care for the health and education of "good socialist children."[95]

The changes that affected women's work and women's place in the family late in the nineteenth and in the twentieth centuries are subjects which are virtually unexplored by historians. They cannot be under-

91. Chatelain, "Migrations,"; McBride, "Rural Tradition," p. 20. Domestic service continued, at the same time, to be the channel of geographic mobility of small rural population groups, sometimes in international migration streams.

92. Tilly, "Women at Work."

93. Holcombe, *Victorian Ladies.*

94. Stearns, "Women in Britain," p. 116.

95. These particular attitudes were expressed in *Le Reveil des Verriers* in an 1893 article, entitled "La Femme socialiste," but they are representative of many such attitudes expressed in the working class press. See M. Guilbert, "La Presence des femmes dans les professions: incidences sur l'action syndicale avant 1914," *Le Mouvement Social* no. 63 (1968): 129. For Italy, see *La Difesa delle Lavoratrici* (a socialist newspaper for women), 11 May 1912, for a socialist view of women's role as mothers. See also Theodore Zeldin, *France, 1850-1950, Ambition, Love and Politics* (Oxford, 1973), 1: 346.

stood, however, apart from the historical context we have presented. It was European peasant and working class families which experienced at first hand the structural changes of the nineteenth century. These experiences were anything but uniform. They were differentiated geographically, ethnically, and temporally, and they involved complex patterns of family dynamics and family decision-making. The first contacts with structural change in all cases, however, involved adjustments of traditional strategies and were informed by values rooted in the family economy. It is only in these terms that we can begin to understand the work of the vast majority of women during the nineteenth century. We must examine *their* experience in the light of *their* familial values and not our individualistic ones. The families whose wives and daughters constituted the bulk of the female labor force in western Europe during most of the nineteenth century simply did not value the "rights and responsibilities of the individual" which Goode invokes. Their values cannot be logically or historically tied to the political enfranchisement of women. The confusion about women's work and women's place begins to be resolved when assumptions are tested against historical data. The evolutionary model which assumes a single and similar experience for all women, an experience in which political and economic factors move together, must be discarded in the light of historical evidence.

ᕁᕂ MICHAEL ZUCKERMAN

DR. SPOCK:

The Confidence Man

In one sense, there is nothing unusual at all in the modern American obsession with child-rearing. Americans have been ill at ease about the younger generation, and preoccupied with it, for centuries.

But in another sense there is something odd indeed about this extravagant anxiety. Few parents anywhere have ever put themselves as hugely and hopefully in the hands of child-care counselors as American parents of the aspiring classes have in the twentieth century. And few parents anywhere have ever had so hard a time raising their children.

These difficulties imply the plausibility of an exploration of the very advice parents attended, but it would be best to be clear at the outset about the logic and the limitations of such an undertaking. For the investigation of advice is, inevitably, a perilous enterprise. We have no clear notion of who heeds such advice, or in what sense. We rarely even know how many parents bought a particular baby-care book, and we virtually never know the social strata from which they came. We do not know whether they ever actually read the book or, if they did, which parts they took to heart. We cannot recover the conditions under which, or the state of mind in which, they sought expert advice, so that, given what we know of selective perception, we cannot be confident of the meaning they made of what they read. And above all we do not know what they really did about what they read.

We do not know, therefore, how to treat the preachments of the past or even those of the present. In any strong sense of knowing, we probably never will. But our ignorance does not dicate on that account a turning to sources other than those of the prescriptive literature, because the fact of the matter is that such sources afford no easier or more reliable access to parent behavior. We can penetrate the process of socialization in the present only for those atypical subjects willing to submit to surveillance in bringing up their children, and in the past only for those atypical elites able—or those aberrant minorities obliged—to leave records of their acts and intentions. The relation between these parents and the wider population is at least as problematic as the relation of advice to audience and action.[1] And in any case we can discover almost nothing, either past or present, of the identificational and imitative transactions we now take to be most elemental in the enculturation of the young, since such modes are so largely nonverbal.[2]

If we would enter at all, then, into the play of parents and children, we must enter inferentially rather than by direct and definitive observation. And as soon as we recognize that, we have also to see that inferences founded on manuals of instruction and idealization are, in principle, exactly as plausible or implausible as any others. The issue is not the propriety of establishing inferences on the basis of advice but the soundness of the particular inferences built on that basis, and the illumination they afford.

Of such inferences, there are three fundamental categories. The first moves backwards from admonition to practice, assuming that parents did, by and large, follow the tuition they were given and that the manuals do, within vague but determinate limits, present realistically the raising of children. The second moves forward from advice to future outcomes, attempting to predict or explain the sorts of adults to be expected from such regimens of rearing if they were indeed imposed. And the third simply moves side-ways, or perhaps never moves at all. It concedes that the guidebooks are evidence only of values and attempts essentially to analyze those values. It focuses, therefore, on parents rather than on children or parent-child interactions.

The first, if it is not entirely tautological, rests on an extremely shaky empirical bottom. We know from a number of studies that there are significant misfittings between parents' knowledge of proper conduct and

1. On the atypicality of contemporary informants, see, for example, Joseph Church, *Three Babies* (New York, 1966), p. vii. On the atypicality of the most widely studied childhood of the past, see Elizabeth Marvick, "The Character of Louis XIII: The Role of his Physician," *Journal of Interdisciplinary History* 4 (1973-4): 347-74.

2. See Jay Mechling, "A Role-Learning Model for the Study of Historical Change in Parent Behavior; with a Test of the Model on the Behavior of American Parents in the Great Depression "(Ph.D. diss., U. of Pennsylvania, 1971).

their actual behavior.[3] And we know from several other studies that, within given families, mother and father often set distinctly different standards for their offspring, so that it hardly seems safe to infer from a single manual to a single parental mode of rearing.[4]

The second suffers all the debilities of the first, since the prediction of future behavior on the basis of present instruction demands that such instruction be indeed acted upon, and it incurs still others all its own. Empirical evidence, again, suggests that there is no simple and straightforward transfer from the attitudes inculcated by books to the actual adoption of such habits of mind by children grown to maturity.[5]

The only sort of inference that seems truly tenable, then, and the only one that will be undertaken in earnest here, is to parental and societal values. For it is, after all, adults who write the baby-care books, adults who publish them, and adults who purchase them. We will wonder, briefly, at the end, about the prospect for the future if the adult values delineated in this essay should be successfully transmitted to the generations to come, in child-rearing or otherwise; but it will be worth our wondering only if we comprehend the values themselves compellingly in the first place.

To gain such comprehension, we will have to confront the advice in its entirety. Parents may or may not have read it that way, but there is

3. The problematic relation of ideals and actualities is proverbial; conceptualization and demonstration that is apposite in this context include Allen Edwards, *The Social Desirability Variable in Personality Assessment and Research* (New York, 1957), and David Marlowe and Douglas Crowne, "Social Desirability and Response to Perceived Situational Demands," *Journal of Consulting Psychology* 25 (1961): 109-15. For specific applications to parent behavior, see, e.g., Daniel Miller and Guy Swanson, *The Changing American Parent* (New York, 1958), p. 223; Marian Yarrow, John Campbell, and Roger Burton, *Child Rearing: An Inquiry into Research and Methods* (San Francisco, 1968), pp. 137-40; Grace Brody, "Relationship between Maternal Attitudes and Behavior," *Journal of Personality and Social Psychology* 2 (1965): 317-23; Michael Zunich, "Relationship between Maternal Behavior and Attitudes toward Children," *Journal of Genetic Psychology* 100 (1962): 155-65.

4. See Kenneth Davidson et al., "Differences between Mothers and Fathers of Low Anxious and High Anxious Children," *Child Development* 29 (1958): 155-60; Leonard Eron et al., "Comparison of Data Obtained from Mothers and Fathers on Childrearing Practices and their Relation to Child Aggression," *Child Development* 32 (1961): 457-75; Donald Peterson et al., "Parental Attitudes and Child Adjustment," *Child Development* 30 (1959): 119-30; M. Kent Jennings and Kenneth Langton, "Mothers versus Fathers: The Formation of Political Orientations among Young Americans," *The Journal of Politics* 31 (1969): 329-58.

5. David McClelland, *The Achieving Society* (Princeton, 1961), pp. 101-2.

almost no way to know. We cannot guess the parts they ignored or rejected if they did ignore or reject any, and we could not trust their answers even if we were able to ask them explicitly.[6] So we must eschew all efforts to divine what parents did see in the advice and address ourselves instead to what was there to be seen. We must seek a reconstruction of the pervading assumptions and injunctions of the text. And we must be content with the conviction that, in so doing, we accept a postulate neither more nor less hazardous, in principle, than what must obtain in more traditional domains. For the problems of interpretation and of imputation to an audience are hardly peculiar to the literature of child-rearing. A Puritan sermon too must have meant different things to its diverse auditors, and a Roosevelt campaign promise to its readers. We cannot get inside the minds of these audiences either, except by interpretation. We have only the texts. Yet if we are not too chary of interpretation—if we admit its inevitability and ask rather about the adequacy of its specific showings and the insight they invite—the texts may be sufficient.

The text to which this essay essentially attends is Benjamin Spock's *Baby and Child Care.* The best-selling handbook for parents ever published, it is a text that would deserve much closer consideration than it has had even if it were manifestly eccentric. But in fact it is by no means odd or unrepresentative. It appeared at a time when any number of similar counsels were emerging in other quarters, and it appeared in a social context common to them all.[7] The argument to be set forth here could almost as readily have been based on those other advices. We will

6. See Lillian Robbins, "The Accuracy of Parental Recall of Aspects of Child Development and of Child-Rearing Practices," *Journal of Abnormal and Social Psychology* 66 (1963): 261-70; Marian Yarrow, John Campbell, and Roger Burton, "Reliability of Maternal Retrospection: A Preliminary Report," *Family Process* 3 (1964): 207-18.

7. See Celia Stendler, "Sixty Years of Child Training Practices," *The Journal of Pediatrics* 36 (1950): 122-34; Clark Vincent, "Trends in Infant Care Ideas," *Child Development* 22 (1951): 199-209; and Martha Wolfenstein, "Fun Morality: An Analysis of Recent American Child-Training Literature," in *Childhood in Contemporary Cultures,* eds. Margaret Mead and Martha Wolfenstein (Chicago, 1955), pp. 168-78. For some striking convergences with actual practices as well, see Urie Bronfenbrenner, "The Changing American Child—A Speculative Analysis," *Journal of Social Issues* 17 (1961): 6-18; Evelyn Duvall, "Conceptions of Parenthood," *American Journal of Sociology* 52 (1946): 193-203; and Sibylle Escalona, "A Commentary upon Some Recent Changes in Child-Rearing Practices." *Child Development* 20 (1949): 157-62.

confine ourselves to Spock primarily to provide, in the integrity of a single text, a concentrated focus for analysis.

But we must begin before Spock if we would understand his impact. We must begin at the beginning of the twentieth century and the advent of formal psychological prescription for parents.[8] For it was then that American mothers and fathers of the ambitious middle classes faced for the first time a distinctively modern problem: the necessity to cope not merely with the immemorial dilemmas of daily attention on their offspring but also with the complications induced by the very advice they sought in the discharge of such duties. In the face of that necessity, their behavior began to be fraught with significances they had scarcely suspected before. They could no longer even cuddle the baby when he cried, or be impatient with him when he soiled his diapers, without worrying about one scientifically authoritative injunction or another. And more, though they dared not do the wrong things, they could not do the right ones.

They dared not do the wrong things because the expects insisted that a child's character could be so "spoiled by bad handling" that it would be impossible to "say that the damage is ever repaired." They could not do the right things because those experts never did agree on what such things were. Conscientious parents of the first decades of the century confronted, in the collective counsels of traditionalists, progressives, Freudians, and Watsonians, a crazyquilt canon that at once required stern discipline and gentle indulgence, detachment and intimacy, prohibition and permissiveness. The more earnest parents were, the more anxious they were bound to be.[9]

Eventually, even the experts could stand back from such work and see that it was not entirely satisfactory. So around the time of the Second World War, a few of them began to add that, in the face of their corroding cares, proper parents ought to relax. The idea was probably about as helpful as a coach telling his team before the big game not to be nervous, but it was where Doctor Spock came in.

Benjamin Spock's first *Baby and Child Care* was published in

8. On the rise of formal psychological guidance over the course of the twentieth century, at the expense of more strictly medical counsel, see Vincent, "Infant Care Ideas."

9. John Watson, *Psychological Care of Infant and Child* (New York, 1928), p. 3. On the quandaries of conscientious parents, Helen Merrell Lynd, *On Shame and the Search for Identity* (New York, 1958), p. 61n.

1946.[10] Through two subsequent revisions, more than two hundred printings, and sales of over twenty million copies, it has remained as it began: a manual of tension-management for parents, premised on a simple little confidence trick. For even as its author acknowledges at the outset the unease of his readers, he diverts it by directing them from doubts about their functional competence to assurances of their instinctual adequacy. "Trust yourself," he tells them, in the celebrated title of his opening passage. "What good mothers and fathers instinctively feel like doing for their babies is usually best."[11]

The equation of inclination and aptness makes a virtue out of everything spontaneous and a vice out of all that is deliberate or controlled. The mother who "feels like" comforting her crying child should go ahead, without fear of spoiling him. Her very desire to give such solace makes it "natural and right." The father who gets angry with his toddler had "better" avow it openly. His prudential calculation of other responses would be "grim" and "unnatural." For simply "on general principle," it is "safer to do things the natural way." Unrelieved irritations and "suppressed" resentments are "not good for" parents, nor for their children either. Easy indulgence of impulse is what the doctor orders.[12]

Moreover, such celebration of hedonic immediacy depends on Spock's most fundamental notions of human nature. His assumption of the benevolence of the instincts underlies his invitation to trust them. His supposition that what wells up from within will be basically benign sustains his incitements to self-confidence. Babies are, by disposition,

10. The first edition was published simultaneously in hardcover, *The Common Sense Book of Baby and Child Care* (New York, Duell, Sloan and Pearce), and paperback, *The Pocket Book of Baby and Child Care* (New York, Pocket Books), in 1946. The second editon, *The Common Sense Book of Baby and Child Care* (New York, Duell, Sloan and Pearce) in hardcover, and *Baby and Child Care* (New York, Pocket Books) in paperback, was published in 1957. The third edition, *Baby and Child Care* (New York, Meredith) in hardcover, and *Baby and Child Care* (New York, Pocket Books) in paper, was issued in 1968. The alterations are more substantial between the first and second editions than between the second and third, but in both cases the changes serve basically to reduce the original realm of "permissiveness" and enlarge the sphere of parental control. For a discussion of the differences, see Lynn Bloom, *Doctor Spock: Biography of a Conservative Radical* (Indianapolis, 1972), ch. 6.

So as not to triplicate citations, all references not otherwise noted will be to the third (1968) edition in its more accessible form, the Pocket Books paperback.

11. *Baby and Child Care*, pp. 3-4. See also p. 9.

12. Ibid., pp. 320, 20-22, 338, 72, 345, 250. See also pp. 4, 19, 61, 186, 190, 192, 193, 222, 253, 262, 271, 275-77, 327, 329, 339, 345, 439. For a variety of ways in which nature knows best, see pp. 72, 81-82, 123-24, 157, 173, 263; though cf. p. 170.

"friendly and reasonable." They are "meant" to be "free, warm, life-loving" people.[13]

They are not, therefore, the dangerous little beasts whose terrifying drives haunted the imaginations of older Americans. They move instead in milder climes, where the heats of erotic excitement and the blasts of savage fury rarely reach.[14] Their sexual pleasures are only satisfactions of a "wholesome curiosity," not consummations of an indomitable itch.[15] Their aggressive impulses spring from misunderstanding or parental ineptitude, not native ferocity.[16] So if a child goes upstairs to "play doctor" with the girl next door, or if he smashes his friend's toy or his little brother's finger, his derelictions do not signify the eruption of untoward impulse or prophesy for him a career of urgent craving. They merely represent episodes of exploratory development.[17]

Spock sets the sweet positivity of these inquisitive little innocents in an environment consistent with, and supremely congenial to, their own dispassion. He refuses to concede that "life is a struggle" and affirms on the contrary the elemental harmony of things. In a cosmos that is "peaceful," amid relations that are "quietly friendly," "fond," and "gentle," he discovers all about him a wondrous concordance of human needs and natural supply.[18]

In the feeding of infants, for example, he finds parables on the reliability of the child's instincts and the safety of indulging them. Studies of "self-demand" show that even new-born babies manage well on their own initiative in eating, so a mother may presume that her child already "knows a lot" about his own nutritional needs. She can trust his vagrant fancies. She "doesn't have to worry" if he suddenly spurns string beans. She can give in "without worrying about the conse-quences" if all at once he has to have ice cream or Queen Anne cherries. He is a satisfactorily self-regulating organism. He will want what he needs and need what he wants, difficult though it is "for us moderns to

13. Ibid., pp. 232, 327. See also pp. 4, 14, 16, 281.

14. For a similar configuration, at almost exactly the same point in time, in the *Infant Care* bulletins of the Children's Bureau of the U.S. Department of Labor, see Wolfen-stein, "Fun Morality."

15. *Baby and Child Care*, p. 372. See also p. 379.

16. Ibid., pp. 233-34, 319. Spock does occasionally concede that aggression is to be ex-pected in early childhood (see pp. 311, 328), but he acknowledges little or none thereafter.

17. In truth, there is nothing that can count against this assumption; any child who *is* "preoccupied with sex" or aggression is dismissed as abnormal and shunted off to see "a good children's psychiatrist." See pp. 311, 319, 372, 373.

18. Ibid., pp. 59, 169-70.

have this kind of confidence in our children's appetites"[19] And in sleeping, walking, bladder control, and a number of other motor controls and sustenance functions, Spock posits a similar coincidence of appetite and ability and advocates an identical confidence in the provision of nature.[20]

In social behavior, everything works out equally well. Just as the child covets what is good for him, so he seeks willingly what is seemly and convenient for society. He has no propensities that stand in any real antagonism to civilized convention. He has no need to disengage himself from his fellows to pursue his own identity. He aims merely at an alignment with his world. "Every hour of every day," he tries to emulate his elders and assimilate grown-up modes. With all his heart, he wishes to "fit into the family's way of doing things." He "wants" to accept obligations. He "prefer[s] to be helpful." For the fact is that "three-quarters of the things that we think we must impose on children as unpleasant duties are things that they enjoy learning to do themselves." If anything, it is the absence of imposition that disturbs children, because they know very well when they are "getting away with too much naughtiness" and would actually "like to be stopped" at such times. Their waywardness is no irresistible expression of an imperial id but only a departure from their dearest ideals.[21]

The success of a book based on premises such as these is more than a little puzzling. Ascetic civilizations do not display such acceptance of instinct. Competitive cultures do not so eagerly embrace a conception of human nature so amiable and mild. And yet Benjamin Spock breaks precisely with that dominant tradition in America which has considered children as scaled-down savages, the tradition which modern sociology sustains when it compares the births of successive generations to recurrent barbarian invasions.[22] His nonpareils do not need to be salvaged for society because they are never unfitted for it in the first place. Their so-

19. Ibid., pp. 58, 279-81. See also pp. 61, 68, 69, 125, 303-4, 436, 439. Spock seems to have been profoundly affected by these studies, which were conducted just a few years before the original publication of *Baby and Child Care*. Here and elsewhere, feeding functions paradigmatically for Spock in his conception of the appetites.

20. See, for example, ibid., pp. 81-82, 157, 166-67, 238, 263, 323.

21. Ibid., pp. 308, 4-5, 326, 324, 247, 330. See also pp. 22-23. Spock imagines the child so perfectly cooperative and companionable that even good manners, the very epitome of artifice, "come naturally" to him; see p. 327.

22. Roger Brown, *Social Psychology* (New York, 1965), p. 193. The specific image is from Talcott Parsons.

cialization is not dependent on the breaking of an obdurate will or the sublimation of a polymorphous penchant. Their growth is not conditional on a gracious escape from depravity. They have only to learn specific roles and routines, because from the moment they draw breath (and as long as they are not undone by adults) they are creative and caring human beings.[23]

The success of the book is also curious because its supposition of the child's perfect endowment is an extraordinarily inconvenient one for the parents of the prodigy. They must bear the fearful burden of preserving his perfection intact through his youth, yet they can claim only the most paltry credit if they manage the task. For theirs is not the Pygmalion part on the Spockian stage. They do not mold the child, nor do they even bring forth his dormant potential.[24] An infant is as inquiring, as expressive, and as good as he will ever be; and his glory is his by birthright. His parents have no portion of it but the blame if he should fall away from it.

Nothing whatever of ill inheres in a child. He does not misbehave unless he is "bossed and disciplined too much." He is not "naturally deceitful," and he does not tell lies unless "under too much pressure." He is "born to be" inquisitive and enthusiastic, and he does not become lazy unless his initial eagerness for life is "trained out of" him. He is a hearty eater at the outset, and he does not desist unless his mother devotes "knowledge and many months of hard work to make a feeding problem." Indeed, even when Spock is obliged to acknowledge the occasional complicity of the little one in a vicious circle of mutual animosity, he never doubts that "the parent starts it." Children are just not naturally ornery. Any of them who act that way must be products of parental ruination.[25]

And Spock does invoke that spectre of ruination often enough to recall parents after all to the portentousness of their responsibility. For it is they who have the ominous power to shatter the child's primal innocence and set the shape of his discontent "forever." It is their word "uttered in a thoughtless or angry moment" that can "destroy the child's confidence," their nagging that can precipitate troubles that

23. *Baby and Child Care*, p. 16.

24. Though cf. the otherwise splendid essay of Philip Slater, *The Pursuit of Loneliness* (Boston, 1970), ch. 3.

25. *Baby and Child Care*, pp. 319, 580, 367, 407, 436, 326. See also pp. 233-34, 263, 279-80, 328-30, 331, 372, 379, and, for further elaboration on the theme of feeding, which serves as a model for other impositions on "natural appetite," pp. 123-24, 439.

"last for years," and their failure to afford the child love and security that can cause "irreparable harm."[26]

In the face of this forbidding awareness, Spock's appeals for confidence fade. He may know that mothers and fathers cannot come to any assurance of their own adequacy if they have to rely on physicians and psychiatrists in every extremity, but he is nonetheless unwilling to leave parents to their own intuitions at such junctures. Before the mother ever brings the baby home from the hospital, he urges her to leave things wholly "in the doctor's hands." As soon as she gets her charge across the threshold, he tells her she "ought" to have a visiting nurse. And as the days go by, he presses her again and again to "ask the doctor" rather than decide for herself, in everything from her choice of baby toys to the baby's own bowel movements.[27]

Of course, the mother who could truly trust herself would not be bothered by these aspersions on her competence. She would never have needed a book to be convinced of it in the first place. But with just those mothers who most require confirmation of their abilities, Spock strains to the limit the confidence he commends. He bids such women be natural, and then, dozens of times over, he lets them see how "easy" it is "to be mistaken" in diagnosis and how "absolutely necessary" therefore to have "close medical supervision" of the child.[28] Or he allows them a nominal autonomy and then compromises it by instructions so specific as the stifle their independence anyway. In his advice on bathing the baby, for instance, he encourages the mother to "enjoy it" but orchestrates her action in such detail that he has even to remind her to take off her wrist watch before beginning. In his directions for cleaning soiled diapers he actually tells her to "hold tight" while she rinses the garments in the toilet.[29]

Moreover, Spock has quite as equivocal a faith, ultimately, in Mother Nature as he has in the mothers of children. And in some sense

---

26. Ibid., pp. 589, 282-83, 567. See also pp. 200, 408, 418, 517, 521, 522.

27. Ibid., pp. 60, 49, 172. For a wider sample of situations in which to consult doctors or psychiatrists, see, e.g., pp. 174, 176-77, 177, 197, 282, 283, 354, 359, 367, 386, 409, 436, 563.

28. Ibid., pp. 205, 199, 190. Spock issues far too many of these injunctions to cite: more than 150 in all, and eighty-six (well over one every other page) on pp. 395-540 alone.

29. Ibid., pp. 155-56, 176. See also pp. 453-57 for five pages of painfully detailed description of the simple procedure of taking the child's temperature, and pp. 266-67 for a list of thirty-six do's and don't's hard on the heels of an insistence that parents "cannot prevent all accidents" and will "only make a child timid" if they try.

he almost has to. If natural processes and predilections were actually as reliable as he often asserts, there would be no need for child psychiatrists or professors of pediatrics. If babies did infallibly do as their parents preferred, and if vitamin deficiencies and gastrocolic reflex irregularities and a hundred other nuisances of flesh and spirit were unknown in nature, there would be no occasion at all for professional expertise or intervention. *Baby and Child Care* would be a contradiction in terms.

As it is, however, Spock hedges on the sanctity of spontaneous inclinations. He does prefer an image of affairs suffused with moral significance, tending always to the optimal in the best of all possible worlds. He does hold forth fulsomely, when he can follow his preference, on "how smoothly Nature works things out."[30] But after all his effulgent rhetoric is spent, he knows that there remain a few matters that cannot be contained so felicitously. The breasts, as an example, are susceptible to a number of ills that a can of condensed milk is not. They engorge, they cake, they get infected. The nipples become sore or cracked, or retract. The baby bites so painfully that "nursing has to be stopped."[31] And all these infirmities signify for Spock a very different image of nature and imply for him a very different attitude toward artificial intervention in her vicissitudes.

Where the complementarities of supply and demand unfailingly inspire Spock to exalt the providence of nature, the disparities never do drive him to reflect on her niggardliness or inefficiency. They elicit from him only an austere normative neutrality, couched in a language itself all at once technical rather than teleological, in which aggravations become straightforward somatic problems devoid of moral meaning or emblematic import.[32] And in such circumstances, Spock's advice shifts even as his diction does. He promotes certain parental efforts to "influence" and indeed to "change" the child's natural feeding and sleeping schedules. He recommends some vitamin supplements, for the

30. Ibid., p. 81. See also pp. 14, 61, 123-24, 263, 281. Needless to say, Spock finds a metaphor for this cosmic conceit in the feeding of infants at their mothers' breasts, the harmony between baby's need and mother's milk supply being both a proof that "Nature" does "provide" and a model of the design of creation; see p. 157. In an even more expansive instance of the doctor's apprehension of nature as morally purposive, Spock supposes that "the reason that the soles of the feet are ticklish and sensitive under the arch is to remind us to keep that part arched up off the ground"; see p. 239.

31. Ibid., p. 99.

32. Ibid., pp. 61, 87, 94-100, 127.

breast-fed baby as well as for the one brought up on a bottle. He sees
circumcision as "a good idea."[33]

If he is nonetheless no apostle of pill and scalpel, it is not because he
has no use at all for these tools of this trade. He does write as one
trained in the infringement of nature's unimpeded course, and his book
owes a part of its authority to its scientific seal. It is, in some measure, a
medical manual. Yet to just the degree that it is, its medium inevitably
violates its message. To just the degree that Spock directs mothers and
fathers to medical specialists who then preempt responsibilities he
promised they could manage, he obstructs the path he wants to clear for
such parents—and their children—to enjoy a ready run of impulse.[34]

Of course, it is no real indictment of Spock's book to cite its internal
incoherences. Its unprecedented popularity puts it far beyond quibbles
about consistency. *Baby and Child Care* is, to the extent that any single
book can be, an embodiment of its culture. And a culture never does re-
solve its focal tensions. It merely oscillates endlessly about them.

But it is just because American culture has not oscillated about these
particular tensions in the past that the very success of the book suggests
a shift in the culture itself. And the suggestion brings us back to the
questions with which we began. Why should American parents of the
mid-twentieth century have been willing, as their ancestors never were,
to take up a psychology so farfetched and a programme so problematic?
Why should they display such overweening concern for self-confidence
in the first place? Why should their thoughts turn so ceaselessly on the
axis of anxiety?

For despite all his divagations, Spock never really swerves from his
transcendent intention to dispel parental anxiety. The easy instinctual
release which he counsels is ultimately just a tactic in a grander strategy
designed to shore up the psyche by inculcating confidence and averting
dread. It is the tactic he celebrates, but it is not the only one he ever ad-

33. Ibid., pp. 66, 166-67, 159-60. See also pp. 65, 87, 127, 172, 192, 322, 323-24, 418,
428-29, 462. On a very few occasions Spock does maintain that parents must afford the
baby "firm guidance" because the little one "doesn't know what's good for him," but even
such uncharacteristic concessions are ordinarily vitiated in definitional assimilation of
such directives to nature ("it's [the child's] nature to expect" parental guidance) and to
the pleasure principle ("this comforts him"). See p. 193 and, similarly, pp. 6-7. Spock's
one truly contemptuous dismissal of nature as an adequate authority is at p. 428. There is
nothing else of the sort in the entire volume, and nothing like it at all in the original
edition of 1946.
34. See, for example, *Baby and Child Care*, p. 59.

vocates. He would far sooner put parents in the care of the technicians than throw them on their own resources if those are inadequate to the occasion, because in the last analysis he is less concerned that mothers and fathers trust in themselves then that they trust, and less insistent that they relax in the amplitude of nature than that they just relax.[35]

So if we would understand why so many parents have embraced an instruction premised on such solicitude for emotional repose, we must move beyond persisting misperceptions of Spock as a subversive or, alternatively, as an author of a great charter for childhood.[36] We must remind ourselves that it is, after all, American parents themselves who have bought the doctor's books and propagated his gospel. And parents presumably relinquish power no more readily than any other ruling class.

We had best begin, therefore, with the primacy of parents. We had best suppose also, if only as a pragmatic postulate of inquiry, that the permissive mode of child-rearing is as serviceable to the book-buying classes of the present day as older modes were to older audiences. Then, exactly on such a supposition, Spock would be neither savior nor saboteur of the rising generation. He would be merely its universal nanny. His would be the expertise to which mothers and fathers might defer, yet he would hold his dominion solely on their sufferance. His would be the office of nursemaid and mentor to millions, yet he would maintain his position only on the thoroughly conservative condition that, in the immortal round of parents and progeny, his strictures aid the elders and smoothe for them their children's inheritance of the ancestral estate.

Indeed, as long as we presume that few parents purposely raise their youngsters to be misfits in society, and that no society encourages them to do so, it is quite unconscionable to condemn—or applaud—*Baby and Child Care* as a spring of revolution before considering it as a source of revelation. At least at the outset, Spock's admonitions and injunctions ought to be taken as functional for parents, and for their social order as well. His departure from traditional precepts ought not to be taken to imply an abandonment of obligation to the social system so

35. See, for example, ibid., pp. 58, 175, 201, 210, 295, 347-48, 480, 517, 521, 522.

36. Among the commentators, it has been primarily the politicians who have seen Spock as subversive, the sociologists who have seen him as a liberator of children. See, e.g., Robert Winch, "Rearing by the Book," in *Sourcebook in Marriage and the Family*, ed. Marvin Sussman (3rd ed., Boston, 1968), p. 340.

much as a different definition of it, as appropriate to the emergent order as past sanctions were to preceding configurations.

By 1946, or 1956 or 1966, the contours of such an emergent order seemed obvious. American children would pass their days, as many American parents already passed theirs, under the auspices of the enormous organizations that dominated the economic life of the nation. And in the society that those organizations shaped, certain prerequisites of personality would prevail.

The prerequisites may be seen most conveniently in terms of production and consumption; and of the two, those of consumption were probably the more powerful and certainly the more pervasive. The centralized structure of power that was conceived in the New Deal and born in the wake of World War II offered vast numbers of people an unprecedented economic security. It flattened the business cycle, blunted the competitive edge of American commerce, and made credible an existence beyond scarcity. At the same time, and for just those reasons, it accentuated emotional disengagment from work. People who no longer ran their own risks and could no longer identify with the elephantine operations that increasingly controlled their occupational destinies turned instead to realms they could still control. They gave up the satisfactions of getting for the pleasures of spending. They grew impatient of their old habits of deferred gratification and embraced an ethic of indulgence for which it was more than a little comforting to be assured that the provenance of nature was dependable.[37]

As Marcuse among others has seen, this nascent hedonism was absolutely essential in an economy of abundance. Such an economy cannot count on any substantial reserve of demand for its goods and services. It has already appeased most men's necessities. It can all too easily produce more than what most of its members, left to their own unaided imaginations, might consider amenities. It must therefore stimulate appetites relentlessly. And to that end, its customers have to be brought to release old inhibitions and accept the appropriateness of desire. "Controlled desublimation," as Marcuse calls it, was a precon-

---

37. There is an intriguing irony in Spock's celebration of indulgence as "natural" and denigration of restraint as "unnatural," since earlier Americans also defined good and evil by the opposition of "natural" and "artifical" yet aimed exactly at the inhibition of "affectional displays." Those patriarchs saw emotional exhibition as "unnatural" and took moderation and control to be much more nearly "natural." See Bernard Farber, *Guardians of Virtue: Salem Families in 1800* (New York, 1972), pp. 30-31.

dition of the administered demand that became a hallmark of the corporate economy after World War II.[38]

Altered circumstances of production did not touch as many men and women as the changed conditions of consumption did, because the mass of Americans could not plausibly aspire to echelons of the great organizations where the alterations were most manifest.[39] But for the strategic cohort that could—and that was in any case likelier to attend earnestly to the child-care counselors—careers in the post-war world of business also implied new terms of conduct and character.[40]

The most suggestive exposition of these terms is still the one put forward fifteen years ago by Miller and Swanson.[41] In it, the two social scientists contrast the isolation of the self-made man and the concern for loyalty, morale, and interpersonal adjustment of the organizational staff. They counterpose the emphasis on aggression, ambition, and active manipulation of risk in the entrepreneurial regime and the promise of steadiness and security in what they call the welfare bu-

38. Herbert Marcuse, *One Dimensional Man* (Boston, 1964), ch. 3. It should be added that the very forces that foster such hedonistic expression also attenuate the resistance to it. For the economy that requires disinhibition to clear its inventories is at the same time an economy that erodes the values that might allow men to stand against the corporate order. It is an economy in which family enterprise plays a steadily shrinking role, so that children grow up steadily less dependent on the family for occupational placement and steadily less subject to the authority of the father. "He has less to offer, and therefore less to prohibit." He becomes "a most unsuitable enemy and a most unsuitable 'ideal,' " because he "no longer shapes the child's economic, emotional, and intellectual future." And the child himself no longer learns the necessity of repression in protracted conflict with the father. Instead, the ego-ideal is "brought to bear on the ego directly and 'from outside.' " The child is "prematurely socialized by a whole system of extra-familial agents and agencies," and his parents' influence in his upbringing is supplanted by that system's "direct management of [his] nascent ego." Herbert Marcuse, *Eros and Civilization* (New York, Vintage ed., 1961), p. 88; Herbert Marcuse, "The Obsolescene of the Freudian Concept of Man," in *Five Lectures* (Boston, 1970), pp. 46-47. For somewhat similar arguments to a similar conclusion, see Fred Weinstein and Gerald Platt, *The Wish to be Free* (Berkeley and Los Angeles, 1969), p. 196.

39. Nonetheless, many Americans could, for it seems to be the case that the bureaucracy of the great corporations facilitates upward mobility. See W. Lloyd Warner and James Abegglen, *Occupational Mobility in American Business and Industry* (Minneapolis, 1955), pp. 150-54, and Seymour M. Lipset and Reinhard Bendix, *Social Mobility in Industrial Society* (Berkeley and Los Angeles, 1962), esp. ch. 4.

40. Orville Brim, *Education for Child Rearing* (New York, 1959).

41. Miller and Swanson, *The Changing American Parent*. See also, among many, William Whyte, *The Organization Man* (New York, 1956), David Riesman et al., *The Lonely Crowd* (New Haven, 1950), and Thomas Cochran, *The American Business System* (Cambridge, 1960).

reaucracy. And, more, they link these attributes of ecological niche in production to practices of child socialization in the family. Maintaining that role requirements of different economic institutions are differentially reflected in the general perspectives of their actors, they attempt to show that these divergent outlooks in turn affect beliefs and behavior in the rearing of children.[42]

At the same time, Miller and Swanson do recognize that there is still substantial pressure to perform in the modern corporation, even if it assumes a somewhat different guise. They shrewdly trace that pressure to the ascendant corporate ethic itself, and to the ambiguity inherent in a system that compels the very license it allows. Giant enterprises depend, in daily routine as well as in deeper structure, upon smooth social relations among members. They can scarcely operate without at least a semblance of amiable intercourse in the ranks. And therefore they require, especially of those who would advance into their administration, a degree of freedom from the inhibitions that might impair such outgoing affability. Individuals who are unduly cool, controlled, or independent are, in those respects, ill-suited to act in bureaucracies which would have their agents cooperative and congenial.

In this light, the significance of Spock's obsession with confidence and the management of anxiety becomes explicable. Confidence is essential to the easy camaraderie necessary for success in corporate society, but on just that account the achievement of such assurance is inevitably problematic among the people who need it most. For letting go which is itself constrained is less than liberating. Spontaneity that is part of the job specifications is no simple effusion of self. And vivacity that is compulsory soon bids to become compulsive. The result is that the organization man is caught in such psychological binds that he is very nearly bound to be tense, bound to be worried about his capacity for relaxation and release, bound to be anxious about the adequacy of his impulses.[43]

42. There are not many systematic studies that bear upon this argument, but for a few that bear it out see Paul Breer and Edwin Locke, *Task Experience as a Source of Attitudes* (Homewood, Ill., 1965), Melvin Kohn, *Class and Conformity* (Homewood, Ill., 1969), and Donald McKinley, *Social Class and Family Life* (New York, 1964). It might be added that Miller and Swanson also extend their assumptions to considerations of consumption. They posit that employees in the welfare bureaucracy are more free to enjoy the present than they ever were under entrepreneurial imperatives to self-denial, and more prone to express their feelings than they every were under mercantile mandates to self-control; and they predict, on just those grounds, that such people are more likely to school their youngsters in similar self-indulgence.

43. Cf. Wolfenstein, "Fun Morality."

Spock's insistence on the benevolence of nature and the dependability of instinct serves in this context to counteract, or at least alleviate, such anxiety. It affords about as much solace as may be mustered for parents whose ability to express an easy-going warmth with others is central rather than peripheral to occupational attainment, and it provides about as much comfort as may be contrived for children who have in prospect a society in which similar psychological demands will be similarly the stuff of life. For in the bureaucracies in which parents work and toward which they point their offspring, the chief accomplishments are interpersonal. They are matters of the management of social relations more than of the movement of merchandise. And because they are, parents must be concerned to instill social savvy in their children, for whom they can hardly anticipate a world any less organized or other-oriented than their own.

Spock's sense of human nature and advantageous character interlaces exquisitely with these parental concerns. It was not the only one that might have done so since it was by no means strictly entailed by the structure of the corporate system, and it may not even have been called forth in the first instance by bureaucratic conditions. Some of its elements were assuredly evident before the war, in areas rather remote from the pressures of big business routine.[44] But if the personality formations promoted in *Baby and Child Care* were not direct responses to the requirements of the corporate colossus, they certainly converged well enough with them. "Without planning by businessmen," as it were, "the new conditioning fitted people for easy and effective participation in an impersonal corporate society where individual eccentricities were suppressed in the interest of harmonious action by the group."[46]

There can be little profit, then, in continuing to conceive Spock as a man gone against the American grain. He is neither an evil genius of degeneracy nor a singular beacon of decency so much as he is a representative man of his epoch, acutely alive to its tendencies and tensions. He may seem more generous in his sympathies than his

44. On the emergence of hedonism as a motif in the settlement of southern California, as long ago as the late nineteenth century, see Robert Fogelson, *The Fragmented Metropolis: Los Angeles, 1850-1930* (Cambridge, 1967), ch. 4. On a more equivocal hedonism, at exactly the same time, much closer to the urban-industrial citadel, see Charles Funnell, "Virgin Strand: Atlantic City, New Jersey, as a Mass Resort and Cultural Symbol," (Ph.D. diss., U. of Pennsylvania, 1973).

45. Thomas Cochran, *Business in American Life* (New York, 1972), p. 273.

predecessors in the tutelary trade, but he is as moralistic in his way as they were in theirs. His tutelage is as fully functional for the oligopolistic economy of the mid-twentieth century as theirs ever was for the dicier enterprise of earlier days. Their teachings, in times of chronic scarcity of capital and commodities, emphasized prudent calculation and the containment of immediate appetite; his, in a period of plenty so remarkable that is must unceasingly exacerbate demand, celebrate impulsiveness and inexhaustible desire. Their counsels, in ages when challenges were essentially environmental, stressed independence and an ardent assault on nature; his, in an era when exigencies are primarily interpersonal, commend social facility and accommodative complaisance.

Baby and Child Care merely marks an alteration of the national course that it did not cause. It differs from the earlier manuals exactly because it shares with them an adaptedness for preparing children to be the adults they must be in a business civilization, and because that civilization itself has changed. The post-industrial order does not need the exaggerated autonomy and aggressiveness that an older mercantile milieu honored. It prefers men and women more mutually supportive, more genial and mild, more benign and bland. And Spock's advice serves its preference superbly.[46]

The most obvious indication of the way *Baby and Child Care* conduces to corporate ends is its unremitting attention to the child's capacity for smooth social exchange. From the first, Spock defines the infant's developmental potential in terms of success in social relations. The baby is "born" for "friendly" fellowship. As long as he has the companionship he needs, he will grow to be "a person who loves people." And his growth will be no mere incident in a larger maturing of environmental or emotional mastery. It is itself "the most important

---

46. It might be objected that the popularity of *Baby and Child Care* reflects less its utility to the corporate regime than its accidental priority in the paperback publishing revolution. As the only child-rearing manual on the early list of Pocket Books, the pioneering firm whose Donald Geddes claimed that he "could sell 'em by the hundred thousands, whether or not the book is any good," Spock's guide was for a time the only such book to be widely available to the American public in an inexpensive edition. Bloom, *Doctor Spock*, p. 101 and, generally, ch. 5. But it is difficult to believe that the book could have capitalized so remarkably on its initial advantage if it did not serve the needs of parents and the business system alike. And certainly the argument for affinity advanced here is strengthened signally by the convergence of Spock's advices with contemporaneous counsels and conduct in a wide variety of other quarters. See footnote 7, above.

job in his life." He simply "can't be happy" unless he acquires such social ease. So his parents have to help him "to be sociable and popular." They literally "owe it to the child to make him likable."[47]

They also owe it to the youngster to teach him confidence in his own innate endowment, because he will never be able to use his talents effectively, whatever they may be, unless he does develop such self-trust. Nineteenth-century authorities of the nursery may have demanded the inculcation of a precocious control, but Spock brands their presumption of the dire origins of impulse "unwise." The child who is "appreciated for what he is" will grow up with "confidence in himself" and "a spirit that will make the best of all the capacities that he has." By way of contrast, "the child who has never been quite accepted by his parents" will "grow up lacking confidence" and "never be able to make full use of what brains, what skills, what physical attractiveness he has." A child must be confident to be competent. He "must feel secure" to be outgoing, and he must be outgoing among his peers to advance in their midst, since his gift for cordiality with them sets the shape of his bureaucratic achievement.[48]

The triune tangle of assurance, sociability, and success that is largely theoretical in Miller and Swanson is thus made tangible in Doctor Spock. His prescriptions rest on an explicit assumption that sanguinity will allow ebullience among fellows and that such ebullience will in turn afford more advantage than any training in the techniques of specific tasks. For in a host of endeavors, it is the child's frame of mind that is more important by far than his actual ability. "The most powerful factor" in a child's performance is "attitude." It is better "to do the supposedly wrong thing with an air of confidence than the supposedly right thing with a hesitant or apologetic manner," because, properly appreciated, almost all things are episodes in interpersonal relations rather than task execution. That is why the father who would have his son an athlete must concentrate less on coaching the boy then on insuring that he feels "approved by his father." Acceptance lets the lad come "around to an interest in sports in good time" where even the most constructive criticism leaves him "uncomfortable inside" and

47. *Baby and Child Care*, pp. 4, 383, 20, 391, 328. See also pp. 4-5., 19, 27, 28, 124, 311, 312, 320-21; though cf. the more spacious vision of such other-orientation at pp. 12-13, 16, 317. Spock holds such sociability as essential as physical health itself, asserting that the child needs it "just as much as he needs vitamins and calories"; see p. 4.

48. Ibid., pp. 430, 5-6, 347. See also pp. 87, 89, 90, 320-21, 563-66, 585, 587.

liable to a "feeling of being no good." And in any number of other activities as well, conciliation of the child's confidence profits parents more than any specific schooling they may provide.[49]

Mothers and fathers must therefore foster a basic trust in their offspring, because the alternatives are dismal indeed. The father who puts undue "pressure" on his child only disposes the youngster to be "hard to get along with." The mother who persists in prodding her baby to eat his last few mouthfuls merely manages to "take away his appetite" and build in him "a balky, suspicious attitude." And "once a child becomes balky" and his parents begin to fret, "the fat's in the fire."[50] Anxiety is aroused. Further fears and doubts are begotten. Existing difficulties are aggravated, and new ones are animated as well. The child seems unable to sleep at night, or shows a diffuse disinclination to behave. He stutters, or wets his bed, or suffers stomach aches. He develops an asthmatic condition, or simply catches a cold. There is no end to the variety of somatic symptoms of such psychic stress.[51]

Though the physician's antibiotics, sedatives, and salves may sometimes "help a little" in these cases, they cannot "do the whole job." No medicaments can. For treatment turns ultimately on uncovering what is "making the child tense," so as to "take away his worry." Parents ought to do this themselves, but if they cannot thus relax the lad or relieve the pressure upon him, they ought to enlist the aid of a psychiatrist who can.[52]

In fact, they ought to seek professional assistance for less than that. The child who is merely "lonely" or "unsociable" must also be ministered to. His estrangement from his peers is debilitating in its own right, and it often marks as well the diagnostic distinction between ordinary growth and pathology. There may be "no cause for concern" when a child with "plenty of . . . playmates" masturbates, but real reason to "find help from someone" when he is "wrapped up in

49. Ibid., pp. 353, 426, 320-21. See also pp. 124, 249, 310, 321, 325, 336, 384-85, 465, 491, 508-9, 509, 553, 555, 567, 569, 571, 571-72, 576-77, 580. Given this priority of social relations to specific task orientations, it is scarely surprising that Spock states plainly in the preface that his book "is not meant to be used for diagnosis or treatment" so much as to give "a general understanding of children"; see p. xv.

50. Ibid., pp. 357, 124, 282-83. Failure of such early "love and security" inevitably occasions "irreparable harm"; see pp. 408, 567.

51. Ibid., pp. 85, 201, 223, 282, 353, 354, 358, 360, 367, 372-73, 374, 381, 382, 408, 410-11, 445-46, 451, 471, 486-87, 487, 510-11, 512, 513-14, 550, 584, 586.

52. Ibid., pp. 353, 515. See also pp. 87, 359, 360, 381, 486-87, 510-11, 513-14, 514. For the remarkable notion of worry as a "psychological emergency" in itself, see p. 201.

himself, or unable to enjoy friendships." There may be nothing untoward when a three-year-old who is "outgoing in general and happy with other children" has imaginary friends, but grounds for misgiving when he is "living largely in his imagination and not adjusting well with other children."[53]

Spock's sovereign "remedy" for excessive isolation is to provide the sufferer more "companionship with his parents" and more "children his own age to play with." At school the refractory child can be drawn "gradually into the group" and enabled to "find a comfortable place" there. At home the little one who overeats, or chews his fingernails, or skips his breakfast, can be plied with attention and affection. Like everyone else, he has to be helped to "feel he really *belongs*."[54]

Just because his belief in his belonging is "necessary" and even "vital," the child must be given no cause at all to suppose "that he is different from" his age mates. He must be permitted to "dress like, talk like, [and] play like" them. He must "have the same allowance and privileges as the other average children in the neighborhood," regardless of whether his parents "approve of the way [such children] are brought up." For parents are not to insist upon their own opinions in the face of antithetical conventions among the child's friends. They are not to set the stamp of their own attitudes so indelibly on the child that he is himself made capable of resistance to the judgment of his peers. Mothers and fathers have instead to be made to see that their values "won't be of much use" to an heir "unable to get along comfortably with anyone," and to understand that the "other average children" are the arbiters of their own child's conduct.[55]

And such subordination of parental standards to prevailing peer usage prefigures as well the final supercession of parental authority itself. Spock warns parents warmly against inordinate subjection in their offspring, but he does not seriously seek to free the youngsters for whom he begs independence. He simply wishes them removed from the intensities of the immediate family to the mildness of their larger society. The independence he actually affirms is little more than a dif-

53. Ibid., pp. 445-46, 395, 372-73, 376, 366-67. See also pp. 319, 360, 447-48. For the overt physical infirmities that may attend the child who does not "get along enjoyably with his fellows" or is not "deeply loved," see pp. 445-46, 486-87, 586.

54. Ibid., pp. 367, 408, 411, 405. See also pp. 350, 359, 360, 383, 384-85, 402, 410-11, 447-48. "The main lesson in school is how to get along in the world"; see p. 400.

55. Ibid., pp. 563, 564, 392. See also pp. 242, 422, 565, 566; though cf. pp. 390, 427, 428-29.

ferent dependence, a due submission to the sentiments of the other fledglings on the block and the styles of the other students in school. The child of six or eight who "becomes more independent of his parents" merely grows "more concerned with what the other kids say and do." His "emancipating himself from his family" is mostly a matter of "shifting to his own age for his models of behavior," and the shift is only extended and exaggerated as he grows older. "Independence" in the adolescent is but a "pleasurable sense of belonging" with peers rather than parents and siblings.[56] And Spock sees nothing disconcerting in this Newspeak notion of autonomy, because the adolescent ideal is his own, too. It finds a fitting expression in his valedictory injunction that the child "must belong completely," by which the book brackets itself in neat symbolic symmetry between its opening invitation to assurance and this ultimate invocation of affiliation.[57]

Men who espouse affiliation so fondly can hardly hail as well the recompense of conflict, and Spock does not. The children of *Baby and Child Care* do not contend for their identities in bitter struggles against their elders. They do not strain for their souls in furious campaigns against their own concupiscence. They do not even fight for their physical safety against the bully on the block. Their peers are all playmates rather than rivals.

If these children experience sporadic antagonism anyway, they experience it simply as they might suffer an occasional constipation or a spill on the jungle gym. They do not discover the recalcitrance of the cosmos in their collisions, but just the differences of an instant. And because such differences are merely "facts of life," without wider ramification, parents can presume that the settlement of strife is always possible. Because broils are never embedded in irreconcilable discordances of desire, parents can be sure that the resolution of childish strife requires only their own adroit management.[58]

Among their other offices, then, parents are the personnel directors of the houses that Spock would have them build. They are the ones who can damp the first flaring of friction. They and they alone are the ones who can fan the flames of animosity by mishandling it. They must therefore be every bit as adept as their corporate counterparts in

56. Ibid., pp. 388, 390, 422. See also pp. 270-71, 385, 388. For monitions against excessive submission to parents, see pp. 170, 186, 193, 270-71, 271, 353.

57. Ibid., p. 589. See also pp. 585, 587.

58. Ibid., p. 340. See also pp. 161, 319, 345, 379.

denying extended expression to aggression. They must know that sentiments of obduracy are as impermissible in the intimacy of the family as
in the bustle of the bureaucracy, and they must know how to make such
sentiments over "into other feelings that are painless and constructive"[59]

The most immediately expedient tactic to alter the child's feeling of
being thwarted is simply to let him have what he wishes. And as long as
his demands "seem sensible" and the mother does not "become a slave"
to them, Spock often urges exactly such submission. Sometimes he suggests that the concessions be made as a matter "of course." Sometimes
he advises only that they be made if the child "insists." But again and
again, in everything from the toddler's choice of teething objects to his
efforts to get out of the playpen, Spock does order that concessions be
made.[60]

Nonetheless, the doctor never exhibits any dogmatic attachment to
his precepts of permissiveness. The deference to puerile importunity
that he encourages is merely a tactic in a grander strategy of conflict
management, not an end in itself; and he promotes it only in specific
situations, on prudential calculation of its costs and benefits. It is never
a principle as much as a ploy. It never proceeds from his devotion to the
dignity of children as much as from his fears that the fallout from
contention could last "for years." And its function is never to provide
children maximal protection as much as to afford animosity minimal
purchase. When parents are asked to "leave [a child] to his
preference," it is primarily because opposition to his inclination would
make him "more antagonistic and obstinate" under the circumstances.[61]

Under other circumstances, Spock is perfectly willing to confess that
the child and his parents alike would be better off for their interdiction
of his demands. A parent can be "a pal at times" without ceasing to be

59. Ibid., p. 340. See also p. 345.
60. Ibid., pp. 4, 122, 271. See also pp. 59, 233-34, 244, 320. For denials of the danger
of spoiling the child, see pp. 61, 189, 191; though cf. pp. 191-92. Again, the justifications
for these concessions emerge most paradigmatically in considerations of feeding. The child
knows his own appetite. His parents can as easily offer him foods he enjoys as others he
cannot abide, within a wide range of nutritional equivalence. And if parents do not ca-
pitulate, their intransiguence may precipitate strife over eating itself. Thus Spock presses
the menu-planner to seek nutritionally similar substitutes for the dishes the child dislikes
and to allow some rather unconventional requests "right away, willingly." He argues
that as long as parents do not force "a battle," their child will eat "a reasonably balanced
diet"; and as along as they instigate no "issue," he may even eat his vegetables. See pp.
304, 283, 299, and also pp. 61, 68, 69, 296, 297, 298, 302, 303-4, 305, 306.
61. Ibid., pp. 282-83, 233-34. See also pp. 228, 244, 319, 327, 514, 520, 537.

"a parent all the time." It simply "isn't necessary," as Spock explains
with some exasperation, "to be a doormat." If grown-ups "can't be
comfortable" with a child who is "doing things [they] dislike," they
should not "ignore" behavior they were "brought up to be disturbed
by." If they are distressed by masturbation or bothered by bad manners,
they should attempt the child's reformation. If they are embarrassed by
obscenity, they should monitor the books and movies they allow the lad,
to be "sure" that such entertainment has "a moral and spiritual tone of
which they approve."[62]

The truth is that "strictness or permissiveness is not the real issue" at
all. "Good-hearted parents" can "get good results with either moderate
strictness or moderate permissiveness." Insecure ones can anticipate
comparably "poor results" with either "a permissiveness that is timid
or vacillating" or "a strictness that comes from harsh feelings." The
"real issue is," accordingly, "the spirit the parent puts into managing
the child."[63]

This spirit cannot be caught in explicit definitions, any more than it
can be epitomized in the crude dichotomy of discipline and indulgence.
Model mothers and fathers may display adamantine intransigence in
some situations and barely dare lift an eyebrow balefully in others.
They may force an assurance they do not feel on some occasions and
then go guilelessly on others. And as often as not they may seem merely
to make do, decisive one day and evasive the next, improvising as they
go.[64] Yet for all that, there are methods in their meanderings. The
expedients which vary so greatly from one incident to another can fi-

62. Ibid., pp. 332, 443, 375, 396. See also pp. 193, 196, 205, 317-18, 332, 356, 361,
364-65, 365-66, 366, 386, 390, 410, 423, 426. For more ambivalent expressions, see pp.
166-67, 303. Between the first edition and the present one, Spock has grown gradually
more appreciative of the place of parental guidance and control in the rearing of children.
The alteration is largely a matter of modifications of nuance, and as such its instances are
at once too numerous and too trifling to cite in themselves. But for some stunning reversals
that indicate, in vastly exaggerated form, the direction of this deeper drift, see the movements from the radically permissive posture of the 1946 edition to the cautiously coercive
stance of the current version in regard to right- and left-handedness (1946: pp. 141-43;
1968: pp. 233-34), toilet-training (1946: pp. 184-93; 1968: pp. 258-59), and fictive violence in play and on movies and television (1946: pp. 240-41; 1968: pp. 313-17). For conflicting findings on the wider generality of this trend, see Nathan Maccoby, "The Communication of Child-Rearing Advice to Parents," *Merrill-Palmer Quarterly* 7 (1961):
200, and Michael Gordon, "*Infant Care* Revisited," *Journal of Marriage and the Family*
30 (1968): 578-83.

63. *Baby and Child Care*, p. 7.

64. Spock does declare that "the main source of good discipline" is "a loving family,"
but he never elaborates the disciplinary manifestations of such mutual affection. See ibid.,
p. 336.

nally be comprised in a few fundamental modes, and those few are all subject to a single standard. Spock's immutable measure of the incessantly shifting disciplinary practices he advises is effectiveness in heading off hostility and preventing pitched battles of the will. The very crux of the parental control on which he insists is its contravention of direct confrontation.

Permissiveness is simply the most straightforward of Spock's elemental modes. It is to be employed in affairs in which something of importance to the youngster is a matter almost of indifference to his elders, and its object is the arrest of needless breaches between parents and children. Mothers and fathers on permissive maneuvers may go no further than to try, "tactfully," to guide the child "if he is willing to be guided." They may not advance beyond such indirection, and, above all, they must not "argue or fight" with the youth.[65]

Evasiveness is another mode in which parents may move, especially when they cannot bend so readily before the child's desires. In this course they try to "distract him" from his intent without exciting his ire, by getting "his mind on something pleasant" in place of the project he cannot consummate. And in this course too, they attempt to prevent asperity even when they cannot so cunningly mask their manipulation. For it is rarely their imposition as such that antagonizes the child, rarely the bare reality of being made to come in for dinner or wash up before bedtime that arouses his wrath. His outbursts are rather the result of insult than of mere injury. So parents must not "scold" their little one lest they spur him "to further balkiness." They must not be "reproachful" lest they "bring out his meanness." They have instead to abandon these moralistic embellishments of their authority for more "matter-of-fact" routines of regulation, in order to escape the corrosive sequels of censoriousness. And they have to carry themselves "cheerfully" in all these operations, and maintain a "breezy" bearing and a facade of "friendly encouragement."[66]

Severity is yet another mode in which parents may proceed, setting themselves against the child's demands without any subterfuge whatever. But even in such strident imposition of their own interests, they still oppose their darling primarily to contain more serious cleavage. For when he implores privileges he cannot be permitted— when he pleads not to be sent to school, say, or not to be separated from

65. Ibid., p. 234. See also pp. 103-7, 282, 410-11.
66. Ibid., pp. 335, 276, 390, 319, 355-56, 223. See also pp. 275, 277, 319-20, 340, 349, 354, 356, 462.

his mother at night—his parents can be sure that their appeasement would only prolong his resistance to a regimen he must ultimately endure anyway. "If parents are firm, children accept; if parents are hesitant, children argue." So parents must sometimes deal "firmly" with the child's appeals. Their puissance may have to be posed, but the pose must be impenetrable if it is to achieve its end in the preservation of domestic tranquility. They themselves may have to bear with "a little unhappiness" in these brushes with belligerence, but they must harden their hearts for a moment if they would not have "the struggle drag on for weeks."[67]

In permissiveness, evasiveness, and severity alike, then, a persistent ambition controls Spock's teachings. For in all these modes of handling the child's inconvenient conduct, the doctor aims unfailingly at the dissipation of friction. Conflict is not, on his account, a normal social process, nor a natural aspect of the ordering of interpersonal relations, nor even a sometimes seasonable instrument in the settlement of differences. It is simply a source of frustration, because it cannot satisfy the desire it arouses to make an adversary "change his mind" or "see the error of his ways." So if parents would "really" avert trouble, they must try to muffle every clash of wills. They must, indeed, give up the very categories of contrariety, because the polarity of domination and docility itself impels them to one extremity or the other, or worse, to one and then the other, in endless escalation. A mother and father may begin, perhaps, by indulging their child. He discovers that he can "take advantage" of their leniency. They discover that "their patience is exhausted" swiftly in such circumstances, and they "turn on him crossly." But because their displeasure is so much stronger than his misbehavior alone would seem to warrant, they make him "feel guilty." And just because they are aware of that, they suffer sufficent consciousness of their own culpability to begin the cycle all over again.[68]

67. Ibid., pp. 559, 195, 355. See also pp. 196, 205, 276, 317-18, 332, 335, 337, 349, 353, 369, 386, 462.

68. Ibid., pp. 276, 275, 331, 369. See also pp. 282-83, 283, 319-20, 439, 512; though cf. pp. 258-59, 562 on the inevitability of conflict. Spock's deep-seated preference for the conciliation of contrariety is revealing in a special sense, since Bloom maintains (*Doctor Spock*, pp. 86-87) that the chief formal sources of Spock's psychological notions were the ideas of Freud and Dewey. Given that Freud always thought conflict inherent in the nature of things, while Dewey devoted his philosophy to the denial of such dualism, it seems clear that Spock's spiritual affinities are far more profoundly with the American pragmatist. For his symptomatically "soft" reading of Freud, see *Baby and Child Care*, pp. 14, 364, 366. (And, in a similar vein, see his domestication of Darwin: pp. 59, 169-70.)

Spock is sensitive to these crescendos of contrition, since guilt is in the end the veritable bogeyman of *Baby and Child Care*. The doctor's New England ancestors may have hailed heartfelt conviction of sin as a condition of salvation, but he does nothing of the sort. He allows only that it "drives" people to do things that are "not sensible." He admits only that it "can cause" somatic afflictions. He acknowledges only that it may attend masturbation, parental overprotection, and a wide variety of other ills. And he adds that it does most of this damage quite gratuitously. The "sense of guilt" appears, all too often, where "there is no realistic need for it."[69]

Parents must, therefore, resist guilt in their own right and refuse to instill it strenuously in their offspring. They must not fight or in any other way force a concussion of purposes, because they must not do anything to stimulate a stricken conscience. They must never feel "too guilty" themselves—their very "guiltiness" could be "harder" on the child than the "irritation" that touched it off—and they must never make the youngster "feel really guilty" either. A "*heavy* sense of guilt" would impair the confidence he has to have to get on among his friends, and it would quicken his susceptibility to the promptings of the still small voice within.[70]

It is to protect the child from the terrors of interiority and to spare him the cares of self-awareness that Spock promotes the values of peer-group play. For the youth must, at all costs, be kept from himself. He has to be outgoing so as never to be alone long with his inmost ideas and imaginings. He has to be "absorbed in games" so as to find no time for "inner fears." And he has to be extroverted and unceasingly busy in the pursuit of popularity so as never even to dream of descending into regions of his being in which "it's risky and it's wrong" to dwell.[71]

The days of the lad's life are, accordingly, to be spent in the emotional shallows. He is to sound no spiritual bottom of his experience, and fathom no sensual one. He is to shun every current that might carry him beyond the safe mooring of his sociability into a more turbulent inner life. He is to know nothing of "deep" distress, or of "deeply" felt doubt, or indeed of any passion that is not passing. He is to be a vessel of affability and ease, and little more.[72]

69. Ibid., pp. 573, 520, 353. See also pp. 375-76, 438, and, because almost every one of these occasions of guilt is linked to tension and anxiety, the whole extensive roster of ill effects attendant on such insecurity: among many, pp. 79, 223, 381, 408, 510-14.

70. Ibid., pp. 26, 517-18, 338. See also pp. 25, 190, 193, 345, 366, 374.

71. Ibid., p. 369.

72. Ibid., pp. 374, 345.

Every intense affect that could lead to a deepening of the child's character has consequently to be made to remain "out in the open," where it can dissipate its potential energy. For desires that are "suppressed" do not disappear. They only enter more profoundly into the unconscious, where their denial "dosen't work out well" at all. The lad who tries to "bottle up his feelings" merely makes himself "more tense than ever." His anxieties "accumulate inside." His fears multiply. And his very possession by such demons—his very possession, that is to say, of a distinctive personality—unsuits him for the camaraderie that will be a measure of his manhood. He must be made, on that account, to see a psychiatrist, who can "clear the air" and dispossess him of his particular tendencies. He must be brought "back to the surface again." His eccentricities must be exorcised, his idiosyncracies "expressed," and his grievances gotten "off his chest."[73]

Americans of an earlier era did not worry so much about the things on a child's chest, because they were more concerned about the things in his heart. They did not strive to scan the child's mind, either, because they were more attentive to the state of his soul. And they certainly did not even contemplate the spiritual search-and-destroy missions that *Baby and Child Care* actually advocates.

Such changes are symptoms of still vaster transformations. Even if only inadvertently, *Baby and Child Care* epitomizes the emergence of a new American ethos, and perhaps the beginning of a new chapter in the history of Western sensibility as well. Though it simply summarizes a traditional American way of life when it invites sociability and a due deference to the opinions of others, it goes much further when it solicits such ends in the context of a concerted effort to detach the youngster from the moral authority of the immediate family. For that family has been, over the last few centuries, the cauldron of the modern conscience and, as such, the very crucible of identity and individuation in the West.[74]

So when *Baby and Child Care* disdains dependence on parents and urges instead an independence defined as an efficacious reliance on peers, it does not just represent reconceived parental prerogatives. When it subordinates the morality of the family to the mores of the "other average children" in the neighborhood, it does not just betoken

73. Ibid., pp. 345, 190, 52, 22, 346-47. See also pp. 21-22, 370.
74. On the emergence of this familial focus of sensibility, see Philippe Ariès, *Centuries of Childhood* (New York, 1962).

the recast claims of the rising generation. And when it aspires to a certain invulnerability to deep-going guilt, it does not just seek to spare the young the anguish of their elders. It is, in addition, a part of a sustained onslaught on the structures of conscience, and on the family in which they are formed. And insofar as such siege is successful—insofar as conscience, guilt, and the absorptive family itself are laid waste—it is hard to see how the inner citadels of individuality that have been the mark of modern man can long survive.

CONTRIBUTORS

Wolfram Eberhard is a professor of sociology at the University of California at Berkeley. He is an internationally renowned authority in the fields of Chinese folklore, culture and social history.

Diane Owen Hughes is a resident fellow of the Centre for Reformation and Renaissance Studies at Victoria College, University of Toronto. Her research interests include social and family history of the medieval and renaissance period.

David Landes is the Robert Walton Goelet Professor of French history at Harvard University. He is the author of several books on European economic history including *Bankers and Pashas* and *The Unbound Prometheus*.

Charles E. Rosenberg is a professor of history at the University of Pennsylvania. He has worked principally in the areas of nineteenth century science and medicine.

Joan Scott is an associate professor of history at the University of North Carolina, Chapel Hill. Her book the *Glassworkers of Carmaux* won the 1974 Herbert Baxter Adams Prize of the American Historical Association.

Lawrence Stone is the Dodge Professor of History at Princeton University and the Director of the Shelby Cullom Davis Center for Historical Studies. His published works have focused on the social history of early modern England.

Louise Tilly is an assistant professor of history at the University of Michigan, Ann Arbor. She is also the director of the Women's Studies Program at Michigan. She has worked extensively in European social history, particularly the role of women in the labor force.

Michael Zuckerman is an associate professor of history at the University of Pennsylvania. He is the author of *Peaceable Kingdoms* and other works in American social history.

STEVEN ALLEN KAPLAN, 1940-1964

This is the first Stephen Allen Kaplan Memorial Symposium in social history. The symposium originated in a series of lectures in the Department of History at the University of Pennsylvania established in the memory of Stephen Allen Kaplan by his parents, Dr. Richard and Reva Stein Kaplan, his grandmother, Mrs. Fannie Berman Stein, and his uncle, Dr. Max B. Kaplan.

I met Stephen in 1960 while we were undergraduates at Cornell University, and we became good friends. A brief outline of his academic career suggests the loss to scholarship occasioned by his tragic death at the age of 24. He was valedictorian of his graduating class at Germantown (Pa.) Academy, received his B.A. with Honors in History from Cornell, and his M.A. in History from the University of California, Berkeley. He was working on his doctoral dissertation at Berkeley when he died March 7, 1964.

It is fitting that his name continues to be associated with distinguished scholarship and humane intellectual concern.

Stephen R. Weissman
University of Texas at Dallas